Armies in the Sand

JOHN SABINI

Armies in the Sand

The Struggle for Mecca and Medina

with 40 illustrations

THAMES AND HUDSON

For Jemima, a good travelling companion

© 1981 Thames and Hudson Ltd, London
First published in the USA in 1981 by Thames and Hudson. Inc.,
500 Fifth Avenue, New York. New York 10110

Library of Congress Catalog Card Number 80–52095

Filmset by August Filmsetting, Reddish, Stockport.
Printed and Bound in Great Britain by the
Fakenham Press Ltd, Norfolk.

Contents

2222284

Acknowledgments

First I wish to thank Miss Elizabeth Monroe, for her encouragement, guidance, and support throughout the writing of this book. Any errors of fact or interpretation that remain should be attributed not to her but to the author. My thanks are also due to Mr and Mrs John Brinton for their hospitality during the early stages of writing and for the use of their fine library on the Middle East. Mr Rodney Searight has been most generous in opening his collection of pictures on Arab and Turkish subjects for use as illustrations. Gratitude is also extended to the following for their help, advice, and encouragement: Mr William Mulligan, formerly of the Arabian American Oil Company; Mr Ritchy Thomas, former librarian of the American University of Beirut; Miss Nawal Na'oum, Mr and Mrs John Fistere, and Mr William Tracy. No writer on the Arabian peninsula in the eighteenth and nineteenth centuries can fail to acknowledge a great debt to the late D. G. Hogarth for his seminal work *The Penetration of Arabia*.

Dhahran – Shemlan – London
1973–1979

Note on the Transliteration of Arabic

The rendering of Arabic words into English letters is an unsatisfactory business. There is no English equivalent for some Arabic sounds, and Arabs make distinctions between letters that sound alike to our ears. There are also variations between spoken and written Arabic and between different dialects. Each of the writers and travellers treated here used his own method, often inconsistently, and I have retained his form in direct quotation. For the rest I have used a system which I hope is at least consistent, if perhaps no more rational than another. Well-known names and words, such as Mecca and Bedouin, are given in their familiar form. The ' or inverted apostrophe represents the letter 'ain, an essential ingredient of some Arabic words like 'ulama, Sa'ud, or Yanbu'; it approximates to a deep growl and often makes a friendly conversation between Arabs sound like a quarrel. Some names, such as Mehmet Ali and Omar, are given in Turkish form where appropriate, to distinguish them from their Arab equivalents. If a name or a word looks unfamiliar on the page, the reader is advised to try saying it aloud – he will probably find he has heard it before.

Note on Currency

During the period covered by this book money from all over the world circulated freely in Arabia and other parts of the Ottoman empire. Piastres, liras, francs, louis d'or, pounds sterling, sovereigns, guineas, dollars, sequins, rupees, riyals, pagodas changed hands or were mentioned in documents, and presumably the people involved at any one time could make quick calculations of their relative values. It is almost impossible to do so today, at least in any consistent and universal way, because the value of each currency kept changing in purchasing power and in the gold and silver content of the coinage. Even if the effort were made to determine par value in terms of pounds sterling or US dollars today, with present rates of inflation the figures would be out of date within a few months. The reader is advised to think of any given amount impressionistically, either as reasonable, extortionate, or a bargain, depending on the context. The Turkish lira contained 100 piastres; in Jiddah in 1814, according to Burckhardt, fifty piastres were worth one pound sterling. The dollar so frequently mentioned was the Maria Theresa thaler, not the US silver dollar.

PART I
PRELUDE

As whirlwinds in the south pass through; so it cometh from the desert, from a terrible land.

Isaiah

CHAPTER 1
A Terrible Land

In the early years of the nineteenth century, the Hijaz – that strip of barren land that lies along the east coast of the Red Sea and contains the holy cities of Mecca and Medina – was the battleground of a hard-fought war between two combatants, both of whom were alien to the country. From Najd in the heart of the Arabian peninsula rode an army of God-inspired warriors calling themselves Unitarians but known to the rest of the world as Wahhabis, under the spiritual guidance of the eighteenth-century Islamic reformer Muḥammad 'Abd al-Wahhab and the military leadership of the House of Sa'ud. Opposing them, a miscellaneous army of mercenaries – Egyptians, Turks, Albanians, Moors, a few Europeans – swarmed across the Red Sea under the command of Mehmet Ali, Pasha of Egypt and viceroy of the Ottoman Sultan. The immediate end for which the two invaders fought was control of Mecca and Medina and the security of the pilgrim caravans that crossed the Arabian desert from the rich and cultivated Muslim lands to the north.

The Egyptian-Wahhabi war was a true holy war, a battle for the soul of Islam, although it concerned territory and politics as well. On one side stood a newly reborn, fully self-conscious puritanism, a protestant revolt against decadent orthodoxy. In the spirit of most protestant movements, the Wahhabis conceived of their reform as a return to the primitive message of the Prophet and the Quran, uncontaminated by 'innovations', animated by a strict code of morality, and enforced by the state. The motives of the other side were less clear-cut and undoubtedly as mixed as the origins and uniforms of the Ottoman-Egyptian troops. Mehmet Ali himself was intent on legitimizing his recent acquisition of Egypt from the Mamluks and extending his influence to other parts of the Ottoman world. A freethinker in religion, he represented a secular, modernizing trend of thought utterly opposed to the theocracy of the Wahhabis. The Ottoman government, too, had political interests in preserving its hegemony over the Hijaz. The Sultan was also the Caliph of Islam, with a duty to stamp out heresy and schism throughout his domains. He earned great prestige as Protector of the Holy Places; and the caravans that set off from Damascus, Baghdad, and Cairo, swollen by tributaries from the furthest reaches of the Muslim world, were state-sponsored affairs of considerable ideological significance. Any interference with them was a challenge to Ottoman authority.

The two combatants thus represented a confused series of polarities: purity versus corruption, fanaticism versus apathy, particularism versus imperialism, simplicity versus civilization. The Wahhabis challenged the complacent orthodoxy of the Ottomans in the name of what they conceived to be an older and purer orthodoxy. They opposed Turkish imperialism, yet they imposed their own form of government on neighbouring towns and tribes with wholly different traditions and institutions. The Ottomans, tied to a system of decayed institutions, were susceptible to modernization through European influence, while the Wahhabis aimed at the reinstatement and preservation of an immutable past.

Caught between the invading armies, the Sharif Ghalib of Mecca tried to preserve his position as nominal ruler of the Hijaz, siding first with the Wahhabis, then with the Egyptians. The Sharif embodied many of the contradictions of the Muslim world in his own person. A reputed descendant of the Prophet, he was a religious leader held in high esteem even by the Wahhabis. Yet he ruled under the suzerainty of the Sultan and held office at the pleasure of the Ottoman Porte, which could, and often did, replace him with another member of his numerous and quarrelsome family. A Turkish prince in education and entourage, he was also a Bedouin shaikh through his connections, both political and personal, with the tribes that grazed in the Hijaz and neighbouring territories. In 1791 he had been ordered by the Sultan to stop the depredations of the Wahhabis against their neighbours; but after years of indecisive desert encounters the Sharif had been compelled to recognize the authority of the Wahhabi leader, 'Abd al-'Aziz ibn Sa'ud, over the northern tribes and his right to interfere in the affairs of the Hijaz.

But the Wahhabis had not been content with this. In 1802 they attacked and massacred almost the entire population of Karbala in Iraq, and the following year they turned back the Syrian and Egyptian caravans. Then they invaded the Hijaz, forcing the Sharif Ghalib to flee to Jiddah. Mecca and Medina were abandoned to the Wahhabis, who tore down the tombs of mere men and uprooted all signs of devotion objectionable to their creed. When a few years later the Wahhabis threatened Damascus, the Porte ordered the Pasha of Egypt to put down these desert upstarts. Mehmet Ali delayed complying with the orders of his sovereign until he had consolidated his hold on Egypt, but in 1811 he felt secure enough to send an army to the Hijaz under command of his seventeen-year-old son Tusun. This was the start of a war that was to last for seven years.

The Egyptian-Wahhabi campaign coincided with the latter stages of a much broader conflict, the near-global war that the French and the English had been waging for more than a century. The overland route from Europe to India, passing through the Red Sea or the Persian Gulf, was only half as long as the sea journey round the Cape of Good Hope, and the Western powers took a keen interest in who controlled that route. Napoleon's invasion of Egypt in 1798 was partly designed to cut England's communications with India and to re-establish French influence there. Although the English fleet, in conjunction with the Ottomans, drove the French out of Egypt, Napoleon's initial success exposed the weakness both of the Mamluks and of the Porte and thereby set the scene for the rise of Mehmet Ali. The English thereafter were vigilant to see that no strong power could block their ready access to India.

The global expansion of European influence also encouraged a new breed of world traveller. The Hijaz, with its Holy Places forbidden to all but Muslims, naturally attracted the curiosity and bravado of adventurers of all stripes. Some were sent as spies for their governments; others came as aimless vagabonds; a few were disinterested explorers well grounded in the useful sciences and necessary languages. Some went openly as Europeans, others in the guise, more or less sincere, of Muslims. The Egyptian-Wahhabi war, its prelude and aftermath, took place under the eyes of a band of intelligent, perceptive, sometimes disreputable European observers, many of whom wrote shrewd and lively accounts of what they saw and heard. The Hijaz, once *terra incognita* in the West, was revealed by them in vivid detail.

It is difficult for worldly eyes to see why anyone should want to fight for possession of this naked, skeletal, rebarbative land. The Hijaz – the name means 'the barrier' – is part of the great geological fault that split Africa from Asia, and splinters from that fault lie dangerously near to the surface of the water that rushed in to fill the resulting chasm. The coastline glitters under a crust of salt overlying lakes of viscous clay that clogs the pads of animals and can bury the wheels of a vehicle to the hub. Much of the year a veil of humidity shrouds the shore, only to be lifted when the hot dry wind blows from the desert. The plain is littered with huge blocks and boulders, and scarred with gullies that are sometimes choked with sand. Vegetation is sparse and juiceless, consisting of thorny acacia barrens or spiky wild palms, sedge and saltbush. The mountains rise abruptly from the plain, and old volcanoes sleep amid the debris of former convulsions, blackening the earth with dead lava flows. Winds scour the plain and raise pillars of sand that scud across it. Lightning flickers on the mountain tops; torrential rains flood the gullies. East of the mountains stretches the vast emptiness of Arabia.

From time immemorial, life in the Hijaz has been as harsh and violent as the environment. Cheated of natural resources, the people have had to wrest what sustenance they could from the sea and the land, and from one another. The nomadic tribes waged almost constant warfare among themselves and with the town dwellers. The cities attacked one another for advantage and defended themselves against the Bedouins by pre-emptive attacks. The inhabitants of the Hijaz, whether nomads or cultivators, considered it their right to exact tribute from anyone crossing their terrain, or to take it by force if necessary. But even the natural poverty of the land was no protection from foreign aggressors, from the Roman legions of Aelius Gallus, Tetrarch of Egypt, to the Crusader Reynald de Châtillon and the Portuguese under Affonso d'Albuquerque. The geographical position of the Hijaz on one of the principal trade routes of the world was enough to ensure its importance.

But surpassing all worldly concerns, the Hijaz has been a source of extraordinary spiritual force. For millions of men and women inhabiting every quarter of the globe, the Hijaz – or that part of it comprising Mecca and Medina – is the Holy Land, the earthly focus of their spiritual lives, more important to them than any other place on earth after their own homes. They study its history and geography; they turn to face Mecca every day in their prayers; and they aspire to visit the Holy Places at least once in their lives. To those who make the journey, the pilgrimage is the spiritual climax of their careers, and ever afterwards the memory colours their existence, adding to their stature and prestige in this world and the next. Whatever occurs in the Hijaz has spiritual significance to a large portion of mankind, and even to those outside Islam this fact gives a dis-tinctive flavour to events that unfold there. Even violence – and the Hijaz has had its share of rebellion, fratricide, massacre, invasion, and murder – takes on a sharper, more ironic edge, whetted on the stone of religion.

Mecca and Medina, which lie so close together on the map and in the mind, are quite different in physical and spiritual character. Both were caravan towns of considerable antiquity, but Medina had the advantage of being set on fertile volcanic soil with sufficient water to support groves and gardens which soften the atmosphere with the benign chemistry of growing things. Mecca, on the contrary, stands in a naked gully with barely enough drinking water for its inhabitants and hardly a shred of green to soothe the weary heart and eye. Travellers without the stimulus of faith have been universally appalled by the grim aspect of Mecca. 'This citie is greatly cursed of God,' observed the Italian Ludovico da Varthema in the sixteenth century, 'as appereth by the great barrennesse thereof, for it is destitute of all maner of fruites and corne.' Three centuries later the Anglo-Indian John F. Keane execrated the place as 'a mangled limb of old mother earth, compound comminuted fracture, bones protruding, exposing the very marrow of the world'. Medina on the other hand appeared to him, as he approached it, like Constantinople as seen from the Sea of Marmora 'or any of the loveliest cities of the world . . . a fresh bright jewel, bounded by the grim barrenness of the desert, an opal and pearl mosaic set in a brilliant border of shining green enamel'. Medina, then, is a natural city resembling many others. But Mecca – for what earthly reason was a city founded in such a forbidding place? If Medina is a natural town, Mecca is a mystery, a sort of miracle.

And that is what the Arabs have always considered Mecca to be. Long before the time of Muhammad the place was thought to be so holy that men were forbidden to build houses there, to cut down trees, or to kill wild animals or one another. Gradually, despite the prohibitions, a town grew up round the Spring, or Well, of Zamzam and the adjoining sanctuary. Periodically, in times of truce from nearly incessant warfare, the pagan tribes came to worship at the sanctuary, to exchange goods at a great fair, and to compete in the recital of poetry, the one true art and palladium of the Arabs. Mecca welcomed the gods of all the tribes, including in later times those of the Jews and Christians; an icon of the Virgin once hung in the sanctuary. But the principal deity, the god of the Meccans, was Allah, who was worshipped at the Ka'ba, or Cube, a large rectangular building of great antiquity. The worshippers stripped naked before they circled the Ka'ba, kissed the black stone set in a corner of the building, ran between two hills as though in search of water, stoned a pillar representing the devil, and cut the throats of sacrificial animals. There was something inexplicable and irrational about the rites at Mecca, as if some ancient thought, pre-cerebral, almost pre-human, was embodied there.

Muhammad was born into the ruling clan of Mecca, the Quraish, around AD 570. As a young man he worked in the caravan trade and may have travelled to the Byzantine province of Syria. At about the age of forty he began to preach the unity of God (Allah) and the necessity of submission (Islam) to Him. This threatened the lucrative position of Mecca as a place of pilgrimage to many gods, and he was driven out of town by his kinsmen and fellow citizens. The more cosmopolitan city of Yathrib to the north – later to be called Medinat an-Nabi, or City of the Prophet – offered him refuge and made him arbiter of disputes among the Arabs and Jews living there. The date of his flight, or *hijrah*, from Mecca in 622 marked the beginning of the Muslim calendar. But although he attained secular authority in Medina, Muhammad still felt the religious call of Mecca. When the Jews failed to support him to the extent that he expected, he turned away from Jerusalem as the direction of prayer and instructed his followers to turn their faces thereafter towards the Ka'ba.

Muhammad deplored the violence he saw around him and tried to curb the warlike spirit of the Arabs. In many ways he succeeded, checking tribal warfare, improving the lot of women and slaves, and creating a spirit of brotherhood among the faithful. But Muhammad was not only a prophet; he was also a statesman and a warrior. As his following grew he began attacking the Meccan caravans, and in 623 at the battle of Badr he defeated the Meccan army and won control of his native town. He cleansed the Ka'ba of idolatry but retained most of the rites performed there. In particular he affirmed the importance of the pilgrimage as one of the five pillars of Islam, or principal duties of all Muslims. But Muhammad continued to live in Medina, governing his people and directing the campaign of conversion and conquest of the Arabs. When he died around the age of sixty-two in the arms of 'Aisha, his favourite wife, he was buried under the floor of her house. Thus Medina acquired a shrine as well, though not one so ancient or so central to Islam as that of Mecca.

The circumstances of Muhammad's death sowed the seeds of dissension among his followers, for he died without male issue and without clearly designating a successor. Leadership was therefore decided by election, and the first two caliphs ('representatives' of God on earth), the Prophet's kinsmen and companions, Abu Bakr and 'Umar, were recognized by all the faithful. But the third election was contested by 'Ali, the Prophet's son-in-law through marriage to Fatimah, Muhammad's daughter by his first wife. 'Ali claimed that he had been named to succeed by the Prophet himself. 'Aisha and her faction would have none of this, and war was declared between those who favoured open elections and those who backed dynastic succession. When 'Ali was killed in battle and later his two sons, Hasan and Husain, died 'martyrs'' deaths, an element of tragic passion entered the Alid cause, diametrically opposed to the spirit of worldly success inspired by the Prophet's own career. The schism between the Shi-ites, or 'partisans' of 'Ali, and the Sunnites, the orthodox followers of tradition, has split Islam to this day.

After Muhammad's death the Muslim armies carried the message of Islam into Syria and Egypt, and later to Persia. When the fourth caliph, Mu'awiyah, was elected in 660, he was governor of Syria at the time and, though Meccan by birth, he established his capital at Damascus. Mecca immediately set up a rival caliph of 'Ali's line and had to be brought back into the orthodox fold by a six months' siege. Medina readily accepted the Umayyid caliphs of Damascus (661–750) and later the Abbasids of Baghdad (750–945), but Mecca chafed under foreign rule, even though the caliphs patronized the pilgrimage and embellished the Holy Places. But in the ninth century the political unity of Islam began to break up under the strain of territorial and cultural expansion. In Spain and North Africa rival caliphs proclaimed themselves. In western Arabia a Shi-ite faction known as the Carmathians broke out of al-Hasa in the early part of the tenth century and swept through the peninsula. They butchered their opponents in the very precincts of the Ka'ba and prised out the Black Stone to send back to al-Hasa. For a time they ruled the Hijaz and even threatened to overrun Syria and Egypt, where another Shi-ite dynasty, the Fatimites (969–1171), claimed the caliphate. The Carmathians were finally pushed back into al-Hasa, and the Fatimites claimed sovereignty over the Hijaz, though local despots seized the Holy Cities and exploited the pilgrim trade.

The disunity of Islam abetted the Crusaders. In the 1170s Saladin, a Kurd, rallied his co-religionists to resist the Christian invasion, and to this end sent his brother to Mecca to replace a rapacious governor and put down the schismatics. But the Crusaders, after establishing themselves in the Christian Holy Land, threatened the sacred places of the Muslims. Despite a truce between the Crusaders and Saladin, Reynald de Châtillon, lord of Oultrejourdain, led his knights to Taymah in the northern Hijaz in 1182 and robbed an Arab caravan travelling to Syria. Saladin sent troops to chase Reynald back into Jordan, but the Frankish bandit refused to relinquish the stolen goods. Encouraged by the success of his raid, Reynald built a fleet of galleys on the Dead Sea and had them dismantled and carried overland to the Gulf of Aqaba, along with a thousand fighting men. Reynald then rampaged down the Red Sea as far as its southern gates, Bab al-Mandib, sinking pilgrim ships, investing the port of Yanbu', and threatening to invade Mecca and Medina. When Saladin repudiated the truce with the Crusaders, Reynald had to return to Oultrejourdain to defend his fiefdom.

Saladin placed the Hijaz in the orbit of Cairo, where he and his descendants, the Ayyubids, ruled till the middle of the thirteenth century. Local despots meanwhile fought for control in the Hijaz. Some of these petty amirs claimed descent from the Prophet and called themselves *sharif*, a word meaning 'noble' and 'generous'. In 1201 the Sharif Qitada, ruler of Yanbu', sent his son at the head of a troop of cavalry against his neighbour, Mecca. The amir of Mecca had taken all his men outside the city to make the lesser pilgrimage (one performed not in the prescribed season), and the Yanbu' horsemen were able to take the town with the loss of a single man. Qitada installed himself in the Holy City and gradually extended his rule over most of the Hijaz, despite attacks from the Ayyubids of Cairo and the Abbasids of Baghdad. On his deathbed he confided to his son the principles by which the ruler of such a poor and weak country could succeed: he should fortify himself within the Hijaz and not risk his limited forces further afield; he should hold a balance between Cairo and Baghdad, depending on Yemen for support; he should allow the name of whichever foreign ruler was strong enough to impose it to be mentioned in prayers at the Holy Mosque in token of sovereignty; he should obtain grants and presents from richer Muslim rulers in order to maintain the Holy Places and the pilgrim routes; and he should keep the exactions on pilgrims within tolerable limits. By sticking more or less to these rules, the descendants of Qitada reigned as Sharifs of Mecca until the Treaty of Versailles in 1919.

Although the Grand Sharif, as the ruler was called, made a show of orthodoxy, many if not most of the sharifian dynasty were suspected of being sectaries of 'Ali. That branch of the family that came to power in Yemen made no secret of being Shi-ite and, according to the nineteenth-century traveller Burckhardt, the sharifs residing abroad did not deny the accusation. The Grand Sharif, though he relied on mercenary troops to keep his throne, did not neglect his connections with the great Bedouin tribes. By family custom he sent his sons to the black tents to be reared by a Bedu foster-mother, thus ensuring that they forged fraternal ties with her children which lasted all their lives. The young sharifs learned how to ride camels and horses, how to live off the desert, and how to fight Bedouin fashion. Curiously enough, the daughters of the Grand Sharif were not used in forming dynastic marriages; according to Burckhardt, they were not allowed to marry at all. Many of the sharifs were astute politicians and soldiers; those that were not were soon replaced by some ambitious relative. That sharifian rule suited the Hijaz was proved by the survival of the dynasty for more than seven centuries.

But the Hijaz continued to bow to the authority of Cairo. There the Ayyubids gradually lost power to their own praetorian guard of white slaves known as Mamluks, or 'owned men'. This extraordinary institution depended on a constant supply of boys bought or captured from Turkic tribes living north of the Black Sea and brought to Alexandria on Genoese ships; later the chief source of supply was Circassia. Whatever their origins, the boys were converted to Islam and trained from childhood in the military arts. They spoke Turkish and Circassian rather than Arabic, wore gorgeous clothes, rode the finest horses and camels, and carried an array of splendid arms. Many of them were tall and fair, and they had a reputation for homosexuality. Organized into military units, each commanded by a bey, they were the élite of Egypt, living in luxury off the labour of the natives. The strongest beys fought pitched battles in the streets of Cairo and on the banks of the Nile for the supreme position of Rais al-Balad, or Sultan of Egypt. In the words of the Egyptian historian Shafiq Ghorbal, 'The corruption and tyranny were relieved by frequent murders, cabals, tumults, and unnatural vices.' Yet this gang of arrogant, rapacious slaves preserved Islamic civilization from the barbarians of both West and East, the Crusaders and the Mongols. They also enhanced that civilization by their patronage of the arts, a patronage which produced the magnificent carpets, glass, illuminated Qurans, and the splendid mosques and tombs of medieval Cairo.

After the Mongols destroyed Baghdad and ended the Abbasid caliphate in the early thirteenth century, Cairo's influence in the Hijaz was unchallenged. The Mamluk Sultan Baybars made the pilgrimage in 1269 travelling in great luxury, with fresh flowers and fruit shipped to him daily from Egypt. Baybars had been sold as a boy in Damascus for 500 pieces of silver but was returned by his purchaser because of a cast in one eye. The young slave, however, had other qualities: tall, strong, brave, and clever, he was tough and unscrupulous enough to rise to the top in a cut-throat profession. As a symbol of his sovereignty in the Hijaz, he brought with him a *kiswah*, an embroidered silk covering for the Ka'ba, which continued to be replaced annually from Cairo up to the early twentieth century. When he departed he left a *wali*, or representative, in Mecca to adjudicate between rival sharifs and to protect foreign pilgrims. Later Mamluk sultans maintained this supervision, sometimes replacing an insubordinate Grand Sharif with a more tractable cousin and bringing the culprit to live in honourable captivity in Cairo. In the fourteenth century Sultan Malik an-Nasr contemplated abolishing the sharifian dynasty altogether but was dissuaded by the learned *'ulama* of al-Azhar on the grounds of respect for the descendants of the Prophet.

The Hijaz prospered from the Egyptian connection. Under the protection of Mamluk arms, pilgrims poured in from all parts of the Muslim world – Moors from Spain and North Africa, Berbers from the Atlas and Libya, Negroes from the Sudan; the ancient semitic peoples of Syria, Palestine, and Iraq; Kurds, Turkomans, Mongols, Circassians; Persians, Baluchis, Afghanis, Punjabis; Sinhalese and Malays. Many pilgrims stayed to trade in the Holy Land, taking local wives and leaving their seed behind to create the rich mixture of races that so struck later travellers. Wealthy pilgrims endowed the mosques, wells, and caravan-serais, and presented gifts to the Sharif and the servants of the shrines. In 1325 a Negro emperor of Mandingo left a trail of gold behind him that was remembered for generations. Ships from India discharged cargoes of cotton and silk, spices, and gems in Jiddah, where customs duties were collected before transhipping the goods to Suez and the Mediterranean world. Coffee ships from Yemen and slave ships from Zanzibar arrived in season. Mecca was a principal mart for black slaves from Africa, both Negro and Ethiopian, the latter highly prized by the Arabs as concubines. So lucrative was the port trade of Jiddah that the Mamluks placed a representative there to supervise the collection of customs duties and pass on a part of them to Cairo. The sharifs often disputed the division of revenues, but they profited from direct grants and stipends from Egypt. When Sultan Kait Bey made the pilgrimage in 1480, Sharif Barakat acknowledged his sovereignty by presenting him with the keys of the Ka'ba and sending his own son and heir to Cairo as hostage in the Sultan's train. The once proud and isolated birthplace of Islam was thus snugly incorporated into an empire of slaves.

But this harmonious, if inverted, arrangement was about to be challenged once more by Christendom. Three centuries after the defeat of the Crusaders, the West again turned acquisitive eyes towards the East. Vasco da Gama's discovery of the sea route round the Cape of Good Hope brought Portuguese galleons directly into the Indian Ocean, by-passing the old trade routes through Arabia. Some historians date the decline of Middle Eastern economies from this discovery. After carving out a commercial empire in the Indies, the Portuguese turned back to try and wrest command over Arab waters. They seized Muslim ships on the high seas, attacked Arab ports, and built forts and colonies on the islands of the Persian Gulf. As devout Catholics, the Portuguese considered all Muslims not only as commercial rivals but as heretics to be exterminated in a perpetual crusade. The great Affonso d'Albuquerque, a hero to his countrymen, behaved with calculated ferocity towards the hated infidel. One of his schemes was to raid Medina, snatch the body of Muhammad from his tomb, and hold it to ransom against the return of the Holy Sepulchre to the Christians. Another was to divert the Nile through Christian Ethiopia, thus destroying Egypt. Luckily his dire imagination exceeded his power.

With the expansion of European navigation and trade, it was inevitable that restless, vagrant, or captive Christians should drift into the Red Sea and land on the Hijazi coast. From the sixteenth century onwards, growing numbers of *renegados* – the word was originally Portuguese – entered the Muslim world in search of wealth or adventure, in flight from troubles at home or at sea, or compelled by shipwreck or capture. Portuguese, Spanish, Greek, Italian, French, German, English, Scottish, Irish, Dutch, they turned up in unexpected places and roles, usually trading on their one qualification, a superior knowledge of arms or seamanship. Many of them 'turned Turk' or 'took the turban' in the parlance of the day, and some rose to positions of prominence in their new world, while others met an obscure death in forgotten battles.

If the story can be believed, a Portuguese sea captain wrecked on the coast of Yemen was one of the first Europeans to visit Medina and cross the Arabian peninsula. Thrown into prison in Yemen, he learned Arabic and became a hatmaker. Later he travelled with a caravan of Muslims to Medina, where he was overcome by religious fervour and publicly declared himself a Christian before the very tomb of Muhammad. Instead of granting him martyrdom there and then, the pilgrims were so impressed by his evident holiness that they helped him to set out across the desert for Persia. Clad in nothing but a loin-cloth, he nearly died of sunburn and thirst but was rescued by a caravan of Arabs and taken to Babylon. From there he made his way to Ormuz and back to Portugal, where he ended his days as a Franciscan monk. Was the whole episode a hallucination brought on by sunstroke, or merely a moral tale erected on the basis of a shipwrecked sailor's invention? It apparently satisfied sixteenth-century standards of credibility and was published as a true story in Albuquerque's *Commentaries*.

Ludovico da Varthema, an Italian renegade, provided the West with its first description of the Holy Cities and the pilgrimage. A true son of the Renaissance, he took the turban voluntarily, wore it with panache, and doffed it as easily as he put it on. After visiting Egypt, he joined the Mamluk corps in Damascus in 1503 and rode guard to a pilgrim caravan as a 'Mamaluchi renegado . . . in familiaritie and friendshyppe with a certayne capitayne Mamaluke'. (The English is that of Richarde Eden, 1576, in Hakluyt's *Voyages*.) The caravan, which consisted of some 40,000 men and 35,000 camels, was attacked by Bedouins more than once with great loss to the attackers but none to itself, as the Mamluks possessed firearms and gunpowder and the Arab tribes did not. For three days and nights the caravan toiled across the Great Nafud, a vast tongue of sand that arches across northern Arabia. Entering the Hijaz, it passed the mountain of the Jews which, although Varthema did not name it, was doubtless Khaybar, a dark forbidding fortress which for centuries had the reputation of being a refuge for Jewish exiles from Jerusalem. According to Varthema, the inhabitants 'wandred in that mountayne, scattered lyke wylde Goates or Prickettes [young bucks], yet durst they not come downe, partly for feare, and partly for hatred agaynst the Mahumetans. . . . They are circumcized, and deny not them selues to bee Iewes. If by chaunce, any Mahumetan come into theire handes, they flaye him alyue.' As the inhabitants stayed on their mountain, this must have been hearsay, as was the information that they were very short, 'fiue or sixe spannes' (a span was about nine inches), had high voices like women, and were black in colour, 'yet some blacker then other'. The Damascus caravan loaded 16,000 camels with water at the spring at the foot of the mountain, which enraged the inhabitants watching from the heights.

In Medina Varthema visited the Prophet's tomb and gave a somewhat inaccurate description of it. The temple, he said, was vaulted, about a hundred paces in length and four score in breadth; it was entered by two gates and borne up by four hundred columns of white brick; the interior was hung with three thousand lamps. (Varthema's figures are largely impressionistic.) The tomb itself was vaulted on every side, covered with silk, and entered by a narrow gate: 'within the sayde gate, is seene a Sepulchre, (that is) a digged place, where they say Mahumet is buried and his felowes, which are these, Nabi, Bubacar, Othomar, Aumar, and Fatoma; but Mahumet was theyre chiefe Captayne, and an Arabian borne.' This is hopelessly muddled: 'Nabi' is the Arabic word for prophet; 'Othomar' is probably 'Uthman, who is not buried there at all, though 'Bubacar' (Abu Bakr) and 'Aumar' ('Umar), the first two caliphs are. 'Fatoma' (Fatimah) has a tomb near her father Muhammad's, as well as one in the cemetery on the outskirts of town. But Varthema passed through the Holy Land with as much comprehension as a Turk at St Peter's, professing nothing but contempt for what he called 'the filthinesse, and lothesomenesse of the trumperyes, deceites, trifles, and hypocrises of the religion of Mahumet'.

Mecca he found 'very fayre and well inhabited', consisting of about six thousand houses 'as well buylded as ours, and some that cost three or foure thousande peeces of golde'. The ruler of Mecca, he noted, was of the race of Muhammad and subject to the Grand Sultan of Cairo, but there was a civil war on at the time among four brothers who fought to be lord of Mecca. The Holy Mosque reminded him of the Colosseum in Rome; that is, it consisted largely of a colonnade surrounding the Ka'ba. The water of Zamzam tasted to him of saltpetre, and he wondered at the pilgrims 'all wette from the headde to the foote, although they be apparelled with sylk. Then the dotying fooles dreame that they are cleane from all theyr synnes, and that theyr synnes are forgeuen them.' One detail which Varthema reported casts doubt on his credibility elsewhere: in a pen inside the Mosque he claimed to have seen two unicorns, dark bay in colour, resembling half-grown colts with heads like stags, legs like goats, and cloven hooves; he even measured the single horn each grew on its forehead.

Varthema followed the pilgrims to Mount Arafat outside the city and heard the qadi preach a sermon to the people below. And he attended the sacrifice at Mina where 'the butcherie sometyme so floweth with bloode that in one sacrifice are slayne aboue three thousande sheepe. They are slayne at the rysyng of the Sunne, and shortly after are distributed to the poore for God's sake.'

When the pilgrimage was over, Varthema sought to escape from the caravan and to proceed eastwards to India. He arranged with a Mamluk resident in Mecca that the latter should take his place in the caravan returning to Syria, while he himself hid in the Mamluk's house until he could join a group of Indian pilgrims leaving for Jiddah. Arriving in Jiddah by this stratagem, he hid himself among a crowd of poor pilgrims in the mosque, feigning illness to discourage inquisitive questions. But he looked about him, noting that the city had no walls but 'fayre houses, somewhat after the buyldyng of Italie' and 'great aboundaunce of all kynd of merchandies, by reason of resorte in maner of all nations thyther'. He described the climate and terrain in terms a visitor would recognize today: 'The soyle is vnfruitfull, and lacketh freshe water. The sea beateth agaynst the towne. . . . The heate is here so great, that men are in a maner dryed vp therewith. And therefor there is euer a great number of sicke folkes.'

After fifteen days Varthema found passage to Yemen and from there sailed on to Persia and Calcutta, where he served against the Portuguese as gunner to an Indian Muslim prince. However, he took the first opportunity to defect to the Christian fleet and thereafter fought against his former employer, being present at a naval battle in which Mamluk warships sent down the Red Sea joined with the Muslims of India against the Portuguese invaders. Varthema later returned to Europe where he was knighted for his services by the Portuguese.

But the Hijaz was soon to pass from the Mamluks to a new master. In 1517 Selim I, known in the West as 'the Grim', but to his own people as 'the Just' because of his suppression of the Shi-ites of Turkey, conquered Egypt and incorporated it into the Ottoman empire. The Grand Sharif Barakat I immediately sent his thirteen-year-old son to Cairo to present the keys of the Ka'ba to Selim and to obtain confirmation of his title. The Ottoman Porte replaced the Mamluks as masters of the Hijaz, bringing to it the benefits of greater protection from the Portuguese, greater security for the pilgrim routes, and the advantages of the larger trading area of the Ottoman empire. The Turkish Sultan's name was mentioned in public prayers, and the Sultan's gold endowed new schools, khans, and water channels. Selim's son, Sulayman the Magnificent, rebuilt and endowed the Holy Places. A Turkish *wali*, or representative, was sent to Jiddah to supervise the collection of revenues, but the money sent to Constantinople was amply replaced by the stipends paid to the Sharif and local officials. The Sharif's sons were now sent to Constantinople rather than to Cairo to complete their education and to stand hostage for their father's loyalty. On the strength of his friendship with the Sultan, the Grand Sharif dominated the desert tribes in his vicinity.

Although Constantinople was further away than Cairo and less able to interfere in local affairs, contingents of Turkish troops were stationed in the Hijaz, while others passed through on their way to Yemen and the Ottoman frontiers to the south. The Turkish soldiery, whose pay was nearly always in arrears, could be counted on to vent their anger on the local populace. In 1631 troops returning from defeat in Yemen mutinied in Mecca and Medina, seizing food supplies and looting the shops and homes. According to Muslim historians, the lustier soldiers raped every virgin and boy they could lay hands on, first forcing the victims to drink wine in order to ease entry. The Porte ordered fresh troops from Egypt to put down the revolt. One of the rebel leaders was let off as he had protected the women of the Grand Sharif. But another was paraded naked through the streets of Mecca seated backwards on a camel. He was then crucified while cuts in his arms and shoulders were stuffed with rags soaked in oil and set alight. Next he was cut down and dragged to the cemetery, where he was suspended from a post with his right hand and left foot transfixed by a hook. There he was left to curse and rage till he died. These grisly details were still the talk of Mecca when Burckhardt visited the city two centuries later.

In the cosmopolitan Ottoman world more and more Westerners came to the Hijaz, either as free men or slaves. A Portuguese slave was taken on the pilgrimage in 1565 and described it in the margins of an Arabic book now in the Vatican. Thirty years later an anonymous Englishman joined a caravan of pilgrims in Cairo and rode forty days to Medina. Early in the seventeenth century a young German named Hans Wild was captured by Turkish soldiers in Hungary, sold into slavery, and taken by his master to Mecca. A few years later a Venetian boy, Marco de Lombardo, was captured at sea on his uncle's ship, and after enslavement and conversion was taken to Mecca as a companion to his owner's son. All of these men returned to Europe with eye-witness reports of the pilgrimage and the sights and sounds of the Holy Cities. But the most informed and sympathetic account of the Muslim Holy Land was brought back by an Englishman, Joseph Pitts of Exeter.

The *Speedwell* was returning from a voyage to the West Indies and Newfoundland in 1679 when it was captured by Algerian pirates led by a Dutch renegade, who sold the entire crew in the slave market in Algiers. The fifteen-year-old cabin boy, Joseph Pitts, was bought by a rich merchant, who, though fond of the boy, thought it his duty to convert him to Islam. As Joseph resisted, the conversion was effected by repeated bastinados of the feet, while the 'patroon' rammed his heel into the young proselyte's mouth to stifle his cries. Taking the revenge of the weak, Joseph continued to read his Bible in private, eat pork whenever he could, and say his prayers in a state of ritual uncleanness. But he remained troubled by his apparent apostasy from 'the English religion' – for he despised the Papists even more than the Mohammedans.

As a converted Muslim the young Pitts was taken on the pilgrimage by his master. Arriving by ship at Jiddah, he found the climate so oppressive 'that people run from one side of the street to the other to get into the shadow', while he himself slept on a roof, wrapped in a wet sheet which he renewed several times during the night. Mecca he considered a place of 'no tolerable entertainment, were it not for the resort of many thousand Hagges, or pilgrims, on whose coming the whole dependence of the town (in a manner) is, for many shops are scarcely open all the year besides'.

The Holy Mosque reminded him of the Royal Exchange in London, but the Ka'ba was unique:

It is built with great stones, all smooth, and plain, without the least bit of carved work on it. It is covered all over from top to bottom with a thick sort of silk. Above the middle of the covering are embroidered all round letters of gold, the meaning of which I cannot well call to mind, but I think they were some devout expressions. . . . Near the lower end . . . are large brass rings fastened into it, through which passeth a great cotton rope; and to this the lower end of the covering is tacked.

He was impressed by the devotion of the pilgrims round the sacred edifice:

At the very first sight of the Beat-Allah [Bait Allah=House of God], the Hagges melt into tears. . . . And I profess I could not chuse but to admire to see these poor creatures so extraordinarily devout, and affectionate, when they were about these superstitions, and with what awe and trembling they were possessed; in so much that I could scarce forbear shedding tears, to see their zeal, though blind and idolatrous.

He found the water of Zamzam brackish but saw others 'drink of it unreasonably; by which means they are not only much purged, but their flesh breaks out in pimples; and this they call purging of their spiritual corruptions'. The pilgrims also bathed in the water, taking off their clothes and covering their lower parts with a thin wrapper while one of the well attendants poured five or six buckets over their heads. 'The person bathing may lawfully wash himself therewith above the middle, and not on his lower parts, because they account that they are not worthy, only letting the water take its way downwards.'

In Medina Pitts visited the Prophet's tomb and counted the lamps there, making them about a hundred, not the three thousand described by Varthema. They were kept alight by eunuchs, who also swept and cleaned the place and demanded alms of the pilgrims. The latter were permitted only to thrust their hands through the brass grate of the tomb and 'to petition the dead juggler, which they do with a wonderful deal of reverence, affection, and zeal'. 'My patroon', he added, 'had his silk handkerchief stole out of his bosom, while he stood at his devotion there.' Pitts thought very little of the morals of the Muslims in any case. ''Tis common for Men there to fall in love with Boys, as 'tis here in England to be in love with Women.'

After his return from the pilgrimage Joseph Pitts longed to see his home and family again. Back in Tunis he sought out the English consul and asked to be ransomed; but only £60 could be raised and his owner wanted £100. Later Pitts changed hands, and his new master, a kindly man, released him, a meritorious act in Islam. Although he was now free to go where he pleased, Pitts remained voluntarily in his former owner's service as a member of the crew of a merchant ship. But his parents were growing old, and at the age of twenty-seven he again approached an English consul, this time at Smyrna, where his ship was docked. The consul arranged for him to board a French ship bound for Italy, and an old acquaintance, a Cornish merchant established at Smyrna, gave him £4 for the passage. He was still beset by doubts, however, and seriously debated whether to stay with his master and Islam. But putting the devil behind him, he doffed his Turkish clothes and went aboard the French ship 'apparell'd as an Englishman, with my beard shaven, a *campaign periwig*, and *cane* in my hand' (the excited italics are his). When the ship reached Leghorn, he leapt out to kiss Christian soil and proceeded overland on foot to Holland to take ship for England.

His arrival at Harwich showed him that life in England could be as harsh as that in Turkish lands. As he sailed into port a press gang seized him in the King's name and, after a night in Colchester jail, he was shipped out to a waiting man-of-war to serve in the King's navy. In desperation he managed to send a letter to Sir William Falkener, a Turkey merchant he had known in Smyrna, who was then in London. Sir William used his influence at the Admiralty and got his young countryman's release. Pitts 'rejoice[d] exceedingly and could not forbear leaping upon the deck' at news of his deliverance. He went first to London to thank his benefactor, then proceeded to Exeter where he had a tearful reunion with his old father, his mother having died the previous year. He was relieved to find that his apostasy was not held against him and indeed ended his account of his sojourn among the Turks with an invocation to the Trinity, a pointed rejection of the rigorous monotheism of Islam.

The Ottoman world in which Joseph Pitts moved so easily seemed as self-contained and confident as that which he left and returned to in England. Yet the Ottoman empire had already begun the slow irreversible decline that was to end with its disappearance in the twentieth century. The defeat of Turkish arms at Vienna in 1683 halted expansion to the west, while in the east the success of European merchant venturers drove the Turks out of the Indian Ocean. Yemen rid itself of the last Ottoman troops by the mid-seventeenth century, and in Egypt the Mamluks began to revive and to dispute the Sultan's authority. Even the Sharif of Mecca felt strong enough to resist the Turkish *wali* in Jiddah and to frustrate Constantinople's attempts to purge the Holy Cities of heretics. The Sharif could afford to take a more independent line because the prosperity created by European traders in the Indies began to wash into the Red Sea. Dutch, English, and French ships discharged their cargoes of India goods in Jiddah; rich Indian princes lavished gifts on the Sharif and the Holy Places; and Eastern pilgrims came in increasing numbers under European protection of the sea routes. The Sultan's name was still mentioned in prayers; Ottoman troops kept the peace on the caravan routes; and subsidies from the Porte helped to support the Holy Cities. But the Hijaz looked increasingly towards the East to offset the influence of Constantinople. It was an East transformed by its own involvement with the West, especially the rival empires of England and France. Even the Muslim Holy Land could not remain free of entanglement in that world-embracing conflict.

CHAPTER 2
Western Intrusions

On the last day of the year 1600 Queen Elizabeth I of England granted a charter to divers of her well-beloved subjects to undertake trading voyages to the East Indies. The first four ships of what was to become the Honourable East India Company sailed from Woolwich early in 1601. They were enjoined to avoid the coast of India, which was considered to be a Portuguese preserve, but on the voyage the English captain was not averse to seizing a Portuguese galleon in the Indian Ocean and trading the prize of plate and jewels for a million pounds of pepper, which he brought back to London. It was not till the Company's third voyage in 1607 that India – and incidentally Arabia – was the goal of the venture. The Company instructed its servants to buy 'oliphauntes teeth' at Mozambique and two or three tons of aloes and ambergris on the island of Socotra off the coast of Arabia. They were also to find a pilot at Socotra to take them to Aden, where coffee had recently become a desired object of trade. The ships, however, did not reach Socotra till spring when the monsoons prevented their going to Aden. The commencement of Anglo-Arabian relations was therefore postponed.

When the first English ships appeared in the Red Sea they did little except disrupt Portuguese shipping and annoy the Turks. In 1610 Sir Henry Middleton, commanding the hopefully named *Trade's Increase*, failed to obtain the Grand Mughal's consent to trade in India and turned back to the Red Sea to seek revenge against the Portuguese. Calling at Mocha, he was detained by the governor, who had orders from Constantinople to 'captivate all Christians who come into these seas', as the Porte was determined to preserve the Muslim monopoly of the Red Sea trade. Middleton and thirty-four of his crew were sent to San'a under guard. A boy from the ship fell ill and apostatized, and one officer escaped, but the rest remained prisoners for six weeks, till they bribed an official to take them back to Mocha. There they were held another thirty days till Middleton escaped to his ship in an empty cask and threatened to shell the city if his men were not released. Before clearing the port the English taught the Turks a lesson by bombarding the town.

The Grand Mughal began to take the English seriously when he saw that, though they had not much to offer in trade, they had the power to damage the Portuguese. He therefore granted them a *firman*, or decree, to trade in his domains. But when four English ships appeared off Surat in 1612, they had to fight their way through a Portuguese blockade of six galleons and fifty smaller craft; several of the enemy were disabled or sunk, while the rest fled, a blow from which Portuguese India never recovered. The Grand Mughal was delighted: unable to control the seas himself, he was concerned for the safe passage of his Muslim subjects to Mecca. The religiously indifferent English were preferable to the crusading Portuguese. English traders were made welcome throughout the Mughal empire.

But the English were not to have it all their own way in India. In 1664 a new rival sailed over the horizon, the Compagnie des Indes Orientales, chartered by Louis XIV. At first the French avoided challenging the English in India. After trying unsuccessfully to found a colony in Madagascar, they succeeded in doing so on two islands of the Indian Ocean, which they named Bourbon and Ile-de-France (later to be known as Réunion and Mauritius). When they acquired Pondicherry, south of Madras, they traded discreetly to avoid offending the English.

The French were not slow in turning to Arabia. From the early years of the eighteenth century a company of merchants from St Malo in Brittany sent ships to Mocha in search of coffee. On the second voyage the French captain received an urgent request from the Imam of San'a to send a physician to treat an abscess. Eager to serve the ruler of the world's only source of the precious new beverage, the captain dispatched his ship's surgeon, Barbier, accompanied by a Major de la Grélaudière of Pondicherry. The two Frenchmen were the first Europeans to penetrate the interior of Yemen voluntarily and to report first-hand on the cultivation of the coffee berry.

The Mughal empire at this period was breaking up under attack by the warlike Sikhs and Marathas, and the English and French were picking up the pieces. For a time they avoided open confrontation, playing a deadly game in which they attacked each other's local allies but not each other. But peace between the rival companies could not last when their nations went to war. During the War of the Austrian Succession (1740–48), the French seized Madras and an English fleet blockaded Pondicherry. The result was a stalemate, and when the war ended, all conquests were restored – St Louis in America to the French, Madras in India to the English. Blood had been drawn, and though France and England kept the peace elsewhere, their agents in India now engaged in open warfare. When the two nations again declared war in 1756, Clive, the English commander in India, seized all French possessions there, but this time, when the treaty of peace again decreed restoration, it was found that all French stations in India had been discreetly razed.

Ripples from these distant disturbances reached the Hijaz. By their conquest of Surat the English stopped the flow of treasure, amounting to 5,000 rupees a year, granted by the Grand Mughal to the Sharif of Mecca. The Sharif complained to Constantinople, and for a time the port of Jiddah was closed to English ships. But in the long run the trade from India carried in English vessels was worth more than the Mughal subvention. By the middle of the eighteenth century India ships commanded by English officers were a common sight in the Red Sea and English traders a fixture in the ports of Jiddah and Aden. The pursuit of trade was not without its dangers, however; in 1743 fourteen English traders from India were killed in Jiddah during a mutiny of the vizir's guards. But the English persevered, not only for trade but also for the sake of communications with India, for it was beginning to be realized in both London and Paris that whoever controlled the overland route across Ottoman domains between Europe and India had the advantage in peace and war.

The quest for trade and empire that propelled Western Europeans into every part of the globe was accompanied by another urge, that of intellectual curiosity. The Age of Imperialism was also the Age of the Enlightenment, when the Western imagination took the world for its oyster. Arabia had always fascinated the West as the source of some of its oldest and most fundamental beliefs. Originally it had been Arabia the Blest, a place of fabulous wealth, of scented groves and carefree people, the haunt of the phoenix and the unicorn, perhaps the site of the Garden of Eden. To Biblical scholars it was the original home of the Hebrews, the fount of the Semitic language, and the primitive source of Judaism and Christianity. But the source had been polluted by the heresy of Islam, and to Arabia the Blest had succeeded Arabia the Curst. Dante placed Muhammad and 'Ali in the ninth circle of Hell among the Sowers of Discord and visited on them the most revolting punishment he ever devised. If Africa was the Dark Continent of the European mind, Arabia was lit by a fitful, lurid light. Varthema and Pitts dispelled a few of the phantoms, but they had both been encumbered by religious prejudice. It was not till the eighteenth century that the light of reason was focused on Arabia.

The intellectual elucidation of Arabia began in an unexpected quarter. Shortly after the start of the new year 1761, a group of scholars from the frozen north of Europe boarded a Danish man-of-war bound for Constantinople and the East. The expedition had been commissioned by King Frederick V of Denmark, who, wishing to contribute to the sum of human knowledge, had agreed to finance the first scientific exploration of a part of the Arabian peninsula. It was typical of the period that the original impetus had come from a theologian, Professor Johann Michaelus of Göttingen University, who had suggested that two missionaries trained in oriental languages should be sent to southern Arabia to investigate certain linguistic problems concerning the interpretation of the Bible. The first two men appointed to the expedition were both sons of clergymen and themselves students of Hebrew and theology. Christian Von Haven, a Dane, was twenty-six at the time of his appointment, but insisted on continuing his studies, to which he now added Arabic, for another five years. Peter Forsskal, though five years younger, was also well grounded in sacred subjects, but to them he added the newly burgeoning science of botany which he studied under the great Linnaeus, whom he idolized. The third man to join the expedition was of a different social class and intellectual stamp. Carsten Niebuhr, a German born in Friesland and the youngest of the group, was not a gentleman but the son of a poor farmer. Because of his poverty he had studied practical subjects, mathematics, surveying, astronomy, and, after being asked to join the expedition, mechanics and geography. He too tried to learn Arabic but was so bad at it that he gave it up.

A physician was added to the group for its protection, Christian Carl Kramer, son of a butler and, on the strength of his only publication, *Canaries and their Care*, considered a zoologist. An artist, George Wilhelm Baurenfeind, was named to record the scenes of the expedition's travels and the specimens of nature and art it was to collect. The party was completed by a servant, an ex-hussar named Berggren. It was an ill-assorted band, and rifts began to appear even before the six men left Denmark, with Von Haven and Forsskal competing for leadership and the support of the others.

The intellectual establishment of northern Europe took a keen interest in the expedition. The faculties of the Danish, Swedish, and German universities submitted questions for the travellers to investigate, particularly in the natural sciences and concerning the customs and habits of the Arabs. But it was fatality that was to change the results, if not the aims, of the expedition from theological and linguistic matters to the physical

33

and social sciences. For despite the years of preparation, royal patronage, and the support of the intellectual community, the expedition was to end in tragedy. Of the six men, five died in the East and the sixth nearly did, victims not of Arab hostility, shipwreck, thirst, or starvation, but of disease. The sole survivor was the farmer-surveyor and mechanic Carsten Niebuhr, and, except for fragmentary diaries and a few natural objects collected by the others, it is from his account that all our knowledge of the expedition comes. Conceived in the spirit of Biblical exegesis, the expedition foreshadowed modern scientific and sociological preoccupations. So modest, practical, and objective were the observations of the non-academic Niebuhr that they became the basis of all subsequent explorations of Arabia.

The goal of the expedition was Yemen, but Niebuhr diligently collected facts about the whole of the Arabian peninsula. Quarrelling violently among themselves – at one point they accused Von Haven of planning to poison them all – the Danes took two years to reach the Red Sea, stopping first in Constantinople and Egypt. In Cairo they donned Turkish dress to avoid curiosity and hostility, but at no time did they pretend to be Muslims. Their passage through the Red Sea was alarming. The pilot of their ship was frequently drunk and asked them daily for a quarter bottle of brandy 'to clear his sight'. Niebuhr had great difficulty in persuading the master of the vessel to remove a large magnet which he had placed between his two compasses so as 'to restore . . . their magnetic virtues to the needles'. In the cabin next to that of the Danes, women and slaves kept up a continual chatter and twice allowed their drying linen to catch fire; the second time the master sent an officer to beat them, which brought screams and then twenty-four hours of silence. In another cabin a rich black eunuch was going to Mecca with his seraglio, 'useless as it was to him'. Niebuhr took a lively interest in sex: he peeked through a chink between the cabins to watch the women bathing, and in Cairo he had closely examined the circumcised pudendum of a slave-girl.

The Danes kept aloof from the other passengers, who were pilgrims and might take offence at the presence of Christians. However, Forsskal foretold an eclipse of the sun to the captain and was thereafter regarded as a learned astrologer and physician, the two professions going hand in hand in the East. When the other passengers pestered him for remedies against various ills he sensibly recommended exercise and diet. When one man complained that he could not see in the dark, Forsskal advised him to light a candle, making the others laugh and securing their approval.

At Yanbu', where some of the pilgrims disembarked, three of the Danes landed to see the town, carrying their swords. An Arab gave them the *sala'am alaikum*, but on learning that they were Christians railed at 'the insolence and audacity of these infidels, who dared to wear arms in Arabia'. But no one seconded him, and they returned safely to the ship. After passing Cape Wardan the pilgrims donned the *ihram*, a white seamless garment enjoined on all pilgrims entering the Holy Land, and the crew took up a collection to mark the happy occasion, afterwards throwing the box overboard but keeping the money.

Approaching Jiddah, the Danes felt a strong apprehension of ill treatment from the inhabitants, recalling the insult at Yanbu' and the contempt shown towards Christians in Cairo. But they were agreeably surprised, for as Niebuhr later remarked, 'We were delighted to find the Arabs more civilised the further we proceeded from Europe.' The citizens of Jiddah were accustomed to seeing Christian merchants in European dress and took little notice of the newcomers. They were free to go anywhere in the city and to enter the markets and coffee-houses, so long as they kept away from the Mecca gate.

Jiddah was in a decayed state. The walls were so ruinous that a man could ride a horse through them in many places, and the guns served only to return the salutes of ships in the harbour. The town was nearly destitute of water, with nothing to drink except what was brought by camels from the hills. The country round about was sandy and barren; according to tradition it had not changed since the Creation, the tomb of Eve on the shore being pointed out as evidence of this. But the scientific Niebuhr noted coral rock at some distance inland and deduced that the sea had receded to expose it. Several fine houses were built of this coral.

The Danes carried letters of recommendation from various notables in Constantinople and Cairo to their counterparts in Jiddah, including the pasha sent by the Porte to supervise the collection of duties and his lieutenant. The Greek goldsmith of the Grand Sharif had been given orders to help them, and through this man they were provided with a comfortable house for the whole of their stay. On hearing of the arrival of such learned men in his domain, the Sharif directed his goldsmith to put a question to them: a brother of the Sharif was advancing with an army to attack Mecca, and the Sharif wanted to know whether he or his brother would win. Von Haven tactfully replied that whichever of the brothers bore the greatest resemblance to Hasan, founder of their line, would be victorious. The answer satisfied the Grand Sharif, who, in the event, retained his throne.

The visitors were politely received by the notables of Jiddah, particularly the pasha's lieutenant, an intelligent man, who asked them questions about the manners and customs of Europe. 'We communicated to him and his friends,' Niebuhr remarked, 'more just and favourable ideas of Europeans, than they seemed to have entertained. The Arabs consider us in the same light in which we regard the Chinese. They esteem themselves the more enlightened and ingenious people; and think they do us great honour, when they rank us in second place.' In some respects Niebuhr himself thought the Arabs superior to Europeans. 'No two things,' he said, 'can differ more than the education of the Arabs and the Europeans. The former strive to hasten the age of maturity, as the latter retard it. The Arabs are never children, but many Europeans continue children all their life.' Coming from a man of the Enlightenment, this was high praise.

Niebuhr constantly delights by his cool and refreshing observations on the Arabs. Although proud of being a European and a Christian, he did not feel the need to denigrate other races and religions. Contrary to his expectations he found the Arabs tolerant in religious matters.

I never saw that the Arabs had any hatred of those of a different religion. They, however, regard them with the same contempt with which Christians look down upon the Jews of Europe. . . . This progress towards general toleration preserves the Arabs from the rage of making proselytes. They seek neither to entice nor to constrain any person, except some times their young slaves, whom they compel to embrace Mahometanism.

The authorities did not even welcome all converts, especially the renegades. Niebuhr gathered information from several Dutch and French renegades about the interior of Arabia and had a low opinion of them.

The converts most commonly offer themselves as deserters from the crews of European ships, who take this shift to escape punishment. As they are known to be mostly very bad subjects, [the Arab] government allows them a very scanty pension, scarcely sufficient for their maintenance. . . . They are not confined, either from intercourse with Christians, or from taking voyage into distant countries. We had in our service in Arabia a French renegade, who, when he left us, went to India.

Nowhere was Niebuhr's independence of judgment so clearly shown as when correcting European ideas of Arab sexuality.

The Europeans are mistaken in thinking that the state of marriage is so different among the Musselmans from what it is with the Christian nations.

36

I could not discern any such difference in Arabia. The women of that country seem to me as free as those of Europe can possibly be. . . . Polygamy is permitted, indeed, among Mahometans, and the delicacy of our ladies is shocked at this idea; but the Arabians rarely avail themselves of marrying four lawful wives, and entertaining at the same time any number of female slaves. None but rich voluptuaries marry so many wives, and their conduct is blamed by all sober men. Men of sense, indeed, think this privilege rather troublesome than convenient.

As for the ease of Muslim divorce, 'Only profligate and impudent men, who have married without consideration, will divorce their wives for slight causes.' Niebuhr scoffed at stories told of the marks of virginity expected in a young bride. 'In cases of such an incident, a son-in-law forces an addition to the dowry from his father-in-law, threatening to send his daughter home again, although he never actually does so.'

The Danes waited in Jiddah more than a month for a coffee ship to take them to Yemen. During this time they investigated the government and trade of the city, the port for Mecca and Tayif. The Grand Sharif was represented there by a vizir, a member of his family, who directed the affairs of all the Sharif's subjects living there. But on the all-important point of revenues from customs duties, the vizir shared authority with the pasha sent out from Constantinople, and frequent disputes arose. The trade of Jiddah would have been trifling if it were not for the ships from India, which were obliged to discharge their cargoes there to be reloaded aboard ships from Suez. Customs dues were fixed at ten per cent of value, but this was arbitrarily estimated by the customs officers, so that the duty paid was usually higher. The English were given more favourable treatment than other nations and paid only eight per cent; they were also allowed to pay in goods, while others had to pay in money. The government was always short of funds and sometimes forced the merchants to advance duties on the following year's shipment. The English refused to do this and were in constant conflict with the authorities. One year an English ship from Surat was driven by winds north of Jiddah and proceeded to Suez, where it discharged its cargo; when it returned to Jiddah the following year, the master was thrown into prison and obliged to pay the full dues on his previous cargo.

The Hijaz lived almost entirely on the revenues from customs and depended on Egypt for its supplies of corn, rice, lentils, sugar, and oil, and for all goods imported from Europe. The only local exports were almonds from Tayif and balm of Mecca gathered from wild plants and used universally as a medicine.

37

Although confined to the port, Niebuhr gathered as much information as he could about the interior of Arabia from many sources, both Arab and renegade. Many of the themes of Arabian life now familiar to the West, were introduced by him, including that of the noble, freedom-loving Bedouin. 'The poverty of the wandering Arabs,' he wrote, 'is plainly voluntary; they prefer liberty to wealth, pastoral simplicity to a life of restraint and toil, which might procure them a greater variety of gratifications.' He allowed that their reputation for robbery was well earned, but he saw their point of view. 'Their pillaging expeditions are commonly considered by themselves as lawful hostilities against enemies who would defraud them of their dues, or against rival tribes, who had undertaken to protect these illegal traders.' Besides, 'the Arabian robbers are not cruel, and do not murder those they rob, unless when travellers stand upon their defensive, and happen to kill a Bedouin, whose death the others are eager to revenge'. Bedouin vengeance, however, was a terrible thing. Their honour 'requires an even greater number of victims. . . . Nothing but blood can wash away the reproach; and not only the blood of the offender, but that of all the males of his family . . . This detestable custom is so expressly forbidden in the Quran, that I should not have been persuaded of its existence, had I not seen instances of it.' But, he added characteristically, 'Men, indeed, act everywhere in direct contradiction to the principles of religion.'

Among the lore that Niebuhr picked up from the interior of Arabia was the first news of the Wahhabi movement to reach Western ears. 'Some time since,' he wrote prophetically, 'a new religion sprang up in the province of El Ared [part of Najd]. It has already produced a revolution in the government of Arabia, and will probably hereafter influence the state of this country still farther.' The Wahhabis, he noted, 'resemble the other Arabs in their moral qualities; they are at once robbers and hospitable . . . of a very warlike character, and are constantly in arms. . . . [But their] Schieks, who had hitherto been almost constantly at war among themselves, were now reconciled by the mediation of Abd ul Wahhab, and agree to undertake nothing in future without consulting their apostle.' Niebuhr recognized the true spirit of the movement, which others took to be anti-Islamic. 'The new religion of Abd ul Wahhab deserves . . . to be regarded as a reformation of Mahometanism, reducing it back to its original simplicity.'

The new religion, or rather the reformation of the old, had been germinating in the fastness of Najd for the past quarter of a century. If the tenets of the sect were simple, its founder was not. Far from being a

38

rough, unlettered Bedu, he was one of the most learned men of his time and place. Born in the Najd town of 'Uyainah around 1705, Muhammad 'Abd al-Wahhab first studied the Law at Medina, where his teachers thought they detected signs of heresy in his views. He then spent many years as a wandering scholar – in Basra, Baghdad, Kurdistan, Isfahan, and Qum – marrying a rich wife and for a time embracing the mystic system of the Sufis. In Qum he returned to the orthodox doctrines of the Hanbali school of Law and especially to the teachings of the thirteenth-century theologian, Ibn Taimiyah.

After two decades of wandering, he returned to 'Uyainah and began to preach a return to the practice and beliefs of the time of Muhammad and the generation of Muslims following his death. All knowledge not based on the Quran or the *sunna*, traditions of the Prophet, was suspect. 'Innovations', a key word in his programme, chiefly designating the veneration of saints, were strictly forbidden. This practice detracted from the unique One-ness of God, so the faithful were forbidden to invoke the names of saints in prayer, make vows to them or visit their tombs. The mystic interpretation of the Quran as developed by the Sufis was also forbidden. Predestination, the absolute non-existence of free will, was an article of faith. Public prayers at set times of day were compulsory for all adult males, and alcohol, tobacco, music, even coffee for a time, as well as the wearing of silk and gold, were proscribed. All Muslims who failed to follow these precepts were condemned as polytheists and liable to punishment, usually whipping, but in flagrant cases death. The affinities with Calvinism made Muhammad 'Abd al-Wahhab's Unitarianism attractive to many European protestants, including Niebuhr.

It did not, however, appeal to the people of 'Uyainah, who drove the reformer and his family out of their home. They fled to the nearby town of Dar'iyah, where the harsh but bracing doctrine of 'Abd al-Wahhab was given a hearing and welcome. Muhammad ibn Sa'ud, the chief of Dar'iyah, made a pact with the preacher to spread the Unitarian creed throughout the neighbouring territories, by force if necessary. If this plan succeeded, the House of Sa'ud was to exercise secular power, while that of 'Abd al-Wahhab would prevail in religion. The compact between the two men, renewed by their descendants and reinforced by inter-marriage among their descendants, was to be a driving force in much of later Saudi Arabian history.

Within a year almost all the inhabitants of Dar'iyah (there were only seventy houses) had accepted the new creed; four families who refused were forced to leave. Muhammad 'Abd al-Wahhab built a mosque with a floor of rough gravel on which his followers willingly kneeled and prostrated themselves. All the rules and proscriptions of the new religion were enforced by the House of Sa'ud, and condign punishment consisting of so many lashes was publicly laid on offenders after the Friday midday prayers. Alms collected from all believers were used to support the government.

Muhammad ibn Sa'ud trained his men in the use of firearms and built up a small army for propagating the creed. The old traditions of desert warfare were sharpened by the edge of faith. Wherever they defeated a village or tribe, the Wahhabis built a fort, garrisoned it with the faithful, and installed a mufti and a qadi to instruct the people in Unitarianism. In 1766 the religious authorities of Mecca summoned a Wahhabi delegation to be examined for heresy, but the Wahhabis were exonerated. By the end of the eighteenth century, after some three decades of conquest and proselytizing, the greater part of the interior of Arabia submitted to the Unitarian faith. For the first time since the early days of Islam, Najd was governed in an orderly fashion. As Niebuhr percipiently remarked, 'Experience will here show, whether a religion so stripped of every thing that might serve to strike the senses, can maintain its ground among so rude and ignorant a people as the Arabs.'

When the coffee ships appeared at Jiddah and discharged their fragrant cargo, Niebuhr and his companions sailed for Yemen, where they found nearly complete freedom to scramble over the hills collecting plants and mineral specimens, sketching and coolly noting the customs and habits of the natives. Had it not been for the illnesses that systematically carried off five of its six members, the expedition would have been deemed a great success. But the collections were lost or left to moulder in the storerooms of the northern universities, and the two Christian humanists Von Haven and Forsskal never completed their reports. Although Niebuhr incorporated many of their observations in his own account, Europe's first systematic and scholarly view of Arabia was seen largely through the down-to-earth eyes of a poor farmer's son from Friesland.

In 1769, six years after the Danes left Jiddah, a traveller of a different stamp blew into port. James Bruce of Kinnaird, a Scottish laird and lately His Majesty's consul in Algiers, was on his way to Ethiopia to seek the source of the Blue Nile. Having sailed from Cairo to the First Cataract, he had crossed the Eastern Desert to Qusair on the Red Sea, whence he embarked on further explorations. His mission was also scientific in a sense, for he constantly took soundings, shot the stars, collected mineral and botanical specimens, and kept a detailed journal. But he claimed to have been commissioned by King George III to make his voyages, and one can detect a political flavour, a whiff of the age of imperialism, in his attitude. Like most important travellers of the period he carried letters of recommendation from such powerful personages as the Ottoman Sultan and Ali Bey, viceroy of Egypt, which served as passports and gave the bearer protection against ill-treatment by local officials.

Bruce was a very superior person, immensely rich, over six feet tall, red-haired, with the face (to judge by a portrait in Edinburgh) of a petulant baby. He believed passionately in degree and was precise about his own rank in the social scale. An English gentleman, as he called himself despite his Scottish origin, was equal to a Turkish bey or an Arabian prince. He treated most natives as barbarians beneath contempt and operated on the principle that the best form of defence was attack. His behaviour was often that of a one-man gunboat.

Bruce's arrival at Yanbu' was typical. He knew the town by reputation: 'The inhabitants of Yambo are deservedly reckoned the most barbarous in the Red Sea, and the janissaries [Turkish infantry] keep pace with them, in every kind of malice and violence.' Hearing shots fired on shore and learning that the janissaries and townspeople had been fighting each other for a week, he ordered the ship to drop anchor in deep water and did not go ashore the first day. 'I was very unwilling to interfere,' he remarked, 'wishing that they might all have the leisure to extirpate one another, if possible.' That evening the captain of the port came aboard accompanied by two janissaries, who demanded gunpowder, tobacco, and spirits, all of which Bruce declined to give them. When he asked how many had been killed in the fighting, they answered indifferently, not many, a hundred a day more or less, chiefly Arabs. They insisted that the ship be brought into port, but Bruce flatly refused, threatening to disarm them and carry them off to Jiddah if they did not leave. The janissaries blustered and demanded to know whether Bruce was a Mamluk, a Turk, or an Arab. The Scot, who spoke Arabic and was dressed like a Turkish sailor, told them they would know on the morrow who he was. After they had left, more firing was heard on shore and lights were seen all over the town. Bruce ordered the ship to shift anchor a few hundred yards, away from the town batteries.

The captain of the port came again during the night, this time accompanied by three officers, 'genteel young men', who asked Bruce if by any chance he was the physician of Ali Bey, whom they were expecting. He admitted modestly to that office (like most European travellers of the time, he carried an extensive pharmacopoeia with which he doctored the natives wholesale). They invited him to come ashore and wait upon their masters, two young agas, slaves of the Sharif, who ruled the town. The genteel young officers told him that the affray in town was over as both sides had used up their ammunition. The older men of both parties had met and decided that the quarrel was no one's fault, but that of a camel which had cursed the Sultan and the Sharif and had threatened to burn the agas' palace and to destroy a shipment of wheat destined for Mecca. They had led the scape-camel out of town, upbraiding him with his sins and crimes while each man thrust a lance through the contumacious beast, cursing him as he died.

Next morning, well armed, Bruce and his men went ashore to call on the two agas, whom they found seated on a dais covered with Persian carpets and surrounded by the principal citizens. The agas behaved with great politeness and enquired whether it was true that the Bey of Egypt was ready to send an army to the Hijaz to punish the people for insubordination. Bruce let them believe he was Ali Bey's man of confidence and so played on their fears that they provided him with a good house and guards. The qadi of Medina, who was in Yanbuʻ on business, came to examine Bruce's scientific instruments, as he had been educated in Constantinople and was 'master of Euclid as far as plain trigonometry'. He confided in Bruce that it was impossible to tell which of the two young agas was the more base and profligate and related how, a short time before, a Frank (European) travelling to India was robbed, thrown into prison, and never seen again. Bruce gave the qadi this message for the agas: 'I now tell them, and the people of Yambo, all and each of them, they had better be in their bed sick of the plague, than touch a hair of my dog, if I had one.'

That night Bruce received an unexpected visit from one of the young profligates.

After many pretended complaints of sickness, and injunctions of secrecy, he at last *modestly* requested me to give him some *slow poison*, that might kill his brother, without suspicion, and after some time should elapse. I told him, such proposals were not to be made to a man like me; that all the gold, and all the silver in the world, would not engage me to poison the poorest vagrant in the street, supposing it never was to be suspected, nor known but to my own heart. All he said was, 'Then your manners are not the same as ours.'—I answered drily, 'Mine, I thank God, are not,' and we parted.

42

Continuing his voyage, Bruce sailed from Yanbu' to Jiddah. He slept very little on the way, having an 'aguish disorder', and in dress and cleanliness resembled a Turkish seaman. Going directly to Bengal House where the English merchants lodged, he encountered a fellow Scot, actually a relative of his, leaning over a staircase leading to his apartment. Bruce saluted him by name. The relative, who completely failed to recognize Bruce, fell into a violent rage; calling Bruce a '*villain, thief* and *renegado rascal*', he threatened to throw the upstart Turk down the stairs. Bruce left without reply, thinking, 'If these are their Indian manners, I shall keep my name and situation to myself while I am at Jiddah.' He stood in no need of his countrymen, having a credit of 1,000 sequins upon the vizir of Jiddah. He allowed himself, however, to be taken to the rooms of an English trader, Captain Thornhill of the *Bengal Merchant*. The captain saw at once that Bruce was British and a sick man, and offered to take him aboard his ship. Bruce declined this invitation but accepted a room in Bengal House. While it was being prepared he went into the courtyard where India goods were being exposed for sale. As Bruce ate his dinner there, several Englishmen off the ships came to look at him, 'and I heard it, in general, agreed among them, that I was a very thief-like fellow, and certainly a Turk, and d—n them if they would like to fall into my hands'.

Meanwhile at the customs house, the vizir of Jiddah, ignoring the protests of Bruce's servants, was breaking into the visitor's luggage for want of a key. The first thing he saw was a *firman* from the Sultan, magnificently written, powdered with gold dust and wrapped in green taffeta; then a white satin bag containing a letter to the Khan of Tartary from the French consul at Smyrna; next a green and gold silk bag with a letter to the vizir himself from Ali Bey 'written with all the superiority of a Prince to a slave', and telling him plainly that the merchants had complained that they had been plundered, terrified, and detained at Jiddah and hinting that if any such thing happened to Bruce, 'he would send and punish the affront at the very gates of Mecca'.

The vizir quickly nailed up the boxes, ordered his horses, and 'attended by a number of naked blackguards (whom they call soldiers) he came down to Bengal House, on which the whole factory took alarm. About twenty-six years before, the English traders from India in Jiddah, fourteen in number, were all murdered, sitting at dinner, by a mutiny of these wild people.' The vizir demanded to see the English nobleman and was told that no one had seen him, but that his servant was drinking coffee in the courtyard. The vizir and his men crowded into the yard and

43

asked the ruffianly fellow sipping coffee, where was his master? In heaven, the man replied. Who was the owner of the baggage? Bruce modestly admitted ownership. Then why, asked the exasperated vizir, did he appear in such dress? 'I believe no prudent man could dress better,' Bruce replied, 'considering the voyage I have made. But, besides, you did not leave it in my power, as every article, but what I have on me, has been these four hours at the customs-house awaiting your pleasure.' Pleased by the astonishment caused by his translation from low to high estate, Bruce went up to Captain Thornhill to reveal himself and apologize. The captain laughed, and thereafter they 'lived in great friendship and confidence'.

Bruce was amazed by the trust with which business deals were conducted in Jiddah. Nine India ships were in port at the time with cargoes worth as much as £200,000. A Turkish merchant living at Mecca offered to buy the cargoes and had them carried off beyond the reach of the English traders. Meanwhile, two Indian brokers, neither Christians nor Muslims, settled the price, one representing the Turkish buyer, one the English captain. The brokers sat with their hands covered by a shawl; without speaking they fingered each other's hands under the shawl and in about twenty minutes the bargain was made without a word having been spoken or pen put to paper. But that was not all. A Moor, with nothing to support him but his character, became responsible for payment. He delivered a number of coarse hempen bags containing coins, each bag marked with the amount of its contents and tied with a string bearing the Moor's seal. The bags were received for the amount marked without being opened, and back in India were current for the value marked on them as long as the hemp lasted.

In the leisurely fashion of his time, Bruce decided to explore the length of the Red Sea before going on to Africa. As he sailed out of the harbour of Jiddah the English ships at anchor hoisted their colours and saluted him with eleven guns each. All, that is, except the vessel commanded by his Scottish relation; he showed his colours but did not fire a gun, only standing on deck and shouting through his trumpet, 'Captain — wishes Mr Bruce a good voyage.' Seizing his trumpet, Bruce replied, '"Mr Bruce wishes Captain — a speedy and perfect return to his understanding," a wish, poor man, that has not yet been accomplished, and very much to my regret, it does not appear probable that it ever will.' Sailing southwards, Bruce broached a jar of brandy that he had kept expressly 'to drink the King's health on arriving at his dominions, the Indian Ocean'. With this grand imperial gesture, the Laird of Kinnaird turned back, leaving the Arab world, to plunge into the nightmare world of the Christian kingdom of Ethiopia.

The arrogant Englishmen of Bengal House sometimes met resistance as they pushed their profitable way into the Red Sea. Several of them complained to Bruce that they were oppressed by the authorities of Jiddah, with duty and fees raised at every voyage, their privileges taken away, and presents demanded for every service. Their ardent wish was to sail straight to Suez to avoid the exactions of Jiddah, and Bruce promised Captain Thornhill that he would plead with the authorities in Egypt, on his return there, to grant that privilege to the *Bengal Merchant*, exceptionally. In 1773 the Governor General of Bengal authorized a group of Calcutta merchants to send a trial ship through to Suez. The ruler of Egypt favoured the project, but the Grand Sharif, seeing the ruin of the Hijaz in such a move, petitioned the Porte to prohibit a change in the existing trade route. The *firman* issued by the Porte in favour of the Sharif provides a Turk's-eye view of the English:

Historians inform us, that the Christians, an enterprising and artful race, have from the earliest times, constantly made use of deceit and violence to effect their ambitious purposes. Under the disguise of merchants, they formerly introduced themselves into Damascus and Jerusalem; in the same manner they have since obtained a footing in Hindustan, where the English have reduced the inhabitants to slavery; so now, likewise encouraged by the Beys, the same people have lately attempted to insinuate themselves into Egypt, with a view no doubt, as soon as they have made maps of the country, and taken plans of the fortifications, to attempt to conquer it.
In order to counteract these their dangerous designs, we enjoined their ambassador to write to his court, desiring their vessels may not be allowed to frequent the port of Suez; which requisition being fully complied with, if any of these vessels presume hereafter to anchor there, the cargo shall be confiscated, and all persons on board be imprisoned, until our further pleasure is known.

The English bowed to the prohibition, but owing to the time lag in communication, some English merchants going from Suez to Cairo were plundered and murdered by a band of Arabs, some of them cut to pieces, others left to perish of hunger and thirst. Or so James Capper, a propagandist for the overland route to India, would have his readers believe. 'Nothing less than the existence of our settlements in India,' he wrote in 1771, 'may some time or other depend upon our possessing the right of passing unmolested through Egypt.'

In 1777 four gentlemen of the East India Company, with their servants and slaves, appeared in the Red Sea en route from Madras to London. One of them, Eyles Irwin, carried dispatches to the Company's agent in Cairo and its principals in London; he was also instructed to report on the feasibility of the route for purposes of regular communication. Although a faithful servant of the Honourable Company, Irwin also had literary pretensions (he later wrote an opera on the Bedouins, which was performed in Dublin), and he wrote a book about the journey couched in the form of letters to 'a Lady', with appropriate appeals to feminine sentiment, rounded off with two odes, one to 'the Desart' and one to the Nile.

The Englishmen entered Bab al-Mandib on 19 April in the snow *Adventure* (*snau* being a Dutch word for a square-rigged ship similar to a brig) under Captain Bacon, propelled by a fine gale and a strong current. It was the season of change in the monsoon, a circumstance responsible for a great part of their misadventures. Stopping at Mocha to take on provisions and water, they met the captain and crew of another English ship, the *Aurora*, which had struck a reef near Yanbu' and gone down. Most of the crew had managed to struggle ashore, but on the beach they had been accosted by a band of Bedouins, who had stripped them and taken them to Yanbu' to sell as slaves. The governor of Yanbu', however, had released the prisoners, given them camels and money, and sent them to Jiddah, where they had found an English ship to take them back to India. Despite this cautionary tale, the passengers on the *Adventure* re-embarked 'cheerfully'.

The moon was full, the wind contrary, but they were able to make thirty miles in one direction during the day, then tacked and stood for the opposite shore during the night. In this way they passed Jiddah and had beaten up to within fifty leagues of Yanbu' when they were alarmed to see breakers ahead. The sky was hazy, but just before sunset it cleared and they saw a line of rocks and shoals which they might have struck 'had not Providence, in this unexpected manner, delivered us from the ravenous deep'. Two boats were sent ahead to feel the way, and at midnight one of them fired a gun in signal of distress; she returned to say she had heard surf breaking although there was no ground for fifty fathoms. Exposed to destruction while in motion and finding no anchorage, Captain Bacon ordered the *Adventure* to head towards land. Irwin retired to his cabin where he secured his money and valuables about him, loaded his pistols, and took from his chest the packet of correspondence entrusted to him by the East India Company. By constant soundings, however, they hit upon a narrow bank at fifty fathoms and dropped anchor at four o'clock in the morning.

The rising sun revealed the mountains of Arabia, and 'to the splendour of that glorious luminary, we were once more indebted for a gleam of hope, to revive our drooping spirits'. Lifting anchor, they sailed towards the shore and soon espied a town, which they took to be Yanbu', where they hoped to find a pilot to lead them through the treacherous rocks. Recalling the kind treatment of the *Aurora*'s crew, they had no doubt of a favourable reception.

As they entered the harbour, two boats approached them, one bearing a venerable Arab shaikh, the other a handsome Abyssinian slave, bringing an invitation to the visitors to wait upon their master, the vizir of Yanbu'. Captain Bacon and the four travellers accordingly went ashore in the longboat, passing under a decayed fortress from which a salute was fired, dislodging a quantity of dust and rubbish. To their surprise, the vizir kept them waiting for an hour and then received them without rising, merely placing his right hand on his breast with a slight inclination of the head and giving his hand to each. The vizir made a favourable impression on them, however: he was the fairest Muslim Irwin had ever seen, with black sparkling eyes, an aquiline nose, and a countenance expressive of 'great sweetness and sensibility'. It was only with hindsight that Irwin declared, 'The powers of Garrick would, if possible, fall short to support the countenance and address of the vizier during an interview . . . in which complicated deceit and villany were used, to throw the crooked politics of Machiavel far behind.'

The vizir expressed great respect for the English nation and regard for the Nawab of Narcot, in whose service the *Adventure* ostensibly sailed. He seemed to acquiesce in the travellers' intention to go to Suez and sent for the chief pilot. The pilot, however, positively refused to sail against the monsoon winds, and although the vizir offered him large rewards and even threatened to send him on board the *Adventure* in chains, Irwin suspected that the scene had been rehearsed beforehand. Finally Captain Bacon abandoned all thought of proceeding further and asked only for a pilot to take him to Jiddah, while the others requested a boat to take them to Suez. The vizir consented and engaged a pilot to fit out a boat for them in five days for a price of fifty dollars.

The Englishmen prepared to return to their vessel, but the vizir had ordered refreshments to be served to them in a house on the harbour. They accepted the invitation – or, in Irwin's words, 'swallowed the bait'. After an hour the vizir summoned their interpreter, who returned with the message that the vizir could render them no assistance until he received orders from his master, the Grand Sharif. He also directed Captain Bacon to order the *Adventure* to be brought into port. On looking out of the window, the Englishmen saw that a guard had been placed on the house. They sent the interpreter back to tell the vizir that they had come ashore at his invitation and that he could not detain them without violating the laws of nations and hospitality; they mentioned the odium that would attend such proceedings towards the Nawab of Narcot, and warned him not to offer insult to the British flag, 'which the most barbarous nation had been taught to respect'. The interpreter returned with a strict injunction to the captain to order his vessel into port.

Their own detention confirmed, they determined on the escape of the *Adventure*. Captain Bacon accordingly wrote out an order to his chief mate telling him to slip anchor with the first favourable wind and make his way to Jiddah to communicate the story of their imprisonment to any English ship which might be there. As the vizir could not read English, he allowed the letter to be sent, believing its contents to be in accordance with his wishes. For two days the north wind prevented the chief mate from complying with the captain's orders. When he could do so, a cable was cut and the ship nearly crashed on the rocks, to the alarm of the prisoners watching from the shore. Somehow during these manoeuvres a musket was fired on the ship either as a warning to other boats or as a signal. The vizir took it as an act of war: he demanded the prisoners' swords, which they had been allowed to keep; troops and ammunition were assembled on the beach; and cannon echoed in the hills, calling the tribes to the fray. Soon the Arab musketry began to play on the *Adventure*, and a band of 'wild Arabs' burst into the prisoners' room to take up stations there. Irwin was convinced that, if the *Adventure* replied and an Arab was shot, their lives would be forfeit.

The Englishmen at last demanded a parley of the vizir and offered to deliver the ship into his hands. The shooting was stopped and a pilot sent to bring the *Adventure* into port. The ship was disarmed, its guns and muskets placed under seal, but the swords of the prisoners were returned as a pledge of amity. The captives were allowed to return to their cabins aboard the ship; the vizir supplied them with fresh provisions, and they were permitted to walk about the port, under guard for their own protection. In return for such favours, they sent to the vizir presents of a diamond ring, a fine cashmere shawl, and a piece of gold cloth, all part of the wealth of the Indies with which the boxes of these rich Anglo-Indian nabobs were crammed.

Just less than a month after their arrival at Yanbu', a boat came from Jiddah bearing letters from the Sharif. Captain Bacon was given permission to go where he pleased after paying the port duties either at Yanbu' or Jiddah. The vizir was ordered to send the travellers by boat to Suez. The whole affair, then, was a question of port duties which the Englishmen, perhaps through ignorance, had sought to avoid. But the matter was not allowed to rest there. Another letter addressed to Captain Bacon informed him that an English sloop-of-war had arrived at Jiddah and that the commander, on hearing of their detention, had demanded satisfaction of the Sharif for the insult offered to the British flag. Irwin and his friends promptly sat down and wrote out the damages they believed they had suffered.

The price of a boat to take them to Suez had risen from 50 to 650 dollars. Because of this, the Englishmen named it the *Imposition*. The boat was without a deck and provided no protection from the sun by day or the heavy dews by night. The crew consisted of an Arab master and three black slaves. The four Englishmen were confined to a space amidships five feet in diameter and had to sleep on their boxes. At first their departure was delayed by contrary winds, then by the realization that one of their number had taken leave of his senses during their confinement and was now convinced that the boat crew planned to murder them as soon as they had sailed. After painful deliberation, his companions agreed to disarm the afflicted man and to send him to Jiddah in care of the vizir's guards, where he might board an English ship and be taken back to India.

The passage up the Red Sea was both dangerous and monotonous. The breeze was constantly against them, forcing them to lay up for many hours and sometimes to run back several miles to find a safe berth for the night. The fierce sun burned them by day, and at night the heavy dews drenched the cloaks they slept in as if they had been dipped in the sea. They bathed in the coves every evening and caught fish and turtles to vary the fare. Irwin took daily observations of the sun – they had a quadrant but no compass – and noted the lay of reefs and shoals, mountains and bays, to correct the charts compiled by previous travellers. They sighted the wrecks of several vessels, including that of the *Aurora*, and saw the ribs of the Jiddah ship to Suez standing on the reef where it had struck the year before. The Englishmen set up their own watch against 'the Buddoos, or wild Arabs', who were known to attack anchored vessels during the night. After a fortnight they were joined by several other boats for mutual protection and thereafter travelled at the speed of the slowest. But this precaution paid off when pirates coming out from an island near the Gulf of Aqaba saw that they were outnumbered and slunk away.

On reaching the Gulf of Aqaba, they realized that something had gone wrong with their reckonings. The island of Tiran, which the pilot pointed out to them, appeared some leagues to the north of its position on their charts. The *Imposition* sailed very deep into the gulf before crossing the open water, which it did exceptionally at night; and the width of the gulf was twice that shown on the charts. But as they rounded what they took to be Cape Muhammad at the tip of Sinai, the Englishmen rejoiced that they were in the Gulf of Suez and so close to their goal.

But then the boat turned unaccountably southwards. Their quadrant observations seemed to be off by several degrees, and the coast now appeared on their right. Though they had no compass, the position of the sun confirmed their growing suspicions. During the night they had crossed, not the Gulf of Aqaba, but the Gulf of Suez and were now sailing southwards down the coast of Africa. The awful truth dawned on them that they were bound, not for Suez, but for Qusair many miles to the south. The vizir of Yanbu' had played them one last trick, probably for reasons of commerce. Instead of taking the short and well-travelled road from Suez, they would be forced to make their way across the Egyptian desert and then sail down the Nile to Cairo. As they landed in Qusair during the night of 9 July, Irwin's thoughts were appropriately black. 'Our fortune was wrapped in doubt, dark as the shades which enveloped creation; and we anxiously looked for the returning light, to dispel the obscurity of the scene!'

CHAPTER 3
Enlightenment

It was even darker in Egypt than Irwin thought. A civil war was raging among the Mamluk beys. One of the strongest, Ali al-Kabir, had seized the capital in 1777 and driven his two most dangerous rivals into Upper Egypt, where they were scouring the countryside for men and galleys to make an assault up-river on Cairo. As the power of Constantinople declined everywhere, that of the Mamluks in Egypt revived, and the Ottoman *wali*, sent to curb the turbulent beys, was insulted, ignored, and frequently imprisoned, while the Turkish troops, sent originally to support him, were never rotated and became assimilated. The new Mamluks were often Armenian, Greek, Polish, Russian, Hungarian, Spanish, Italian, or Maltese. Irwin saw a recent recruit to the corps at Qena on the upper Nile. 'A very fine Georgian boy was in the train, whose beautiful features and fair complexion easily distinguished him from the Turks. He is a slave, and, we understand, is in high favor with his master. . . . The chief of the Turks rode on a fine dun camel, and was followed on another by the spritely Georgian, well accoutred with scimitar and matchlock.'

Unable to find a boat to take them to Cairo, Irwin and his companions joined a caravan heading northwards and arranged with a Bedouin shaikh for protection. The citizens of the towns of Upper Egypt did their best to relieve the Englishmen of their treasures, but the 'wild Buddoos' surprised them by their generosity and humanity. After many adventures which inspired Irwin to compose his 'Ode to the Desart', beginning

Thou Waste! from human sight retir'd,
By nought esteem'd, invok'd, desir'd;
Where stony hills and sterile plains,
And ever sullen silence reigns,

they reached Cairo in mid-September and were kindly received by Mr Baldwin, the East India Company's agent there.

The Company had signed a treaty of commerce with the ruling bey a few years earlier, but the incessant warfare between rival beys had made it a dead letter. Mr Baldwin had little to do but forward packets between

London and Bombay. French trade was in an equally consumptive state, and the French consulate had been closed following a bloody incident still fresh on everyone's tongue. Three young men of the French factory in Alexandria were out shooting pigeons one day when they were accosted by three Arabs who demanded their fowling-pieces. The Frenchmen refused, and in the ensuing struggle one of the Arabs was shot dead. The Frenchman responsible fled to a nearby village, hired a mule there, and galloped off to Damietta, where he caught a ship leaving directly for Constantinople. One of his companions tried to hide in the factory, but a mob stormed the building and dragged him out to a tree, where they hanged him, cut the body into pieces, and exposed the limbs throughout the city. The French consul thought it wise to confine himself in his house for two months, then, thinking the matter forgotten, ventured to take the air accompanied by his janissary guard. An Arab approached and, after asking the janissary who the consul was, discharged a pistol into his back, killing him outright. The French government sent two frigates to demand satisfaction but, to Irwin's disgust, they gave up after a time and sailed away.

The foreign colony was demoralized and spent the time in gambling and dissipation. But Irwin was delighted to taste once more the pleasures of European society. The English visitors were entertained by the Venetian and Genoese factors, played cards with the wife of the French factor, walked in the gardens of the Franciscan monastery, and flirted with the half-Greek daughter of a French merchant from Marseilles. Irwin noted with satisfaction that an English sloop, the *Swallow*, mounted with twenty guns, had put into Suez, the first European warship to have been seen there since the Portuguese had been expelled from the Red Sea. Irwin was also pleased that his own expedition had proved the Red Sea route to be feasible, taking about half the time, despite dangers and delays, of that round the Cape. He felt hopeful enough to conclude his Ode on an optimistic note:

> *And on thy furthest sandy shore,*
> *Which heard the Red-sea's billows roar,*
> *May commerce smile, her sails unfold,*
> *And change thine iron age to gold!*

But it was neither smiling commerce nor English sloops-of-war that brought the light of progress to the Red Sea's shore. It was the French invasion of Egypt led by the young general Napoleon Bonaparte in 1798.

The American War of Independence and the French Revolution had rearranged the world with incalculable consequences, but they had not abated Anglo-French rivalry for world domination. Indeed, the wars in India, the American Indian Wars, and the French invasion of Egypt can all be seen as episodes in that contest. The eighteenth-century world was inextricably bound in a vast cat's-cradle of men and events from the Ganges to the Mississippi. St Louis was traded for Madras in the peace of 1748; the tea that was dumped into Boston harbour was produced, packed, and shipped by the East India Company; General Cornwallis lost the Battle of Yorktown but won the war of Travancore. The French Revolution interrupted but did not deflect the old rivalry between the two nations. The Directory pursued the same aims in the East as Louis XV: to defeat the English, recover India, and dismember the Ottoman empire.

Napoleon Bonaparte was twenty-six years old in 1798, freshly crowned with victories in Italy and Austria, his eagle eye fixed on greater glory. 'Europe is a molehill,' he told his secretary Bourrienne. 'Everything wears out; my glory is already past; this tiny Europe does not offer enough of it. We must go to the East; all great glory has always been gained there.' But even in the East, England was the enemy. She had ousted the French from India, and her power at sea had proved unchallengeable. The Directory considered mounting a direct invasion of the British Isles through Ireland but dropped the plan as too ambitious. The alternative was to strike at England's links with India. Egypt appeared to be the weak point in that chain and would provide the field for a land war, which Napoleon was sure he could win. The Directory, already nervous about Napoleon's political ambitions, was happy to send him on an expedition far from France.

Talleyrand, foreign minister of the Directory, undertook to conciliate the Porte by representing the French invasion as directed against the rebellious beys and not against Ottoman rule. Together, he and Napoleon concerted the expedition. The young general wrote to the foreign minister on 13 September 1797, 'If it happens when we make peace with England we have to give up the Cape of Good Hope, we must occupy Egypt.' Talleyrand replied, 'Egypt as a colony would compensate for the loss of the Antilles and open up the road for us to obtaining the trade of India.' When Napoleon asked for 25,000 men and eight or ten ships of the line to carry them to Egypt, Talleyrand raised the stakes by asking the Directory for 35,000 men, adding that ships to carry them to India should be sent from Mauritius to Suez. In the end the Directory exceeded even this request, supplying over 50,000 men, 300 transport ships, and a fleet of thirteen ships of the line and seven frigates to protect them. The Directory's secret decree to General Bonaparte dated 12 April 1798 instructed him to lead the land and sea forces under his command to Egypt to take possession of that country; to drive the English from all their oriental stations that he could reach and notably to destroy their settlements in the Red Sea; and to cause a canal to be cut through the isthmus of Suez and take all necessary measures to ensure to the Republic the free and exclusive possession of the Red Sea.

The eager young general supervised every detail of the military preparations in the harbour of Toulon. But as a son of the Enlightenment, he also prepared to bring the benefits of Western civilization to the East and at the same time to rescue the ancient civilization of the Nile from the darkness in which it had lain for so long. Consequently he arranged to have attached to the expedition 500 of the most distinguished savants of the day under the direction of Gaspar Monge, mathematician and founder of the Ecole Polytechnique. They included civil and military engineers, surveyors and cartographers, astronomers, mathematicians, chemists, botanists, physicists, architects, archaeologists, epigraphers, physicians, surgeons, artists, writers, and professors of Arabic, Turkish, and Persian. Scientific instruments of all kinds were collected, as well as printing presses in Latin, Arabic, and Greek characters, the first to be seen in the East. The library carried on the expedition contained scientific treatises on all subjects, several copies of the Quran, and travellers' accounts of the Levant, Egypt, Turkey, Greece, the Black Sea, and the Caspian. A copy of Niebuhr's *Travels through Arabia* formed part of Napoleon's own personal library. His concept of military intelligence was modern in its thoroughness and scope.

The naval and military activity in the port of Toulon did not escape the ears of the British Admiralty, which ordered Captain Horatio Nelson into the Mediterranean to keep watch on the French port. But Napoleon managed to slip out of the harbour on 19 May and, eluding the English squadron, sailed eastwards. His first stop was Malta, where the Knights of St John of Jerusalem, already suborned by French agents, surrendered the island on 12 June without a shot being fired in its defence. Napoleon reorganized the government along republican lines and loaded the treasures of the Knights and of the Maltese churches aboard his flagship, *L'Orient*.

Within a week, the fleet was back under sail. For much of the time Napoleon lay seasick in a bed mounted on castors to counteract the rolling of the ship. He read the Quran and discussed science and religion with Monge and the other savants. 'With armies like ours,' he had written to Talleyrand, 'for whom all religions are the same, Mahometans, Cophts, Arabs, pagans, etc. all is to us indifferent, we will respect them each and all.' During the voyage he worked on a proclamation to the people of Egypt, assuring them of his sympathies with Islam and calling on them to renounce the Mamluks. One day he came to breakfast dressed *à la turque* in turban and pelisse, but his staff laughed at him and he never wore the costume again. Later he seemed to consider seriously adopting Islam, but to Bourrienne he confessed that 'his principle was . . . to look upon religions as the work of men, but to respect them every-where as a powerful means of government. . . . All he said about Mahom-et, Islam, and the Koran he laughed at himself.'

Meanwhile, aboard the *Vanguard*, Nelson was scouring the Mediter-ranean. From time to time he brought his officers aboard the flagship to debate the tactics to be used when once they met and engaged the French navy. During the night of 22/23 June, the two fleets passed each other off the coast of Crete, but Nelson could not see his quarry in the dark. The faster English ships reached Alexandria on 29 June, but seeing no sign of the French, Nelson immediately set sail for the Levant.

Twenty-four hours later the French fleet appeared off the Egyptian coast. Napoleon immediately sent a letter to the French consul at Alexandria inviting all French residents to come aboard the ships as protection against possible reprisals from the local populace. He then landed his troops at Marabout beach and took Alexandria, Rosetta, and Damanhour within forty-eight hours against the feeble resistance of their garrisons. The fabled city of Alexander, Napoleon's hero and model, was a grave disappointment – a paltry heap of ruins with hovels of mud and straw leaning against fragments of former glory. Leaving the fleet at Aboukir Bay under the command of Admiral Brueys, Napoleon directed his army towards Cairo.

Immediately after the landing Napoleon issued the proclamation to the Egyptian people which he had composed aboard *L'Orient*. It was an astonishing document, attempting to combine the principles of the Republic with those of Islam:

In the name of God, the clement and merciful. There is no divinity save Allah; He has no son and shares His power with no one.
In the name of the French Republic, founded in liberty and equality, the commander-in-chief of the French armies, Bonaparte, lets it be known to the whole population of Egypt that the beys who govern Egypt have insulted the

French nation and oppressed the French merchants long enough, the hour of their punishment has come.
For too many years, that gang of slaves, purchased in Georgia and the Caucasus, has tyrannized over the most beautiful region in the world. But God Almighty, who rules the universe, has decreed that their reign shall come to an end.
People of Egypt, you will be told that I have come to destroy your religion. This is an obvious lie! do not believe it! Answer back to those imposters that I have come to restore to you your rights and to punish the usurpers; that I worship God more than the Mamluks do; and that I respect the Prophet Mahomet and the admirable Quran.

The reply of Egypt was a sullen silence signalling fear and incomprehension. As they marched through the Delta the French soldiers encountered hardly a soul, only a few wretched dogs. 'The most beautiful region in the world' appeared to them a bleak and arid waste, not the lush colonial paradise they had been led to expect. The crisscrossing of canals made the march difficult; the heat of the Egyptian July was intense, the flies and mosquitoes voracious, the food and water sparse and bad. Almost the only thing they found to eat were watermelons, which gave them dysentery. Bands of Bedouin horsemen harried the rear columns and picked off stragglers, whom they stripped and abused, sending them back naked and humiliated to the ranks. The soldiers grumbled against their beloved Bonaparte, and two of them, crazed with fatigue and despair, reportedly threw themselves into the Nile before his eyes. There was not even the excitement of battle, for the enemy was elusive. On 14 July they met a body of Mamluks for the first time, but after a few skirmishes the bravely arrayed horsemen scampered away under a barrage of French fire-power.

The main army of Mamluks awaited the French at Embaba within sight of the pyramids of Giza, entrenched on both sides of the Nile. The defenders consisted of twenty-three beys with their private armies of 12,000 lesser Mamluks, each with two or three servants, supported by 20,000 janissaries on foot and about 8,000 Bedouins. The bulk of the defenders under Mourad Bey faced the advancing French army on the left bank of the Nile, while a reserve under Ibrahim Bey stood by on the right. The French, numbering some 25,000, took up positions facing Mourad Bey in battalion squares, with their baggage in the middle of the squares and their artillery stationed at the intervals between.

The Battle of the Pyramids, as the ensuing massacre was named, pitted medieval chivalry against a modern war machine. Some of the Mamluks were armed with English carbines, but the majority relied on their time-honoured weapons of lance and scimitar, with perhaps five or six pistols tucked into their sashes. Mourad Bey ordered his *corps d'élite* to charge, and the Mamluks bravely obeyed. The well-trained French carbineers coolly held fire till the galloping horsemen were within fifty paces, then let fly with volleys that brought down the front riders. Those behind rushed into the gaps between the French squares and were raked by deadly crossfire. When the charge had been stopped, Napoleon brought up one of his reserve battalions to attack the fortifications of Embaba, while another battalion prevented the surviving horsemen from entering the ramparts. The fleeing Mamluks were forced to drive their horses into the Nile and many of them drowned. The French artillery went into action and soon reduced Embaba. Meanwhile a sand-storm blew up and blinded Ibrahim Bey and his reserves on the right bank. When he realized that the main force of Mamluks had been destroyed, Ibrahim withdrew first to Cairo and then fled northwards into the Sinai desert. Mourad Bey, collecting the remnants of his defeated army, fled south into Upper Egypt. Napoleon sent a contingent under General Desaix southwards in pursuit. Meanwhile the French soldiers began to pillage the bodies of the fallen Mamluks and were astonished by the wealth they carried into battle – purses of 300 to 500 louis d'or, arms encrusted with ivory and precious stones, and fine muslin garments under their chain-mail.

Napoleon entered Cairo in triumph. But in contrast to the personal wealth of the Mamluks, the capital seemed a squalid town. The French were disgusted by the narrow stinking streets, the dungeon-like public buildings, the shops like stables; the people in the streets were blind, begging, and in rags, the children covered with sores and flies, the women hiding their fleshless faces under dirty rags while exposing their pendulous breasts through rents in their gowns. Napoleon, however, installed himself in the comfortable house of a rich Mamluk, Elfi Bey, and set about improving conditions for his men, petitioning Paris to send out gardeners, theatrical troupes, and dancing girls, and to find a substitute for hops that could be grown in Egypt for the flavouring of beer. The savants were kept busy too, swarming over the country, exploring, measuring, sketching, collecting, deciphering, and compiling material for the magnificent publication, *Description de l'Egypte*, which revolutionized the West's comprehension of a half-forgotten civilization and incidentally created a new European taste for *le style empire*.

Bonaparte also tried to improve the lot of the modern Egyptians, creating far-reaching economic reforms and reorganizing the administration along modern bureaucratic lines. To win the trust of the Egyptians he appealed to the religion of the people, representing himself and the French Republic as 'true Muslims', and citing his victories over the Pope and the Knights of Malta as proof of this. He especially cultivated the shaikhs of al-Azhar as keepers of the religious conscience of Cairo, and appeared as a celebrant at the Prophet's birthday ceremonies. He even conceived a plan to make the pilgrimage to Mecca and, perhaps to pave the way, sent a letter of friendship to the Grand Sharif. The only reply was the arrival of armed bands from the Hijaz to join Mourad in Upper Egypt in action to expel the foreign conqueror.

The English meanwhile sought to nullify the French *fait accompli*. If they could not drive Napoleon out of Egypt, they might at least bottle him up there. After learning of the French landing, Captain Nelson hurried back to Alexandria, arriving on the afternoon of 1 August. Admiral Brueys was off his guard: his offshore guns were unmanned, some of his men had gone ashore to collect water, and others were detailed to repaint *L'Orient*. Though only a few hours of daylight remained, Nelson ordered an immediate attack before the French could make ready. His own captains knew from the briefings aboard the *Vanguard* what they had to do. Thirteen French ships of the line lay in a bow across the bay. Five of the English ships passed inside the line, while Nelson's flagship led the attack from the sea. Each of the English ships engaged its French counterpart.

The English sailors, the best of their day, outfought the French and disabled several of the enemy ships. But *L'Orient* was both larger and better armed than any of the English vessels and beat off all attacks. The painters, however, had left some jars of paint oil on deck, which caught fire. An English ship, the *Alexander*, seeing this, directed her fire towards the blaze. At ten o'clock that night, with a shattering explosion, *L'Orient* blew up, lighting the night sky and showering flaming rope and timber over the rest of the fleet. Her crew was thrown into the water, and those not killed by the blast swam about in the dark amidst the burning spars; among them were the French commodore Casabianca and his ten-year-old son. Admiral Brueys himself had been killed some two hours earlier, cut in two by a cannon ball. An unofficial cease-fire followed the explosion and a profound silence fell over the bay. Nelson, who had been wounded in the face, was brought on deck to see the blazing wreck of *L'Orient*, still loaded with the treasures of Malta, sink to the bottom. The *Franklin*, provocatively named after the American rebel, took over as flagship of the French fleet. But at half-past eleven the French commander ordered the colours struck, though sporadic fighting continued till dawn. The rising sun showed the surface of the bay covered with wreckage and the scorched and broken bodies of the dead. English boats were sent out to pick up those still alive, including a great number of French sailors who clung to the bows of the silenced ships. The entire French fleet was either sunk or captured.

The Battle of the Nile succeeded in trapping the French army in Egypt, with no avenue of retreat and no hopes of reinforcements. Napoleon's winning streak was beginning to falter. The religious leaders of Cairo, unimpressed by his protestations of Islamic sympathies, encouraged an uprising of the people against an infidel occupation that opened taverns for the consumption of intoxicating drinks, allowed its soldiers to court Muslim women, and shook the established order with its ideals of liberty and equality. Napoleon retaliated by shelling al-Azhar and chopping off about thirty heads a night, just like any Mamluk bey. Meanwhile his men were being struck down by the diseases endemic along the Nile, especially the dreaded ophthalmia, which rendered many of them temporarily blind.

The English victory over the French fleet was the signal for the Tsar of Russia and the Ottoman Sultan to declare war on France. The Porte, looking to its defences, ordered its representative in Jiddah to repair the ramparts of the city and to give the citizens military training. The representative in turn sent a request to the English commander at Aden for help in repelling a French invasion of the Hijaz, while in India the English began to collect military supplies and pack animals for a Red Sea expedition.

But Napoleon decided to break out of the trap of Egypt by attacking northwards, into Syria. 'Now, gentlemen,' he told his staff, 'we are obliged to accomplish great things. The seas, of which we are no longer masters, separate us from our homeland, but no sea separates us from either Africa or Asia.' He still had confidence in the supremacy of his men as land fighters, and the example of Alexander the Great beckoned him eastwards. In bold, hubristic terms he wrote to Talleyrand recommending the use of Syria as a springboard from which to threaten Constantinople and to march across the desert towards the Indus.

Guessing his intentions, the Porte reinforced its troops in Syria and placed the defences in the hands of a former Bosnian Mamluk, Ahmad al-Jazzar, known with some justification as the Butcher. As Pasha of Damascus he had led a pilgrim caravan to Mecca, barely escaping with his life from a Bedouin attack, and ever afterwards he had claimed pure sharifian descent. Now, over seventy years old, he was still a doughty fighter, dominating the Palestinian coast from his heavily fortified castle at St Jean d'Acre. To give him support, the English sent a squadron of ships under Sidney Smith to stand by off Acre.

In February 1799 Napoleon led a part of his army out of Cairo and occupied al-Arish on the frontier of Sinai. Continuing up the coast he took the ports of Gaza and Jaffa by storm. Despite these successes, a note of desperation now appeared in his conduct. At Jaffa, where 3,000 Ottoman troops surrendered to him, he had them separated by nationality – Egyptian, Turkish, and Moroccan. The next morning the Moors were driven to the seashore where they were gunned down by two French battalions; those who tried to escape by jumping into the sea were shot in the water, and French boats were put out to pick them off the rocks. The following day 1,200 Turkish artillerymen, who had been kept without food or water for two days, were dispatched by bayonets to save ammunition. The massacre of unarmed men was probably intended to cow al-Jazzar into surrender, or it may have been designed to relieve the pressure on short supplies of food. In a sort of nemesis, bubonic plague, encouraged by the putrefying bodies of the unburied victims, broke out and decimated the French ranks.

Sidney Smith's squadron intercepted the French siege guns coming from Alexandria by sea. Nothing daunted, Napoleon ordered the investment of Acre. Al-Jazzar's men fought off the French attacks with the ferocity of beasts condemned to slaughter, but they would doubtless have been overcome by French fire-power had not Sidney Smith's guns destroyed some French positions. As the plague raged within the walled town, Napoleon raised the siege after two months, citing the danger of the spread of the disease among his troops. But the French were not spared; returning to Jaffa, Napoleon found the occupying forces he had left there widely infected. With characteristic *sang froid*, he ordered his chief physician to kill the sick with massive doses of opium, as he could neither transport them nor leave them undefended to the vengeance of the Turks. To his credit, the physician refused to carry out the order. The retreat to the south was a nightmare of heat, disease, and constant attacks from the English gunboats at sea and the Bedouins of Sinai by land. Leaving a trail of their dead behind them, the remnants of the French army struggled into Cairo on 14 June. Napoleon declared the Syrian campaign a great victory.

In Egypt the French now had to defend themselves on every front. General Desaix failed to dislodge the Mamluks from Upper Egypt. The

English blockade of the Mediterranean coast prevented the arrival of supplies and reinforcements. In the Red Sea the arrival of an English squadron from India forced Napoleon to send a detachment of troops across the desert to occupy the port of Qusair; although the English bombarded the town, they were prevented from landing. In July 1799 Ottoman troops supported by English ships landed at Aboukir Bay, where they held a beachhead for two weeks till the French drove them back into the sea.

Throughout the summer of 1799 the news from Europe was bad for Napoleon's interests. Talleyrand resigned as foreign minister; the Directory was torn by dissension. Austria invaded Italy; the Russians entered the Adriatic. The English blockade of Malta prevented a French fleet intended for Egypt from leaving Toulon. Napoleon decided to cut his losses and return to France. Without notifying his second-in-command, General Kléber, of his intentions, he slipped out of Cairo at midnight on 17/18 August, accompanied by a few trusted officers and his Mamluk servant Roustan. Five days later he set sail from Alexandria. Although his ship was sighted by an English cruiser, it was mistaken for an English vessel and slipped through the net. On 9 October Napoleon landed at Fréjus and a month later staged the *coup d'état* that ended the Directory and began the first Consulate.

General Kléber, a blunt and honest soldier, disliked Napoleon and disapproved of his colonial policy. His chief aim was to get the French army out of Egypt with its honour intact. He sent representatives to meet the officials of the Porte aboard Sidney Smith's flagship off al-Arish, where a convention was signed permitting the peaceful departure of the French troops. The British government, however, rejected these terms and demanded the unconditional surrender of the French forces. Kléber prepared to resist such dishonour and in fact turned back an Ottoman invading force at Heliopolis on the outskirts of Cairo. But shortly afterwards he was assassinated by a young student from al-Azhar university, and General Abdullah Menou, a French convert to Islam, took over the command.

By the end of 1800, the English, in concert with the Ottoman government, were ready to drive the remaining French out of Egypt. An army of 15,000 English soldiers with Turkish reserves landed at Aboukir Bay on 8 March 1801 under the command of General Abercromby. The French forces defended Alexandria desperately; Abercromby and three French generals were killed in action; but, although Rosetta and Damietta fell to the invaders, Alexandria held out. Meanwhile an English contingent from Bombay landed at Qusair and marched on Cairo and the Delta. It arrived after the Anglo-Turkish forces had taken the capital, with the capture of 13,000 French troops. After two more months of heavy fighting, the French in Alexandria surrendered under the same terms that Kléber had agreed to at al-Arish the previous year. The French army was allowed to leave Egypt and return unmolested to France, the last troops embarking at Rosetta on 7 August 1801. A few Frenchmen, however, elected to stay on and try their fortunes in the new Egypt of the post-occupation.

Monarchical England, the decadent Ottoman government, and the unrepentant Mamluk beys combined to frustrate Napoleon's attempt to force enlightenment upon Egypt. But the French invasion had illuminated some dark corners. It had shown that the Mamluks alone were incapable of holding Egypt against a strong challenger and that the Ottoman empire itself could not prevent the amputation of its members. It had shown that the West, with its modern arms and efficient military organization, could triumph over the traditional arms and tactics of the East, and suggested that Western science and inventions, including the printing press, might effect profound changes in the structure of Eastern society. And it had shown England that the security of its communications with India required vigilance and greater involvement in the Middle East.

One student of the French invasion who learned these lessons was a young officer in the Turkish forces, Mehmet Ali, who took part in the Anglo-Ottoman landing at Aboukir Bay in the spring of 1801. Born in the same year as Napoleon at Kavala in Thrace, he was orphaned at an early age and brought up by an uncle named Tusun, who was beheaded for some alleged crime by order of the Porte. The twice-orphaned youth was then taken into the home of the governor of Kavala as a companion for his son Ali Aga. Although strong in arm and mentally agile, Mehmet Ali did not learn to read and write till he was forty. This was no bar, however, to his joining the local militia and earning a name for himself as a tax collector with an aptitude for extorting money from recalcitrant Greek villages. In recognition of his talents, he was married to one of the governor's relations, a rich widow or divorcee, whose wealth enabled him to set up in the tobacco business. When the Porte began to raise levies to expel the French from Egypt, the governor sent a troop of 300 horse under the command of his son Ali Aga with Mehmet Ali as his lieutenant. The Macedonian contingent, as it was called, was attached to the 6,000-strong Albanian regiment committed against the French at Aboukir Bay. When the French left Egypt, Ali Aga went home to Kavala, but Mehmet Ali stayed on as chief of the Macedonian troops. Through his skill and intelligence, he had risen by 1803 to be second-in-command of the entire Albanian regiment.

It was a good position from which to observe and profit by the struggle for power that followed the French evacuation. The Porte wished to impose direct rule over Egypt and appointed a *wali* with full powers and the support of the Turkish forces of occupation. The Mamluks, on the other hand, were determined to regain the power they had lost to Napoleon; the two most powerful beys to emerge from the French occupation, Osman Bardissy and Mehmet Elfi, were prepared to resort to the old methods of intrigue and murder to decide which of them should be Rais al-Balad. The English on the whole favoured restoration of Mamluk rule and between Bardissy and Elfi backed the latter. In 1802 Elfi Bey attacked and defeated the Ottoman *wali* but allowed him to remain in office. When, a year later, the English commander, General Stuart, evacuated his troops, he took Elfi Bey with him to London for consultations. Shortly after the departure of the English, the Albanian regiment mutinied for the usual reason of arrears in pay, forcing the *wali* to take refuge in Damietta. Tahir, the Albanian commander, now held the balance of power and petitioned the Porte to send a replacement for the *wali*. But within a few weeks, loyal Turkish troops defeated the Albanians and murdered Tahir. Mehmet Ali succeeded him as chief of the Arnauts, or Albanian contingent.

Mehmet Ali was a practical man. It is not clear when he first set his sights on winning possession of Egypt. In retrospect the events of 1802 and 1803 take the form of a diabolically clever game in which every move was designed to eliminate his rivals; but there must have been an element of luck, or at least opportunism, in the play. At first he helped the Mamluks to stave off the claims of a pretender from Medina named Ahmad Pasha. Then he supported Bardissy Bey when in the summer of 1803 the Mamluk imprisoned the Turkish *wali* and murdered his replacement. When Elfi Bey returned from England in 1804, Mehmet Ali again supported Bardissy in driving his rival into Upper Egypt, the eternal refuge of exiled beys. But now he demanded payment for his services, namely settlement of the arrears owed to his Arnauts. Being short of funds, Bardissy imposed a special tax on the citizens of Cairo to meet Mehmet Ali's claim. But the tax-payers resisted, and Mehmet Ali, assuming the role of champion of the people, rallied popular support to expel Bardissy from Cairo. When the two exiled beys joined forces in an attempt to take the capital, Mehmet Ali rallied to the *wali*, throwing his Albanians into battle at Minieh to defeat the Mamluks.

The field was now clear of all rivals except the representative of the Porte. When the *wali* received troop reinforcements from Syria, Mehmet Ali took it as a threat to his own position. Prevailing on the people of Cairo and the shaikhs of al-Azhar to support him, he laid siege to the *wali* in the Citadel, the fortified castle built by Saladin on a hill east of Cairo, and called on the Porte to choose between himself and the *wali*. The envoy sent hastily from Constantinople to settle the dispute decided in favour of the stronger, and in 1805 the Porte recognized Mehmet Ali as the Sultan's viceroy in Egypt. His luck held out when both Bardissy and Elfi Bey died within a year and when a British landing at Rosetta in support of Mamluk rule was beaten off. Mehmet Ali had reached his goal as master of Egypt.

But the position of a Turkish pasha was only as strong as his power to defend it. The remaining Mamluks were still a threat to Mehmet Ali's régime, in Upper Egypt and even in Cairo and the Delta. Mehmet Ali sent his eldest son Ibrahim (or perhaps stepson: Mehmet Ali's first wife was said to have been pregnant at the time of their marriage) to deal with the beys who were prowling about Upper Egypt and Nubia. And the Porte, which did not like strong men as governors of its provinces, had only reluctantly accepted a *fait accompli* in recognizing the Macedonian upstart as its viceroy in Egypt. Mehmet Ali was offered pashaliks elsewhere in the Ottoman empire, but though willing to consider an extension of his power, he was not ready to give up control of what was potentially the richest province of all. The Porte then played its trump card by offering Mehmet Ali military adventure in Arabia and the opportunity to enhance his prestige throughout the Muslim world. It ordered him to put down the Wahhabis and to check their threat to the Holy Cities. As the Sultan's viceroy he had a duty to defend his sovereign's interest, and military success in the Hijaz would bring him not only prestige but the possibility of increasing his wealth and influence at the expense of the Porte. But first his hold over Egypt must be consolidated. Mehmet Ali did not refuse to obey the orders of the Sultan, but he played for time.

CHAPTER 4
The Cleansing of the Ka'ba

During the last quarter of the eighteenth century the House of Sa'ud consolidated its rule over Najd, bringing law and order to central Arabia for the first time since the days of the Prophet. The Saudi state was a kind of Bedouin commonwealth in which tribal chiefs were allowed to keep their hereditary rights and privileges so long as they submitted to the Unitarian faith, paid tithes to the central government, and provided levies of able-bodied men to take the field against heretics and infidels. For the first time the tribes were at peace, and a traveller could cross the desert in security. Collective responsibility made every Arab liable for any crime committed by his tribe; even bystanders who failed to prevent a crime were liable to punishment. Fixed tribunals administered the law impartially. Most crimes could be atoned for by payment of a fine, usually in livestock. Capital punishment was rare. The worst punishment that could be imposed on a shaikh was to have his beard shaved off and many went to great expense in payment of presents to avoid this humiliation. One crime, however, was severely punished: intercourse with heretics, by whom the Wahhabis meant all those, including Muslims, who did not abide by their doctrines. For example, any Arab found on the road to Damascus or Baghdad carrying goods for trade was liable to having them confiscated. An exception was made for the protection and transport of pilgrims, as this was a major source of revenue for the state.

But this situation created a problem. Like the cities of their origin – Damascus, Baghdad, Cairo, Isfahan – the caravans reflected all the vices and virtues of contemporary society. The caravans contained rich and poor, the devout and the frivolous, saints and sinners. They were organized and led by an Amir al-Hajj, an Ottoman official, and guarded by troops of Irregular cavalry, Turks, Albanians, Moors, and other nationalities. Sellers of hashish and intoxicating *bouza* peddled their wares, and prostitutes from the brothels of the Levant sought their fortune among men separated from their families. This aspect of the pilgrimage shocked and disgusted pious Muslims, among them the Wahhabis, who arrogated the right to prevent such infamous conduct in their own territory. As the caravans passed through Najd, they were often stopped by bands of armed men and not allowed to proceed until they had sent back their troops of cavalry, bands of musicians, and light women, and agreed to continue as simple pilgrims. Many of the Amirs al-Hajj rejected these conditions and ordered the entire caravan to turn about and go home, causing consternation and dismay among the disappointed pilgrims. Some amirs exaggerated the fanaticism of the Wahhabis in order to justify their own willingness to abandon an expensive and arduous undertaking.

After the tithing of the faithful, the most fruitful source of income of the Saudi state was the plundering of heretics. The Wahhabis made two or three plundering raids a year against their richer neighbours. The land around Basra, rich in cattle and dates, was especially attractive. The raids were swift and brutal. If an enemy surrendered he was stripped and allowed to go in peace; if he resisted or was captured under arms, he was put to death. The Wahhabis held a particular hatred for the Turks and rarely allowed one to escape alive. But they were chivalrous towards women; when plundering a Bedouin camp, they drove off all the cattle, seized the very cooking pots from the tents, and made the women strip naked, taking their clothing and jewels as booty, but turning their eyes away and throwing them a few rags for the sake of decency. If their men had been killed, the women were allowed to join the Wahhabi column for safety till they reached relations. When a Saudi chief gave safe-conduct to an enemy, his word was never broken; the good faith of the Wahhabis contrasted in their eyes with the treachery of the Turks.

The raids into Iraq and the interference with the pilgrim caravans forced the Porte to take action, and in 1790 it ordered the Sharif of Mecca to take the field against the desert upstarts. Ghalib had inherited the title from his brother but had had to defend his right to it by driving off several of his contentious relatives. Physically, Ghalib was an enormous man; some found him sweet natured and circumspect, others said he was secretive and egotistical. It was his misfortune to be pitted against two leaders – Sa'ud the Wahhabi and Mehmet Ali of Egypt – who were more powerful than he. As a milk brother of Bedouins, he knew what to expect of desert warfare: the seasonal forays into enemy territory, the capture of cattle and interdiction of wells, the shifting allegiance of tribal allies. But his mercenary army of Moors and Negroes officered by members of the sharifian clan was no match for the inspired Wahhabis, who cheerfully faced death for their faith. After nearly a decade of indecisive encounters, Ghalib led his motley army, supported by some Bedouin allies, against the Wahhabis at Khurmah in March 1798, where he suffered a humiliating defeat, with thousands of his men lost and some forty sharifs killed. Ghalib was forced to submit and to invite the Wahhabi chief, 'Abd al-'Aziz, to make the pilgrimage. At the hajj, or pilgrimage, of 1800 Mecca saw hordes of Wahhabi warriors, accompanied by their women and children, swarming through its streets like streams from the hills following rain and praying with unaccustomed fervour at the Holy Places.

Meanwhile the Porte, more determined than ever to put down the Wahhabis, ordered the Pasha of Baghdad to act. In 1799 he sent an army of 5,000 Turks and 10,000 Arab tribesmen to lay siege to al-Hasa on the Persian Gulf, the richest of the Saudi domains. The townsmen held off the invaders for a month until a column of Wahhabis under Sa'ud, son of 'Abd al-'Aziz, arrived to lift the siege. The Arab allies of Baghdad melted into the desert, but the Turks found their retreat cut off at Thaj, where Sa'ud had dumped several camel-loads of salt into one well and fortified the other. For three days the two armies faced each other, the Turks dying of thirst, the Wahhabis unable to attack for fear of the Turkish artillery. A parley was held and a truce between the Saudi state and the pashalik of Baghdad agreed for six years. The next hajj the pilgrim caravan from Baghdad crossed Najd under the personal escort of Sa'ud ibn 'Abd al-'Aziz.

But the truce was soon broken. In 1801 a Persian caravan travelling under Wahhabi protection was plundered by Arabs under the jurisdiction of Baghdad. In March 1802 the Wahhabis rode into central Iraq and attacked the town of Karbala, where the tomb of the Prophet's grandson Husain was the centre of Shi-ite pilgrimage. The raiders scaled the walls and rampaged through the streets, massacring almost the entire male population of 5,000, sparing only the old men, women, and children. Then, in a religious frenzy, they destroyed the dome over Husain's tomb and the graves of other Shi-ite saints before they withdrew.

The sack of Karbala shocked the entire Muslim world and awakened it to the danger of the Unitarian movement. The Porte again ordered a punitive expedition from Baghdad, but the Bedouin shaikh in charge of the campaign was murdered at al-Hasa by a Wahhabi slave, and, when Sa'ud approached in force, the Bedouins again vanished into the desert. This time the Turks were not so fortunate: they wandered in the desert, unfamiliar with the tracks and wells, and when they came in for water the Wahhabis, after allowing them a few sips, butchered them one by one. A few local people, faithful to the code of the desert, gave them water and allowed them to go on their way.

Meanwhile the southern Wahhabis invaded the Hijaz. Ghalib sent his Bedouin brother-in-law, Othman al-Madhaifi, to parley with Sa'ud, but Othman went over to the Wahhabis and attacked the town of Tayif in the mountains above Mecca in 1802. Without any religious excuse, Othman massacred the inhabitants, not sparing the infirm, women and children, and those who took refuge in the mosque. Sa'ud now marched on Mecca, easily frustrating Ghalib's attempts to stop him. Mecca was without walls and could be taken by storm. But Sa'ud had a dream in which the Prophet warned him that he would not survive three days if he took a single grain of corn from the Holy City by force. Instead of attacking the town directly, he set up a blockade and cut off the sweet water canal from Arafat. The people of Mecca were reduced to eating cats and dogs and drinking from the brackish wells in town. Judging the situation hopeless, Ghalib fled to the safety of the walls of Jiddah.

The next day the people of Mecca went out to welcome Sa'ud. The Wahhabis entered the Holy City in pilgrim garb and immediately made the *umrah*, or lesser pilgrimage. Sa'ud ordered his men to commit no outrages and to pay for anything they required. The Meccans outwardly became Unitarians, abjuring worldly pleasures, praying regularly, and behaving with unaccustomed humility and decorum in the Holy Places. At Sa'ud's orders they brought their water-pipes and tobacco to a piece of waste ground where they were set on fire. But when told that some Meccans still smoked in private, Sa'ud admonished the informer, 'Is it not written, Do not spy on the secrets of the houses of the faithful?' He appointed a brother of Ghalib as governor, named a qadi of the Unitarian faith, and prohibited the mention of the Sultan's name in public prayers.

The Wahhabis could not conquer Jiddah, although Othman al-Madhaifi attacked it several times. Its inhabitants, aided by foreign traders and pilgrims, stoutly defended the walls. Ghalib, however, had little faith and loaded his treasures aboard ships in the harbour, preparing to embark for India. It was said that he offered 5,000 dollars to Sa'ud if he would withdraw from Mecca. Whatever the cause, Sa'ud did leave the Holy City with most of his troops, leaving only a small garrison. Ghalib unloaded his goods and returned to Mecca, where he resumed the government under a new master.

Sa'ud was received by his father in Dar'iyah in triumph. But the celebrations did not last long. One morning in October 1803 at public prayers a man who had come to the Saudi capital as a dervish to study the doctrines of Unitarianism stabbed 'Abd al-'Aziz and was himself cut down by Saudi swords. The assassin, it turned out, was a native of Karbala whose entire family had died in the massacre the previous year. Sa'ud, who had led the Wahhabi army to victory in the field, succeeded his father as head of the House and defender of the Unitarian faith.

The conquest of the Hijaz continued. Yanbu' and Medina fell to the Wahhabis in 1804. Sa'ud ordered his men to strip the Prophet's Mosque of its treasures and to tear down the dome over the Prophet's tomb. But after several of the zealots who swarmed over the roof were injured in falls, the project was abandoned, and the Wahhabis contented themselves with wrecking the tombs of Muhammad's family and companions in the cemetery. Sa'ud's men patrolled the streets with staves, driving reluctant worshippers into the mosques, where a roll was called of the names of all citizens. All Turks were ordered to leave the city, and some who were slow to obey had their beards cut off.

Although Ghalib retained his title, he lost control of Medina and in Mecca had to share his authority with the Wahhabis. In Jiddah, he still reigned, checked only by the *wali* appointed annually by the Porte. The pilgrimage never entirely ceased; pilgrims arrived by sea from Africa and India, and a few came from Syria by way of Egypt. They were all obliged to leave their arms in Jiddah and to comply with Wahhabi codes of dress and behaviour. The *mahmal* – the splendid litter carried by camel to represent the Sultan – was brought by ship from Suez, guarded by 400 soldiers under the command of the new *wali*. But the *mahmal* remained in Jiddah, and the *wali* died, possibly poisoned by order of Ghalib. For Ghalib, in bowing to Sa'ud, was beginning to defy the Porte; it was a dangerous game, though Ghalib played it with skill. When Sa'ud made the pilgrimage, Ghalib sent a caravan to meet him laden with presents of Indian muslin for the *ihrams* of the men, clothing for the women, and sweetmeats for the children.

An English visitor caught a glimpse of life in Jiddah during this uncertain time. George Viscount Valentia, later Earl of Mountnorris, commanding his own ship on a voyage to Egypt, Abyssinia, India, and Ceylon, stopped in the Hijaz for provisions in December 1805. Because of the Saudi blockade he found foodstuffs scarce and extremely dear. Sheep were not to be had, goats were eight or nine dollars apiece, and bullocks thirty or forty. Valentia tried to purchase two large pigs he saw at the vizir's gate, urging that they were improper inhabitants for so holy a town, but was told that the smell of them did the horses good. The vizir, 'a stupid looking eunuch', whose train was held up by attendants as he entered the audience chamber to receive his guests, served coffee and rosewater though it was Ramadan. The noble lord was not impressed:

The Arab character seems to have declined rapidly in the Hedjas, for in 1763, when Niebuhr was at Jiddah, a sheriffe was always Vizier there, because, as he says, no descendant of Mohammed could, in so holy a country, be judged by one of an inferior race. . . . [Now] the descendants of the Prophet . . . are shut up in four wretched towns, whence they behold their country devastated . . . and instead of receiving that respect, which for twelve centuries they have claimed throughout Asia, they are obliged to submit to the mandates of an Abyssinian slave, who has no real merit except valour, but who is recommended to his master by his willingness to commit every crime.

The Wahhabis kept the town in a state of alarm every night. Valentia was asked to stay and help defend the city, or at least to leave four or five men as cannoneers and armourers, but he refused. 'The martial spirit of the Arabs,' he reckoned, 'seems to have subsided with their religious zeal. The larger proportion of their soldiers, and many of their officers, are slaves, purchased from Africa.' The ship's doctor was asked to see some of these slave-soldiers who were wounded in action against the Wahhabis; their wounds were filthy, so the treatment he recommended was that they be cleaned. Valentia learned that there were European renegades fighting for both the Sharif and Sa'ud. Enquiring of a French renegade at Jiddah the fate of some English deserters from Mocha, he was told that 'they had gone to the devil in different ways; that two of them had been killed in battle, one had been blown to pieces by the bursting of a gun, some had deserted to the Wahabee; and Thomas, whom I had known at Mocha, had gone off with the Sherriffe of Mecca, and had not since been heard of'.

Many merchants were leaving Jiddah; the English had all departed, not so much because of the war as because of the exactions of the Sharif and his servants. Valentia thought the Sharif very short-sighted:

When Egypt was torn by internal strife . . . and when the Wahabee power arose, and cut off communications between Constantinople and Mecca; the Sherriffe became disinclined to give half his receipts to a person he no longer feared. . . . Ghalib, the present sovereign, attacked the Pacha in the citadel and nearly destroyed it; and got rid of him by the more secret means of poison. At present, no representative of the protector of the holy places (for so the Sultan is considered throughout his dominions) is to be found in Arabia.

But Ghalib reaped little benefit from this: 'Without the walls of this town, the Sherriffe cannot be considered as having a subject. Every Arab, who falls into the control of Saud, adopts his religion, and receives permission to plunder those who have not done the same. . . . Unless supported by Turkish power, Ghalib must at length resign Mecca, Yambo, Medina, and Jiddah to the Wahabees.'

A year later another visitor landed at Jiddah, different in almost every way to Lord Valentia. He travelled as a pilgrim and, instead of viewing the country from the deck of his own comfortable ship, threw himself into the life of the people. He claimed to be a Moor from the Maghrib but called himself Ali Bey al-Abbassi, implying descent from the caliphs of Baghdad. Evidently a man of means, he travelled in style with a large retinue of slaves and servants, and spent money with an open hand.

But who was Ali Bey? A mystery surrounded his origins and identity and is not entirely resolved to this day. The Swiss traveller Burckhardt, who followed him to the Hijaz a decade later, came across him in Aleppo and suspected that he was a Spaniard named Badia who had been in London in 1802. Burckhardt described him as a man of middling size with a long thin head, black eyes and beard, a large nose, and feet that showed he had formerly worn tight European shoes. In Aleppo he professed to have been born of Tunisian parents in Spain. Spanish appeared to be his native tongue, though he also knew a little French and Italian and spoke a Maghrabi dialect of Arabic, though Burckhardt thought badly. A Syrian dervish told Burckhardt that there had been a good deal of talk about Ali Bey in Hama and Damascus; 'they suspected him of being a Christian, but his great liberality and the pressing letters he brought to all people of consequence, stopped all further enquiry'. His ostentatious mode of life was an odd disguise for a Christian passing as a Muslim, the opposite of the rags and inconspicuous poverty affected by later travellers such as Burckhardt and Burton.

William John Bankes, an Englishman who toured the Levant later in the century, stated categorically:

Ali Bey was a Spaniard from Catalonia, of the name Badia. I found some particulars among his original papers, to which I had access in Constantinople, which induced me to suspect him to have been secretly brought up a Jew, but I have in my possession authentic proof of his having been employed by the French government as a spy, the original draft in his own handwriting of a memorial to Bonaparte, reciting his services and claiming his reward.

Burckhardt thought he was an agent of the Spanish government: 'from the manner in which it was known that he was afterwards received by the Spanish ambassador at his arrival in Constantinople, he must have been a man of distinction'.

Nor was Ali Bey al-Abbassi – or Domingo Badia y Leblich – unknown to European society of letters and science. On his visit to England in 1802 he made the acquaintance of Sir Joseph Banks, president of the African Association, and became intimate enough to leave a miniature of himself with the Englishman. Chateaubriand, running into him in Alexandria, took him to be a rich Turk, *'le plus savant et le plus poli au monde'*, and was much flattered that a Turk should know his works so well as to salute him *'Ah mon cher Atala, et chere Renee!'* The Prussian naturalist Von Humboldt recommended him highly to an Englishwoman living in Paris. His English publishers revealed these contacts with society, being at evident pains to prove the authenticity of his travels, if not to betray his identity, for his books were published under his Arab pseudonym.

Christian, Morisco, Jew, or Turk – and the evidence contradicts none of these, except the last – Ali Bey travelled as a Muslim and was accepted as one by nearly all he met. He himself gave a simple reason for his Eastern travels.

After having passed many years in the Christian states, studying the sciences of nature, and the arts most useful to man in society, whatever be his faith or the religion of his heart, I determined at last to visit the Mahometan countries; and, while engaged in performing the pilgrimage to Mecca, to observe the manners, customs, and nature of the countries through which I should pass, in order that I might make the laborious journey of some utility to the country which I at last select for my abode.

Ali Bey first entered the Muslim countries by slipping across the Straits of Gibraltar from Spain into the domains of the Sultan of Morocco. He was almost immediately accepted by the best society of Tangiers: 'My liberality and intellectual force . . . contributed to fix on me the general attention, and in a very short time, I attained a decided superiority over all strangers, and even over persons of distinction in the town.' The Sultan himself was so impressed by Ali Bey's attainments – including the ability, so useful to explorers, of predicting the eclipse of heavenly bodies – that he gave him an estate near Marrakesh and two women, one white and one black, whom he received with every mark of respect but with whom he declined to cohabit. Swanning about the country, he received the homage of the Moroccans, a people disposed towards wonder-working saints. In Fez, 'they kissed my beard several hundred times', and when he left the city, 'I was pressed on all sides, that they might touch me, and ask for my prayers. . . . They kissed my hands, stirrups, anything they could lay hold of. . . . How interesting was this simplicity. The mothers were watching me how I should receive their children.' He even had an umbrella carried over his head, a prerogative hitherto reserved for the Sultan. After two years, the Sultan abruptly withdrew his favours and expelled Ali Bey from his domains. Forced to leave his goods and servants behind, Ali Bey sailed alone on a ship bound for African Tripoli, reflecting bitterly on the fickleness of princes.

But his luck and his apparently inexhaustible funds held out. Before his disgrace he had obtained a letter from the Sultan recommending him to all persons he might meet on a proposed pilgrimage to Mecca. In Tripoli he consorted with the ruler and with the admiral of the Tripolitanian fleet, an Englishman married to a relative of the ruler. Arriving in Alexandria, he joined the society of North African grandees, which included an exiled brother of the Sultan of Morocco, and thereafter he posed as a Maghrabi. When he left on the pilgrimage, his noble friends in Egypt sent him off with recommendations to their correspondents in the Hijaz. Ali Bey had raised social climbing to a fine art.

Thanks to one of his letters of recommendation, Ali Bey, on his arrival in Jiddah, was promptly lodged in a comfortable apartment. For four days he was indisposed with fever, but on Friday he went to the mosque for midday prayers. There he had a disagreeable encounter with the governor, the same Negro slave who had so displeased Lord Valentia. This man's soldiers forced Ali Bey to cede his place and even his carpet, which his servant had laid in a position of honour next to the imam. Everyone looked with astonishment to see if the newcomer would take offence. But the governor's men were armed, and rather than provoke an incident Ali Bey ceded. When the prayers were finished, however, he rose and said to his servant in a loud voice, 'Take up that carpet, carry it to the Imam, and tell him I present it to him for the use of the mosque; for I will never make use of it for my prayers.' The people 'applauded this action; but the black governor and his officers remained petrified. I presented alms to the mosque and the poor and, accompanied by several persons, returned home, where I went to bed, tormented by a strong fever.'

Notwithstanding his bad health, Ali Bey explored Jiddah and determined for the first time its longitude and latitude. He thought it a pretty town and was pleased to find the air perfumed by incense carried in small chafing-dishes by the water-sellers. But he found the climate appalling. 'The north wind, traversing the deserts of Arabia, arrives in such a state of dryness, that the skin is parched; paper cracks as if it were in the mouth of an oven; and the air is always loaded with sand. If the wind changes to the south, everything is in an opposite extreme; the air is damp; and everything that they handle feels of a clammy wet.' He saw no Europeans but a few Christian Copts, who were confined to barracks near the port. The garrison of 200 Turkish and Arab soldiers spent their time in the coffee-houses drinking, smoking, and playing chess. The rich showed great luxury in their houses and dress, but there were many poor living in great misery. The mixture of races, noted by all visitors to the Hijaz, Ali Bey ascribed to the prevalence of slavery. On the day of his arrival his landlord asked him if he could purchase an Abyssinian woman for him; Ali Bey declined on the grounds that he was under a state of penance during the pilgrimage.

Though still weak from fever, he set out for Mecca riding for the first time in his life on a camel, in a *shugduf*, or litter, made of sticks covered with cushions and roofed with boughs. Although this allowed him to sit or lie down at will, the motion of the camel exhausted him. His Arab guides started quarrelling before they left the town, but when the moon shone – they travelled at night as all caravans were wont to do – they danced and sang by its light. At last he fell asleep only to awake in a fever, vomiting blood. The Arabs had also fallen asleep and lost the way, but with his usual proficiency Ali Bey woke them and put them back on the track. Sleepless and ill, he consoled himself by noting the geology and terrain by moonlight. It also amused him to watch the camels eat when the caravan stopped: each animal ate his own share placed before him, and if any camel left his place 'his companion at his side appeared to scold him in a friendly manner, which made the other feel his fault, and return to it again'.

At midnight on the fourth day the caravan reached the first houses of Mecca. Several Maghrabis came out to meet it with pitchers of water from the Well of Zamzam; some of them offered to supply Ali Bey's house, telling him secretly never to drink the water which the chief of the well might offer him. He was to learn why later. He went to his lodgings, made a general ablution, and was taken to the temple on the arms of his servants. As he entered the Holy Mosque, he was awe-struck.

The crowd that surrounded me; the porticos of columns half hid from view; the immense size of the temple; the Kaaba, or house of God, covered with the black cloth from top to bottom, and surrounded with a circle of lamps or lanterns; the hour; the silence of the night; and this man speaking in a solemn tone, as if he had been inspired; all served to form an imposing picture, which will never be effaced from my memory.

Whatever his origins, Ali Bey always spoke with respect of the religion of Muhammad, and his comments on the rites and beliefs of Islam were expressed in accents of faith. His definition of Islam is both sympathetic and exact: 'The Mahometan religion is extremely simple; it has no mysteries, no sacraments, no intermediate persons between God and man, known by the name of priests or ministers; no altars, no images, or ornaments. God is invisible, the heart of man is his altar, and every Mussulman is a high priest.'

In this spirit he made the seven-fold *tawaf*, or circuit of the Kaʿba, kissed the Black Stone, and submitted to having his head shaven. While drinking at Zamzam he made the acquaintance of the chief of the well, whom he had been warned against. He was 'a young man, about 25 or 24 years of age, extremely handsome, with very fine eyes. He dresses remarkably well, and is very polished. He has an air of sweetness, which is seducing, and appears to be endowed with all the qualities which render a person amiable. As he possesses the entire confidence of the Scherif, he fills the most important place. His title is the Poisoner.'

Nevertheless Ali Bey accepted the attentions of this dangerous young man, who sent him two pitchers of water every day and came 'running with the most winning grace and sweetness to present me with a handsome cup filled with the same water, which I drank to the last drop'. He seemed pleased by his own recklessness, for he had been warned that 'upon the slightest suspicion, or at the least caprice that may arise in the mind of the Scherif, he orders, the other obeys, and the unhappy stranger ceases to exist. As it is reckoned impious not to accept the sacred water presented by the chief of the well, this man is the arbiter of the lives of every one, and has already sacrificed many victims.' It was charming of Ali Bey to allow himself to become infatuated with this alarming young man, but it is hard to believe that even the Sharif Ghalib would commit a sacrilege of such Borgian dimensions as using the sacred well to poison his enemies. In any case, Ali Bey always kept in his pocket a dose of vitriolated zinc, a powerful emetic, to take the minute he suspected treachery.

It was the Poisoner who took Ali Bey to call upon his master. Ghalib was withdrawn and uncommunicative, as well he might be with Saʿud watching his every move. Ali Bey observed with interest that the Sharif smoked tobacco, despite the Wahhabi prohibition, but kept the pipe in an adjoining room with a leather tube passed through a hole in the wall.

Ali Bey was European at least in his passion for measuring things. He found the great courtyard of the Holy Mosque to be a parallelogram 536 feet long, and the Ka'ba, or Cube, to be actually a trapezium in plan, one side being 38 feet 4 inches, the other 29 feet, and the height 34 feet 4 inches. He found it to be built of square-hewn stone composed of quartz, schorl, and mica, resting on a base of marble. A single door six feet above the pavement was made of bronze covered with a thin layer of silver. The Black Stone set in a silver collar in a corner of the Ka'ba moved him to a strange mixture of faith and science:

We believe that this miraculous stone was a transparent hyacinth, brought from heaven to Abraham by the angel Gabriel, as a pledge of his divinity; and, being touched by an impure woman, became black and opaque. The stone is a fragment of volcanic basalt, which is sprinkled throughout its circumference with small pointed coloured crystals, and varied with red fieldspath, upon a dark background like coal, except one of its protuberances, which is a little reddish. The continual kisses and touchings of the faithful have worn the surface uneven, so that it now has a muscular appearance. It has nearly fifteen muscles, and one deep hollow.

Ali Bey had the privilege of entering the Ka'ba, not once but twice. It was opened only three days in the year, the third day being reserved for women. On the first occasion he mounted by means of wooden stairs rolled up to the door, prayed in each corner of the bare room, and on leaving kissed the silver key which a child of the Sharif presented. Five days later he assisted at the annual washing of the Ka'ba. The staircase was not in place, and the Sharif entered on the heads and shoulders of the multitude. All the water-carriers of Mecca crowded round with vessels filled with water, which they passed from hand to hand into the Ka'ba along with a number of small brooms made of palm leaves. The black eunuchs of the temple, who were also inside the sacred building, threw the water on the floor; as it flowed through a hole under the door, it was caught by the faithful who drank and washed in it. Ali Bey, who was waiting on the side, was given a small pitcher of it; he drank as much as he could and threw the rest over him, 'for although the water is very dirty, it is a benediction of God, and is besides much perfumed with rose water'. He was then lifted upon the heads of the crowd and handed to the door, where he joined the Sharif in sweeping the floor. He was then given a silver cup filled with a paste of sandalwood dust and essence of roses, which he spread on the wall and the tapestry hangings. The Sharif then declared him a 'Servant of the House of God' and he received the congratulations of the eunuchs. He paid for these favours 'in the best manner I could'.

Ali Bey did not think much of the Meccans: 'There are no people more dull and melancholy than these. I never once heard the sound of a musical instrument or song during my whole stay.' As this contradicts the impressions of other travellers both before and after Ali Bey, it can probably be ascribed to Wahhabi influence, or to fear of Wahhabi interference. Whatever the cause, the Meccans vented their resentment on others. 'Plunged into a continual melancholy, the least contradiction irritates them; and the few slaves they have are the most unhappy and wretched of all the Mussulman slaves, in consequence of the bad treatment they experience.' The arts and sciences were totally neglected. There were no locksmiths or gunsmiths, no stone cutters, shoemakers, or cutlers. The whole knowledge of the Meccans was confined to reading the Quran and writing very badly; the Qurans written in Mecca were so full of errors that they were not worth obtaining. The chief astronomer knew nothing about astronomy, and Ali Bey met only two physicians, or 'two who dared to take the name', and both employed only prayers and superstitions in their cures.

The women of Mecca enjoyed more liberty than any others Ali Bey had seen; in fact, he was tempted to call their freedom effrontery. 'I saw several of them that lived in neighbouring houses present themselves continually at the windows, and some of them entirely undressed.' He must have meant *déshabillée*. 'A lady, who occupied the upper storey of the house in which I lived, used to make me a thousand courtesies and compliments, with her face entirely uncovered, every time I went upon the terrace to make my astronomical observations; and I began to suspect that the women themselves might perhaps be a branch of the speculation of their poor husbands.' The appearance of these bold women was highly exotic.

All the women I saw had a great deal of grace and very fine eyes; but their hollow cheeks, painted a greenish yellow, gave them the appearance of having jaundice. Their noses are regular, but they have large mouths. They speak very well, and express themselves with great feeling. They engrave indelible drawings upon their skin, and stain their eyelids black, their teeth yellow, and their lips, feet, and hands a red tile colour.

The men had an equally eccentric style of ornament, perhaps of African origin. It was the custom among male Meccans to make three perpendicular incisions on each cheek, leaving scars which remained for life. Ali Bey heard two different accounts of the purpose of this custom: that it was a form of medical bleeding, or that it was a mark to distinguish them as slaves of the House of God.

From such signs of almost morbid sophistication, it was a relief to Ali Bey to turn to the Wahhabis. For the Spaniard was the first Westerner to witness an eruption of the Unitarian hordes into the Hijaz. While walking in one of the principal streets of Mecca one morning, he saw a huge crowd of men approaching, five or six thousand, he estimated, pressed together and filling the street like a torrent. They were preceded by three or four horsemen and followed by another fifteen or twenty men riding camels or horses, all armed with twelve-foot lances. Ali Bey mounted a rubbish heap to see them better. They were naked, except for a scrap of cloth round their waists and a pad that passed over the left shoulder and under the right arm, and had matchlocks on their shoulders and daggers at their waists. He was struck by their handsome features; they were copper coloured, well made, and very well proportioned, though of short stature. Their heads reminded him of classical Greek sculpture, and he praised their lively eyes and expressive countenances. Some were uttering cries of holy joy, others reciting prayers in loud voices. They had come to pray at the Ka'ba, a right that the Sharif, no matter how apprehensive, could no longer deny them.

The people of Mecca fled at the sight of this torrent of naked savages, leaving the streets deserted. A handful of children, however, who were often used as pilgrim guides, went out to meet them, so avid were the Meccans to make money. The Wahhabis swarmed into the Holy Mosque. The first group had begun to make their turns round the Ka'ba when others entered in a tumult and mixed among the first. The voices of the young guides were lost in the confusion. As all wished to kiss the Black Stone at once, they threw themselves on the spot, many making their way by dint of the sticks they carried in their hands. Their chiefs climbed on the base near the Stone to restore order, but the noise of the crowd prevented their voices being heard. The movement of the circle increased by mutual impulse, and in the tumult the guns carried on the shoulders of the mob broke all the lamps surrounding the Ka'ba.

Then they rushed upon the Well of Zamzam, and in a few moments the ropes, buckets, and pulleys were all broken. The Poisoner and his assistants fled, and the Wahhabis took over the well, forming a human chain to descend to the bottom and pass the water up from hand to hand. They had no money to pay the guides or to leave as alms at the well, but they left a few grains of gunpowder, pieces of lead, or a handful of coffee-beans to discharge their debts.

As fresh contingents of Wahhabis arrived daily to perform the hajj, the Sharif hid in his castle; the fortresses were all provisioned and garrisoned, sentinels posted on the ramparts, and several gates walled up. Although the caravans from Egypt and the East had arrived, the Damascus caravan, which included that from Constantinople, was stopped. It had set out bravely with troops, artillery, and a great number of women, carrying the rich carpet that was sent by the Porte every year to adorn the tomb of Muhammad. Sa'ud's men, however, had met it before Medina and informed the Amir al-Hajj that the carpet could not be received and that he must send back the troops and women if he wished to continue to Mecca as a true pilgrim. The Amir refused and the caravan returned to Damascus.

Still, the variety of believers from all over the Muslim world was impressive:

An innumerable crowd of men from all nations, of all colours, coming from the extremities of the earth, through a thousand dangers, and encountering fatigue of every description, to adore the same God, the God of nature. The native of Circassia presents his hand in a friendly manner to the Ethiopian, or the Negro of Guinea; the Indian and the Persian embrace among the inhabitants of Barbary and Morocco; all looking upon each other as brothers, or individuals of the same family united by the bonds of religion.

A rosy picture perhaps, but it moved Ali Bey to a panegyric of his faith. 'No, there is not any religion that presents to the senses a spectacle more simple, affecting, and majestic! Philosophers of the earth! permit me, Ali Bey, to defend my religion, as you defend spiritual things from those which are material, the plenum from the vacuum, and the necessary existence of creation.' The thought may be obscure, but the emotion is transparent.

Nevertheless, the Wahhabis dominated the pilgrimage of 1807. On the plain of Arafat an army of 45,000 of them, with their camels and horses, passed before Ali Bey's eyes and set up their camp at the foot of the Mount of Mercy. Sa'ud was present, but Ali Bey could not distinguish him from the rest. He thought a venerable old man with a long white beard might have been he, as he was preceded by a green standard bearing in white letters the confession of the faith: *La illaha illa Allah*, 'There is no divinity but God.' Despite the remonstrances of his people, Ali Bey penetrated the ranks of the Wahhabis and spoke to several of them, discovering much reason and moderation among them. He did not seek an introduction to Sa'ud for fear of offending the Sharif.

The Wahhabis showed their power at Arafat. When an imam of the Sharif came to preach the sermon, Sa'ud sent him back and had one of his own imams preach instead. That was not all. On 26 February Sa'ud had published in all public places an order that all Turkish and Maghrabi soldiers should quit Mecca the following day, in preparation for leaving the country. The interdiction included the *wali* sent by the Porte to Jiddah, as well as the qadis sent from Constantinople, so that not a single Turk would be left in the country. It was rumoured that Sa'ud would establish his residence at Mecca, or at least give the government of the Hijaz to one of his sons.

All the Turkish soldiers retired to Jiddah during the night. The members of a small caravan from African Tripoli packed their tents at noon and set off with so little preparation that fears were entertained for their safety. During the night 250 of the soldiers of the Sharif went over to Sa'ud; all the rest left Mecca within a few days. Contrary to expectations, Sa'ud led his troops out of Mecca and towards Medina, leaving only a small garrison, his own qadis installed in place of the Turks, and a present of 35,000 francs for the servants of the Holy Mosque and the poor of Mecca. Not wishing to prolong his stay under such unsettled conditions, Ali Bey returned to Jiddah on 2 March.

Sa'ud, rightly called the Great by his countrymen, was a man cast in the mould of the Prophet, noted for the dignity of his bearing and the simplicity of his manners. His fine countenance was adorned by a luxuriant beard, an exceptional feature among the desert Arabs, and he was affectionately known as Abu Shuwarib, Father of Moustaches. He dressed in Bedouin garb, a belted shirt covered by a woollen cloak, or *aba*, on his head a *kaffiyah*, or headcloth, scrupulously clean and scented with civet. His manners were those of a Bedouin shaikh, simple and grave. He allowed all to address him as 'O Sa'ud' or 'O Father of Moustaches', desired all to remain seated when he appeared, and exchanged the kiss of peace with visiting shaikhs. At home in Dar'iyah he resided in a large mansion built by his father on the hill of Turaif, surrounded by his large family, including his brothers and married sons, each of whom had an apartment of his own. Besides his wives, he kept several Abyssinian concubines, as was the custom of the great men of Najd. He owned a large number of *dalouls*, swift, well-bred camels, and some 2,000 horses and mares that were his personal property. He once paid £600 for a mare, and his subjects complained that if someone owned a fine mare Sa'ud was sure to find that the owner had committed some trespass for which the mare should be forfeited.

In Dar'iyah he received all the shaikhs of Najd who came to pay him homage. They were lodged in his house, while visitors of lower rank were fed and sent a daily allowance of fodder for their animals. He held public audience three times a day, early in the morning, between three and six in the afternoon, and late in the evening, to which everyone was admitted. Yet he lived in fear of being assassinated like his father, wearing a coat of mail under his shirt and rarely leaving his house except to attend Friday prayers at the mosque. Although there was no question of his bravery, after his accession he never took the field at the head of his troops but directed their operations from the rear.

Sa'ud's mother was a daughter of the great reformer Muhammad 'Abd al-Wahhab, so he inherited the mantle of religious authority as well as the sword of government. He prayed regularly and made the pilgrimage every year he could. In Dar'iyah after supper he assembled all his visitors, his sons, and retainers in the great hall, where one of the *'ulama* read a few pages of the Quran or the traditions of the Prophet and interpreted the texts by means of the commentaries of the best writers. Sa'ud himself closed the meeting by taking the book and explaining the difficult passages. His voice was sonorous and sweet and his eloquence much admired. But he could be stern: he hated lies and had to be forcibly restrained from hitting someone he thought to be lying. However, if an honest argument arose over an interpretation of a sacred text, he closed the discussion by saying, 'God knows best.'

Ali Bey had another encounter with the Wahhabis, which was more frightening than his first one. Having no wish to linger in Arabia under the harsh rule of Sa'ud, he took ship from Jiddah for Suez as soon as he could. The ship stopped at Yanbu', however, and Ali Bey could not resist the temptation to visit Medina. As the ship's captain had his family at Yanbu' he agreed to wait there, and Ali Bey persuaded several of his fellow pilgrims, both Arabs and Turks, to undertake the journey with him. They left Yanbu' on the evening of 31 March, a small caravan of fifty dromedaries. Ali Bey took with him only a small trunk containing his instruments and collections, and three of his servants, leaving the others on the ship to guard his things. He was soon exhausted from riding in a wooden saddle without stirrups and was twice violently sick before the first daybreak. Nevertheless, he took bearings, noted the terrain, and collected a number of rocks and plants. On the second stage of the march the caravan reached Jadaidah, sixteen leagues from Medina, and, no longer able to endure the pace of the dromedaries, Ali Bey allowed the caravan to go on without him, while he spent the day resting, guarded by his three servants.

The following day he set out to rejoin the caravan. Within a couple of hours two Wahhabis rode down from the mountain, stopped him, and asked him where he was going. To Medina, he replied. For answer he was told he could not continue. A chief and two officers then came up and questioned him anew. He answered very coolly but could not help recalling a rumour he had heard at Jiddah that all the Turks who had left Mecca had been strangled on the road. The Wahhabis ordered him to hand over his money, and he gave them four Spanish piastres he had in his pocket. They accused him of having more in his belt; he denied it; they insisted; and he began to undress. They stopped him but, seeing the chain of his watch, relieved him of his time-piece by force. Then they told the camel driver to proceed to another spot to await their orders.

While the Wahhabis remained behind to divide the spoils, Ali Bey quickly rearranged his affairs. He destroyed a case of insects that he had collected, along with the plants and fossils gathered on the road from Yanbu'. He swallowed a letter from Prince Moulay Hassan of Morocco which he thought might compromise him. And he gave some piastres which he had in his trunk to his steward and ordered his servants to hide their tobacco under a stone. A moment later the Wahhabis came up to guard them. After two hours, messengers arrived from the Wahhabi amir to demand 500 francs for the prisoner's release. Ali Bey told them that he had no money, and they withdrew. Soon the order came to move and, going behind a mountain, Ali Bey found the rest of his caravan, also taken prisoner. The Wahhabis had ominously separated the Turks from the Arabs, and Ali Bey went to join the latter. The prisoners were heavily guarded and some were pale and trembling with fear. When it was announced that every pilgrim was to pay 500 francs, they all uttered cries of anguish and begged for mercy. Towards sunset word arrived that the price had been reduced to 200 francs. This produced fresh tears, for the travellers really had no money on them. After sunset they were led into a hollow and made to sit in two separate groups. There was much coming and going among the Wahhabis, which filled the prisoners with terror. Ali Bey feared not for his own safety, as he was considered to be a Maghrabi, but he expected to witness a bloody scene for which the Turks would furnish the victims. He was deeply afflicted, as he had urged his fellow pilgrims to make the journey to Medina.

During the night they were moved back along the road to Yanbu', and in the morning reached an encampment which turned out to be the caravan of the imams, servants, and slaves of the Prophet's Mosque, whom Sa'ud had ordered out of Arabia. While they were filling their water-skins at a well, Ali Bey's servant, who was leading his master's camel, broke and ran towards the encampment to place himself under the protection of the people of the temple. As he kept hold of the camel's halter, the animal was forced to run, with Ali Bey on its back. A Wahhabi guard chased them, struck the servant to the ground, kicked him several times, and led the camel and its rider back to the caravan, without saying a word.

At the next halt new discussions were held concerning the ransom. The Wahhabis examined their prisoners' effects and at length made each Turk pay twenty francs and each Maghrabi a cloak and a sack of biscuits. From Ali Bey they took three piastres they found in his writing-desk and from his steward a caftan. They extracted from each camel driver fifteen piastres, but Ali Bey's man refused to pay and was taken off to the amir and never seen again. The pilgrims were then solemnly informed of the order of Sa'ud forbidding any pilgrim to go to Medina. Then, still guarded by Wahhabi soldiers, they began the march back to Yanbu'. When they arrived, the people on the ship expressed great joy at Ali Bey's deliverance.

Ali Bey did not blame the Wahhabis. They were the effective government, and he and his party had wilfully disobeyed a general order to pilgrims not to go to Medina. The exactions were only a fine for the infraction of the standing order; the Wahhabis could have taken all they possessed but had refrained from this. Their menaces towards the Turks were due to their resentment and hatred of that nation, the very name of which aroused them to fury. Ali Bey thought the adventure had ended happily, though he regretted the loss of an interesting journey to Medina and of his watch.

Ali Bey's expulsion by the Wahhabis marked the end of his sojourn in Arabia. On his way home he went to Jerusalem, where he was received as a Muslim at the Dome of the Rock. In 1818 he started out again for the Hijaz but got no further than Syria, where he died suddenly and mysteriously. Because of the reputed connection with Napoleon, it was widely supposed that he was poisoned by the English, but it seems more likely that his death was caused by one of the illnesses constantly suffered by nineteenth-century travellers. In the Spanish edition of his travels, it was claimed that a cross was found under his clothing after his death. But the Spanish editors, or the Badia family, may have had their own reasons for wishing this story to be believed, for in Spain Muslims and Jews were still proscribed. Whatever his origins or political sympathies, Ali Bey appears to have been a true Muslim in his beliefs.

For four years no great caravan reached the Holy Cities from the north. Sa'ud continued to send raiding parties into Mesopotamia and even into

Syria. The southern Wahhabis also made lightning plunder raids into Yemen. But they suffered losses as well. In 1809 an English naval squadron bombarded the Wahhabi port of Ras al-Khaimah, a notorious pirate lair on the Persian Gulf; a ship's heliograph was trained on the reed huts of which the town largely consisted, burning them to the ground. In 1810 the sudden appearance of 6,000 Wahhabi warriors in the plain of Hauran struck terror into the heart of Syria. The raiders had ridden thirty-five days by circuitous routes so secretly that the victims had only two days' notice of the danger. They sacked thirty-five villages, burning the corn, killing the defenders, and taking prisoners. One woman, a Christian carried off as a slave, was later released on Sa'ud's orders. The inhabitants of Damascus sent their valuables into the mountains of Lebanon for safety and prepared to follow themselves. Had he known the terror he inspired, Sa'ud might easily have taken one of the richest cities of Islam. But he withdrew his men with considerable booty.

The Porte looked on helplessly as its authority was flouted, and the very foundations of the Ottoman empire seemed to be crumbling under the onslaught of the Wahhabis. All attempts emanating from Mecca or Baghdad to stop them had failed. Constantinople itself was too concerned over the upheavals of the Napoleonic wars in Europe to diminish its own defences by mounting a war in Arabia. It therefore had no choice but to turn once more to Mehmet Ali, Pasha of Egypt.

PART II
CATASTROPHE

*Your country is desolate, your cities are burned with fire:
your land, strangers devour it in your presence, and it is
desolate, as overthrown by strangers.*

Isaiah

CHAPTER 5
Men of Blood

Mehmet Ali could procrastinate no longer. For nearly four years he had put off responding to his sovereign's commands. During that time he had strengthened his hold over Egypt and begun modernizing his army and administration with the help of French advisers left over from the Napoleonic invasion. His son Ibrahim had subdued the Mamluks of Upper Egypt, killing as many of their leaders as fell into his hands and disarming their followers. His beloved Albanians, while personally loyal to their Pasha, were undisciplined and jealous of their privileges, and hindered his plans to improve the efficiency of the army; they would be better employed outside Egypt in a foreign war. The Porte for its part promised its support in the form of men, arms, transport, and supplies. In 1809, therefore, Mehmet Ali began serious preparations for a campaign against the Wahhabis, naming his youngest son, Tusun, then only seventeen years old but already a veteran in the field, to command the expedition. For two years, 1,000 workmen, mostly Greeks and other Europeans, were employed at Suez building a fleet of transport ships. Volunteers from all over the Ottoman empire and beyond poured into Egypt, attracted by the promise of booty and military adventure.

To celebrate the investiture of Tusun as commander-in-chief of the expedition, Mehmet Ali invited the notables of Cairo to a ceremony at the Citadel. Among the guests were those Mamluks who had remained in the capital or who had returned there under a safe-conduct granted by Ibrahim. Twenty-five beys, sixty *kashifs*, or lieutenants, and four hundred lesser Mamluks mounted on their fine ponies were led by Shahin Bey, successor to Bardissy and Elfi, up the steep lane, enclosed between high walls or overlooking sheer drops, that leads to the castle.

When the ceremony was over, a guard of honour and a military band preceded the Mamluks down the narrow passage. Albanian soldiers armed with muskets stood at attention on the enclosing walls. When the vanguard passed through the lower gate, the doors were swung shut in the face of the Mamluks; at the same moment the gate above them clanged shut, cutting off all escape. The Albanians on the walls raised their muskets and mowed down the shouting Mamluks on their rearing horses. All were killed but one man, Hasan Bey, a brother of Elfi, who spurred his mount over a parapet, plunging sixty feet to the rocks below; the horse died on impact, but Hasan Bey jumped from the saddle and limped off to asylum among the Bedouins of the Eastern Desert. For six days the city rang with shots and cries as the remaining Mamluks were hunted down and slaughtered by the Albanians, who were allowed to keep whatever treasures, horses, or slaves they found in the chase. The Mamluk corps, which had ruled and exploited Egypt for centuries, was effectively crushed, and Mehmet Ali felt ready to face the enemy abroad.

One of the Albanian guards stationed at the Citadel that day was in fact an Italian. Giovanni Finati, a deserter from Napoleon's conscript army in Italy, had made his way to Egypt and once there, for want of anything better to do, had joined Mehmet Ali's forces. Characteristically, he claimed to have had no part in the killing. 'For myself,' he wrote, 'I have reason to be thankful that, though I was one of the soldiers stationed at the citadel that morning, I shed none of the blood of those unhappy men, having had the good fortune to be posted at an avenue where none of them attempted to pass, or come near me, so that my pistol and musket were never fired.' He also denied complicity in the hunting-down of the remaining Mamluks.

Though present at many of these scenes . . . I bore little part in them, and shall hardly be accused of having laid hands on a very large share of plunder, when I mention that, with the exception of a saddle, which I brought home, richly mounted in silver gilt – a piece of magnificence in great estimation with the Beys – and a slave girl that had belonged to one of them, I took no advantage of the permission given to make prize of whatever we found in their houses. . . . The girl was young and pretty, and, as it happened, did not come empty-handed, for she had contrived to secret about her some trinkets and money from the harem which she had belonged to. I lodged her first in the house of an acquaintance . . . and went often to visit her; but, by-and-by, a proclamation coming out from the citadel, that such soldiers as should deliver up any woman taken from the Mamelukes should receive the full equivalent in money, I consulted my little slave, and gave her her choice; to which she answering that she preferred to continue with me, I was so pleased with her, that I determined on making her my wife, and was married accordingly after the Turkish form, which is purely a civil contract.

Finati had come a long way from his boyhood home in Ferrara, where he had studied for the priesthood under the care of an ecclesiastical uncle. He was one of those renegades who drifted like flotsam on the currents of Islam, but he is one of the few renegades whose motives – or lack of them – are known to us. For towards the end of his life he wrote a little book of memoirs with the help of William John Bankes, an Englishman whose dragoman he became. A kind of shiftless opportunism carried him along – to Arabia, the First Cataract of the Nile, Meroë, Jerusalem – while constant subterfuge and excuse enabled him to evade responsibility for the actions in which he was engaged. But thanks to his enlistment as a private soldier in Tusun's army, we have a worm's-eye view of some of the early battles of the Egyptian-Wahhabi war.

After deserting from Napoleon's army, Finati had fled to Scutari in Turkish Albania, where, along with thirteen other deserters (including a sergeant's wife, who immediately disappeared into a Turkish officer's harem), he had casually embraced Islam in order to escape slavery in the quarries. The Italian converts were fortunate in being spared the rite of circumcision – a dangerous operation for adult males in those days – until they should become more proficient in their new religion. Making his way to Egypt, Finati enlisted as a private soldier in a small Albanian company and soon rose to the rank of *balik-bashi*, or corporal. He saw active service in Upper Egypt chasing the Mamluks and returned to Cairo just in time for the massacre at the Citadel.

Finati willingly joined the expedition under Tusun's command, for he had reason to be grateful to the young bey. The Italian had accidentally killed a comrade in arms, mistaking him for a thief in the night. Tusun pardoned him and paid the blood-money from his own treasury to fore-stall the revenge of the dead man's friends. 'Kind, generous, humane, and affable,' Finati said of his benefactor, 'he conciliated the esteem and affection of all who approached or served under him. Nay, he was capable of doing good to his very enemies.' Long after the massacre at the Citadel when some lurking Mamluk was surprised by soldiers and put to death, the Mamluk's family would come and throw themselves at Tusun's feet, often bringing with them the headless body of husband or father to confirm their tale and move him to pity. 'In no instance did he turn away their entreaties or withhold what relief was in his power; – and he protected and provided for the widow, and became a father to the children.' But it was not for his tender feelings that Tusun was chosen to lead an important military expedition. While yet a mere boy he had shown extraordinary courage in his father's war against the Mamluks.

As second-in-command of the expedition Mehmet Ali appointed an Albanian officer who rejoiced in the name of Ahmad Bonaparte. His utter disregard for human life and contempt for moral principles added to his boasting had earned him his surname, which he used even in official signatures. He was a brave soldier, but, according to Burckhardt, drunkenness and lusts of the vilest kind had deprived his mind of all energy and judgment. One of the leading merchants of Cairo, Muhammad al-Mahrouki, was entrusted with the political conduct of the war and with making financial arrangements with the Bedouins whom Mehmet Ali hoped to win over. Two of the learned *'ulama* of al-Azhar university accompanied the troops to try to convince the Wahhabis of the errors of their faith.

When Sharif Ghalib heard of the preparations afoot in Egypt, he communicated secretly with Mehmet Ali, saying that circumstances beyond his control had forced him to adopt Wahhabism but that he was ready to cast it off at the first appearance of a respectable army in the Hijaz. He also supplied information about the strength and disposition of the Wahhabis, the sympathies and forces of the tribes, and the best mode of attack. Mehmet Ali had little faith in Ghalib, but he wanted his help. He therefore made promises that the Sharif's authority would be respected and that the customs duties of Jiddah would be left in his hands. To encourage the Egyptian forces, he had the story spread about that the Sharif's army would join them on arrival.

Throughout the early summer of 1811, the road to Suez was thronged with troops, their baggage, and hangers-on. In August, 15,000 to 20,000 of the infantry embarked on ships bound for Yanbu'. The cavalry, consisting of some 800 Turkish horsemen with Tusun himself at their head, rode by land across Sinai and down the Red Sea coast. Armed Bedouins of the Hawaitat tribe rode with them. The castles along the pilgrim road had been repaired and stocked with supplies, and garrisoned with Maghrabi soldiers accustomed to dealing with Bedouins. Those who lived near the castles had been hired to take their camels into Egypt and return with provisions for the Turkish cavalry.

The infantry was delayed by storms at sea. Finati, who was among the infantry, piously remarked that such storms were caused by Pharaoh's host who had been drowned here while pursuing the Israelites and who were still trying to draw down all seafarers to their destruction. But the infantry still arrived before the cavalry, landing on the coast a short way from Yanbu'. The town's defences had recently been strengthened with a battery erected by an engineer in the service of the Sharif, who kept about a hundred soldiers in Yanbu'. But these soldiers did not go over to Tusun's forces, and the people of Yanbu', though not Wahhabis, defended their homes against the new pharaoh's host. The invaders invested the town and bombarded it by land and sea. The people gallantly resisted until the engineer was killed by a ball and the battery rendered useless. While the defence continued, those not employed on the wall gathered whatever was portable and of value and retired to a small postern gate in the direction of Medina, where the attack was light. At nightfall, as the invaders were scaling the walls, the defenders fell back on signal and got out by the postern gate. Tusun's victorious troops entered a nearly empty town and began pillaging what had been left.

Tusun sent dispatches to his father reporting the taking of Yanbu' as a great victory and a favourable omen. But he failed to follow up his success and allowed his troops to remain idle while he negotiated with the Bedouins and the Sharif. The Bedouins were too overawed by the might of Sa'ud to join the Turks till they had gained some important advantage. As for Ghalib, he excused himself for not joining the invaders because of his small resources and his fear of Sa'ud, but promised to throw off the mask once the Turks had won over the Bedouins. Meanwhile, Tusun's idle army wasted the town water until the wells failed; new ones were dug outside the walls, but Wahhabi raiding parties harassed the water carriers. The woollen-clad soldiers fainted in the heat and were tormented by insects; some of them died of scorpion bites, while others climbed the palm trees at night to escape this danger.

In January 1812, Tusun, having obtained no satisfaction from the Sharif or the Bedouins, decided to march on Medina. The road lay through a defile, called by the Turks Jadeed Boghaz and by the Arabs al-Khaif, which at some points was only wide enough for ten men to walk abreast. Unknown to the Turks, the Wahhabis awaited them behind hastily built breastworks on the heights. A contingent of Harb Bedouin guarded another pass in case the invaders took an alternative route.

Tusun harangued his men on the honour that would accrue to them from the redemption of Medina, and his orders to force the pass were instantly obeyed. The mass of troops pushed forward under sharp firing from both sides. They gained possession of several of the Wahhabi positions, but these were commanded by other positions, and the Wahhabi bullets poured down with deadly effect. At midday the sun, reflected from the bare mountains, grew intensely hot and a mutual truce was declared. The Turks lay down under some palm trees and refreshed themselves with dates, but no one had thought to bring water, and their thirst became intolerable. Tusun's signal for action at four o'clock was received with a desperation bordering on joy. Both sides fought ferociously till two hours after sunset. Then occurred one of those inexplicable changes of fortune, or of heart, that bedevilled the Turks in battle. 'All at once,' Finati reported, 'some panic or disaster turned the fortune of the battle, and we were put completely to the rout. There was a flight and pursuit, but in such disorder and confusion, nothing being discerned and distinguished, that many of the foremost Wahabees were killed by their own party among our troops, of whom a vast proportion perished at every step.'

Tusun, accompanied by two horsemen, tried to rally his troops. 'Will none of you stand by me?' he cried with tears in his eyes. The three men galloped to the rear and plunged into the enemy ranks to stop the retreat. Luckily the Wahhabis stopped to seize the Turkish baggage, four field-pieces, and the booty in the girdles of the Albanian dead. The remnants of Tusun's army fled to the Turkish camp, but finding it untenable, without fortifications or trenches, they set fire to all the tents, abandoning even the military chest in their haste. They then ran to the shore to board the little squadron of ships that had followed the advance along the coast. Some of the vessels waited in one place, others coasted to pick up the fleeing men. Signal guns were fired to guide the stragglers, who arrived singly or in groups for three days. Tusun, aboard one of the ships, encouraged the broken spirits of his men by his own manful bearing.

As for Finati, he and a companion found themselves intermixed with the enemy and cut off from their own side. They scrambled to the heights, where they scarcely dared stand upright for fear of discovery. They could hear cries and shouts in the distance and saw fires kindling on the heights, which they assumed to be lit by the Wahhabis as signals or as flares to help in the pursuit of the fugitives. Further off, a much wider expanse of flame showed the firing of the Turkish camp.

Tired, hungry, and thirsty, Finati and his companion started for their camp about midnight, crawling on all fours to avoid detection. Several times they passed within sight and hearing of Wahhabi search parties looking for stragglers or stripping the dead. They found the Turkish camp a mass of ashes and embers and partly plundered. Finati managed to find some food, but no water, and about 400 gold crowns scattered on the ground, which he picked up though they were of no use to him. Recalling a spring about five miles away, the two men hurried there, drank, and bathed, then made for the shore. On the way they came upon some comrades sitting despondently round a well whose water was too low to be reached; one of the men threw himself into the well and drowned before their eyes. At daylight they discovered tracks leading in all directions. They separated, and Finati chose a track that led him to the sea. The Egyptian ships were still waiting, and he threw himself into the water and swam out to the ship where Tusun sat contemplating the wreckage of his army. Some cavalrymen came up to the shore, and their thirsty horses drank the salt water and died.

When the Egyptian forces arrived back at Yanbu' a general muster was taken, revealing that the army was reduced by half, and that those who remained were mostly without clothing or arms. Tusun hardly dared send his father the news of his defeat. According to one source, the Turks lost that day 4,000 men, the Arabs only 600. Ghalib, on learning of the Turkish rout, joined the Wahhabis in person at their camp near Badr. But the Wahhabis, assuming that the Egyptians had more troops in reserve, did not pursue them.

Finati was not the only European renegade among the invading Egyptian ranks. One of the brave horsemen who had stuck with Tusun when he tried to rally his men at the pass was one Ibrahim Aga, born Thomas Keith in Edinburgh. A gunsmith in the 72nd Highlanders, he had been taken prisoner during the English landing at Rosetta in 1807, eventually being sold into the service of Tusun. Tusun soon recognized the qualities of his Highland slave and made him chief of his Mamluks, or cavalry. After his proof of loyalty at Jadeed Boghaz, Tusun appointed him treasurer, the second ranking post at the court of a pasha.

After the defeat at Jadeed Boghaz many of the disheartened troops returned to Egypt, a move Tusun could not oppose as all Turkish soldiers served as volunteers. Leading the exodus were two chiefs of infantry, Salih and Omar Aga. They sailed to Qusair and led their discontented troops on a march to Cairo, pillaging the countryside along the way. Mehmet Ali locked himself up in the Citadel and had to give the rebels large presents to persuade them to sail from Alexandria to Constantinople.

Meanwhile Mehmet Ali set about recruiting fresh troops for Arabia. Men and ammunition arrived daily at Yanbu' during the spring and summer of 1812. By distributing large sums of money among the Bedouins, Sayyid Muhammad al-Mahrouki, the expedition's financier, won over some branches of the great tribe of Harb. The tergiversating Ghalib, convinced that Mehmet Ali meant business, promised to open the gates of Mecca and Jiddah if the Turks captured Medina.

The second attempt on the Prophet's city was led by Ahmad Bonaparte in October. The Turkish army passed unmolested through the mountains and arrived under the city walls without hindrance from the

Wahhabis. Sa'ud remained unaccountably inactive in Najd; perhaps the cowardice of the Turks at Jadeed Boghaz made him over-confident. At any rate the Wahhabi garrison at Medina was prepared for a long siege with stocks of provisions behind the protective walls and castle of the inner town. For a fortnight the Turks laid mines and the Wahhabis made sorties, without advantage to either side. In mid-November, when the Wahhabis were at midday prayers, a Turkish mine blew a large gap in the wall, and the Arnauts rushed into the breach, Thomas Keith at their head. The surprised Wahhabis made a dash to the castle; 1,500 of them reached safety, while 1,000 were butchered by the Arnauts, who lost only 50 men. The city was given over to plunder.

The Wahhabis trapped in the castle parleyed for terms, and Ahmad Bonaparte gave them fair promises of safe conduct with 300 camels to carry their baggage into Najd. But when the Wahhabis left the castle they found only fifty animals had been provided and they had to abandon most of their goods. No sooner had they left the town when horsemen pursued and killed as many as they could catch. A Harb chieftain allied to Sa'ud was also promised safe conduct, but the Turks killed his son, plundered his house, and sent him off in chains to Cairo and Constantinople, where he was finally beheaded. In true Vandal style Ahmad Bonaparte had a tower constructed of the skulls of dead Wahhabis on the road to Yanbu'; despite his guards, the Arabs removed these grisly trophies one by one for burial.

Ghalib now redeemed his promise to open the gates of Mecca and Jiddah to the victors. The customary savagery of Turkish troops on entering a defeated town was prohibited by order of Mehmet Ali, and the lives and property of the Meccans were spared. Ghalib joined the victors and led an army of Arabs and black slaves to recover Tayif, which he had lost ten years before. His disloyal brother-in-law, Othman al-Madaifi, fled to the desert where he harassed Turkish transport until a reward of 5,000 dollars to the Bedouins delivered him into Ghalib's hands. He was sent in chains to Constantinople, where he was presented to the Sultan along with the keys to the Holy City, and publicly beheaded as a traitor.

The chief cities of the Hijaz were now in Turkish hands, but the power of the Wahhabis was unbroken. Sa'ud's authority was still acknowledged by the tribes east of the mountains, and even in the Hijaz Wahhabi flying squads menaced the roads and attacked Turkish supply trains. The loyalty of the Sharif was doubtful; he had turned and could turn again. The pilgrim caravan from Cairo arrived in November 1812, but the

Syrian hajj was afraid to start out from Damascus. To break the stalemate and give new heart to the campaign, Mehmet Ali decided to come to the conquered territory in person. To mark the importance of the occasion, the Pasha of Egypt embarked at Suez with 2,000 fresh foot soldiers, while an equal number of cavalry, accompanied by a badly needed train of camels, left for the Hijaz by land.

Ghalib went to Jiddah to greet Mehmet Ali in September 1813, going aboard the Pasha's vessel before he landed. The two rulers swore on the Quran to attempt nothing that was contrary to the interest, safety, or life of the other, a vow that was publicly renewed at the Ka'ba a few weeks later. Mehmet Ali made his headquarters at Mecca in a large *madrasah*, or school-house, near the Holy Mosque. Throughout his stay in the Holy City the Pasha of Egypt comported himself as a devout Muslim, attending public prayers and regularly visiting the Ka'ba.

At first the Sharif and the Pasha visited each other on friendly terms, but gradually their relations cooled. Ghalib complained that the customs duties of Jiddah were withheld, while Mehmet Ali accused the Sharif of failing to persuade the Bedouins to supply him with the required numbers of baggage camels. The Sultan had issued a *firman* permitting Mehmet Ali to act towards the Sharif as he saw fit, either to retain him as head of the government of the Hijaz, or to arrest and depose him. But Ghalib was not in a helpless position. He resided on a hill commanding Mecca in a strongly built palace garrisoned with 800 men, protected by twelve heavy guns, well stocked with provisions and water, and connected by means of an underground passage to the castle. Moreover he commanded 1,500 fighting men in Mecca and more in Tayif and Jiddah. And the Bedouin tribes preferred him to the foreign Pasha.

But Mehmet Ali determined to win by guile what he could not take by force. When Ghalib visited him accompanied by several hundred soldiers, the Pasha of Egypt repaid the visit with only a few officers, hoping to produce a similar response. Soon, however, all visits ceased, the Sharif never leaving his palace except to attend Friday prayers in the Holy Mosque. Mehmet Ali considered seizing him at prayers but was dissuaded by the newly arrived qadi from Constantinople, who maintained the inviolability of the sacred asylum. After some time the Pasha devised a stratagem. He directed his son, Tusun, who was then governor of Jiddah, to come to Mecca late one evening. Etiquette required that the Sharif come to greet him, and at an early hour the next morning Ghalib appeared with only a small party. He was told that Tusun was resting in an upper room and prevailed upon to go up alone. After conversing a few minutes with Tusun, the Sharif rose to leave. At that moment soldiers rushed into the room and the captain of the Arnauts told him that he was a prisoner. Ghalib was obliged to show himself at a window and order his officers to return to the palace.

When the arrest was known, Ghalib's sons and supporters took refuge in the castle and prepared for its defence. But Mehmet Ali obliged the Sharif to write a letter commanding them to surrender. He then pro-duced a *firman*, perhaps forged, requiring the Sharif's presence in Con-stantinople. Ghalib, with his sons and a few dozen slaves and servants, was put on a ship bound for Qusair; his women joined him later in Cairo. Throughout the journey he was treated with respect and behaved with dignity, playing chess a good part of the time. From Cairo he was sent to Constantinople where the Porte placed him on pension and exiled him to Salonika. He and all his family died from the plague in 1816. Mehmet Ali appointed a distant relative, Yahyah, a puppet without talent or reputation, to be Grand Sharif, and himself took over all sources of the Sharif's revenue, allowing Yahyah only a monthly stipend like any member of his court.

Ghalib's allies took refuge with the southern Wahhabis at Taraba in the mountains east of Tayif. The Buqum Arabs of that district had the distinction of being ruled by a woman named Ghaliyah. She was the widow of their former chief and was celebrated for her sound judgment and accurate knowledge of the surrounding tribes. Her family was the richest in the area; she distributed money and provisions to the poor, and her table was always open to the Wahhabis and others willing to fight the Turks. Under her guidance the Buqum had already repulsed an attack by the invaders, and as a consequence the reputation of Ghaliyah had grown to mythical proportions among the Turkish soldiers. They re-garded her as chief of all the Wahhabis and a sorceress who by bestowing her favours on the Wahhabi leaders had rendered them invincible.

Mehmet Ali sent his son to take Taraba in November 1813. Tusun led 1,000 men out of Tayif with provisions for thirty days. But the march took twenty-seven days, as the Arabs, incensed by the treachery shown to the Sharif, engaged Tusun's column in running battles. Tusun tried to take the town by storm, but the people of Taraba, incited by Ghaliyah, repulsed him. The following day, Tusun's men, fatigued by their pre-vious march and frightened by the myth of Ghaliyah's magical powers, openly refused to obey his order to attack, forcing him to call a retreat. Seeing the Turks on the run, the Arabs pursued them, obliging them to abandon baggage, provisions, and guns. At a dangerous mountain pass,

Thomas Keith recaptured a gun and held off the Arabs till the fugitives got through the defile. More than 700 Turks were lost during the retreat from enemy fire, or from exhaustion and thirst. This reverse marked the end of Tusun's active service for his father, who henceforth kept him inactive at Mecca.

The pilgrimage of 1813 was celebrated by Mehmet Ali with great pomp. The Damascus caravan arrived for the first time in a decade, though the Bedouins obliged it to pay passage money for the entire ten years of suspension. Pilgrims also came from Constantinople and Asia Minor, travelling by ship via Suez. Badly needed camels arrived by sea from Egypt to replenish the depleted transport corps. The revived trade brought profits unknown for years to the merchants of Jiddah and the citizens of the Holy Cities.

But while celebrating victory in the Hijaz, Mehmet Ali received a stab in the back. He had entrusted the delivery of Sharif Ghalib to Constantinople to a Mamluk named Latif Bey. Latif made a favourable impression at the Porte and was created a pasha of three tails, equal in rank to Mehmet Ali. On his return to Cairo he let it be known that he had the tacit support of Constantinople to oust Mehmet Ali and supplant him as viceroy of Egypt. But Ibrahim and the two other regents of Mehmet Ali moved swiftly to invest Latif Bey's house one morning before dawn. Violence immediately flickered in other parts of the city, where power was always open to dispute. Ibrahim's men forced their way into Latif's house but found that the pretender had taken flight across his neighbours' roofs. The regents scoured the quarter and set guards on every exit. Latif had hidden in an oven, a large brick and plaster structure which the Egyptians commonly built outside their homes. An Albanian posted near the oven was bribed to permit Latif to escape; but the ambitious Mamluk was captured, and his head soon decorated the city gate.

With such able lieutenants to safeguard his interests in Egypt, Mehmet Ali stayed on to direct the campaign in Arabia. Having failed to dislodge the southern Wahhabis from Taraba by a land force, he decided, early in 1814, to direct a naval attack against the port of Qunfudah, which the Wahhabis held. If taken it would provide not only a base for further operations in the interior, but also a possible gateway to Yemen, where the profitable coffee trade attracted the interest of the Pasha of Egypt. The attacking force was placed under Zaim Oglou, an Albanian notorious for his bloodlust. Finati was again a member of the expedition.

1 Carsten Niebuhr, the first modern explorer of Arabia, in the Turkish dress he wore during his travels.

2, 3 Two eighteenth-century visitors to the Hijaz: (*above*) James Bruce of Kinnaird, who stopped at Yanbuʻ and Jiddah on his way to Ethiopia, and (*right*) Eyles Irwin of the Honourable East India Company.

4 View of Mecca at the beginning of the nineteenth century, showing the
Holy Mosque with the Ka'ba in the centre of the city and a procession of
pilgrims.

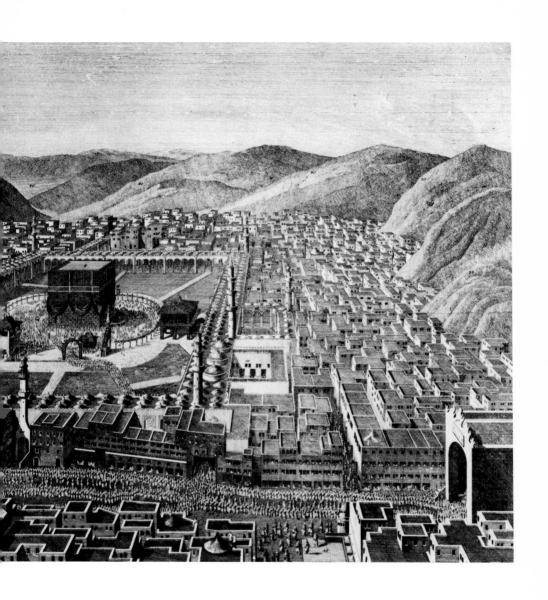

5–7 Three of the principal cities of the Hijaz: (*above left*) the Holy City of Medina showing the Prophet's Tomb; (*below left*) Jiddah, the port of Mecca; (*above right*) Yanbu', the port of Medina.

8 Napoleon Bonaparte depicted shortly after his return to Europe from
Egypt in 1799.
9 A Mamluk bey mounted on a fine Arab stallion and fully armed and
accoutred for combat.

10–12 Egypt at the time of
the French occupation:
(*above left*) the headquarters
of Napoleon's army at Cairo,
from *Description de l'Egypte*;
(*below right*) the Red Sea
port of Qusair showing the
landing of British troops
from India, July 1801; (*above
right*) the Citadel of Cairo
built by Saladin in the
twelfth century, from
Description de l'Egypte.

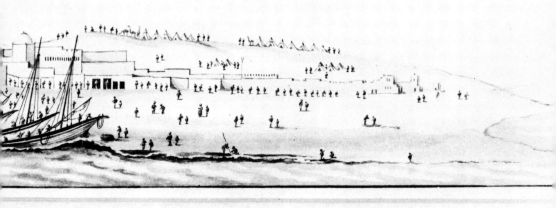

13 Mehmet Ali,
viceroy of Egypt, in
the 1830s at the
height of his power.

14 George Viscount
Valentia, second Earl
Mountnorris, who
visited Jiddah in 1805
during the Wahhabi
occupation of the
Hijaz.

15 Ali Bey al-Abbassi, alias the Spanish traveller Domingo Badia y Leblich, in Arab dress.

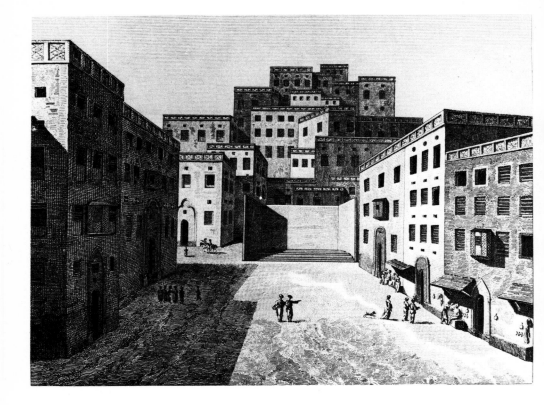

1   2

16–18 Three Meccan scenes sketched by Ali Bey al-Abbassi: (*above left*) a square with barbers' shops on the right; (*below left*) two views of the Ka'ba covered with the embroidered black silk *kiswah* sent annually from Cairo; (*below*) the exterior and interior of the holy Well of Zamzam.

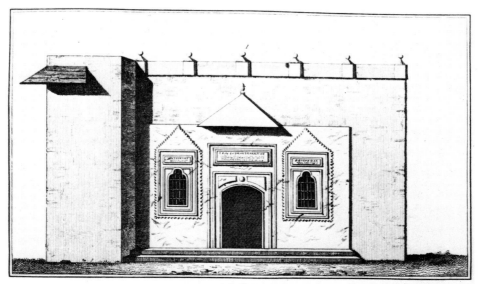

19, 20 Costumes from D'Ohsson's *Tableau Général de l'Empire Othoman*: (*left*) the Grand Sharif of Mecca and (*below*) the chief eunuch of the Prophet's Tomb at Medina.

21 Sketch by or after Ali Bey of his encampment at Mina during the pilgrimage.

22 Mehmet Ali presiding over the massacre of the Mamluks in the Citadel of Cairo, March 1811.

23 *(below)* A Wahhabi Bedouin with a more elaborately dressed Arab of the Azami tribe.

24 *(right)* Two Arnauts, Albanian mercenary soldiers in the army of Mehmet Ali.

25 John Lewis Burckhardt as he looked on the pilgrimage, from a sketch by Henry Salt, British Consul General at Cairo, 1817.

26 A typical *majlis* or sitting-room in Jiddah in the early nineteenth century.

27 View of Suez, port of embarkation for ships from Egypt sailing to the Hijaz.

28 (*left*) Ibrahim Pasha, eldest son of the viceroy of Egypt and conqueror of Wahhabis at Dar'iyah.

29 (*above*) 'Abd Allah ibn Sa'ud, the defeated Wahhabi chief, during his captivity in Cairo, 1818.

30–33 Scenes from the pilgrimage based on sketches by Richard Burton: (*above left*) a grandee's travelling litter, more comfortable than the *shugduf* slung on the back of a single camel; (*below left*) male and female pilgrims in the *ihram* or seamless white garb of the devout hajji; (*above right*) the Mount of Mercy on the plain of Arafat; (*below right*) pilgrims stoning the Devil at Muzdalifah.

123

34, 35 Two illustrations from Burton's *Pilgrimage*: an Arab shaikh in travelling dress and a Bedouin girl with facial tattoos.

36 (*right*) Portrait of Richard Burton by Lord Leighton, painted in 1876 but purporting to show the explorer as a young man.

37 (*below*) The dying pilgrim.

38, 39 (*far right*) Sea travel during the pilgrimage: an Arab dhow in the Gulf of Suez, and pilgrims in the hold of a dhow.

40 The *mahmal*, the richly decorated litter containing a copy of the Quran
sent on the pilgrimage, returning to Cairo from Mecca in 1865.

128

On its arrival at Qunfudah, the Egyptian fleet immediately captured two small ships that supplied the Wahhabi garrison with provisions and ammunition. The attackers trained their guns on the castle, which was built of mud, but the balls merely sank in the unbaked brick and lodged there. The Wahhabis responded by firing through the scarcely perceptible loopholes, scoring several direct hits. Zaim Oglou ordered siege works to be thrown up against the castle to starve the defenders out. On the fourth day the Wahhabis attempted a sortie. The Albanians gave way, caught the enemy between two fires, and secured the castle gate. Within the castle the defenders fought desperately in the narrow staircase and passages, using swords, knives, teeth, and nails, tearing several Albanians to pieces. But not one Wahhabi escaped the castle alive. Zaim Oglou offered a bounty of 200 piastres for every head or pair of ears brought to him. 'Upon which,' reported Finati, who took part in the action, 'the Albanians, who are naturally greedy, went about in every direction to reap their bloody harvest. It was in vain for the younger to plead for their lives, but the old, found lurking in their miserable huts, had their lives spared at the expense of their ears.'

The victorious Albanians, however, failed to secure their position. The water so carefully collected by the late defenders was expended freely in cleaning the castle of blood, and the remainder was consumed. The nearest wells were three hours away; a guard of 200 men, among them Finati, was stationed at the wells, but these were not fortified. After about a month of inactivity a force of several thousand Wahhabis appeared out of the desert and attacked the wells. The Albanian guards sent for reinforcements, for they were in desperate straits, as Finati noted.

Our cavalry, so unfit for action as it was, could do but little, and no sooner was it hotly pressed, than it gave way and took to flight; but the two-hundred infantry, nevertheless, stood their ground manfully, in the expectation of being momentarily relieved, or reinforced; but after three-fourths of them had been killed, the small remainder was at last compelled to fly, the Wahabees cutting them down, so that very few of them indeed made their retreat.

The fleeing cavalrymen ran into the relief force and by their confused and terrified accounts spread such panic that the whole body turned and joined in the flight. This body in turn carried the contagion into the castle, so that the garrison, fearing to be cut off from the water supply, made a rush towards the ships.

When the rout began, Finati took to his heels with the rest. He lost his shoes in the loose sand, however, and his feet were soon scorched and blistered. Just as he had flung himself down in despair, a cavalryman galloped by, his horse so tired and slow that Finati was able to run after it and catch hold of its tail. The rider fired at him; Finati, enraged, fired back; both missed. Finati threw his pistol at the horseman's head. Unable to speak, he was dragged along till they were in sight of Qunfudah. Then he loosened his grip and crawled to the shore.

All was panic and confusion in the castle. The ships were swarming with troops, while other soldiers waded out into the sea with bundles of baggage. Finati threw off his clothes and flung himself into the water. By error he swam to a ship containing Wahhabi prisoners, who struck him senseless with some sharp and heavy instrument. When he came to, he found he had been drawn into a boat of comrades, who fired on the Wahhabi prisoners, causing great losses in their crowded ranks.

On shore Zaim Oglou, seeing his men outnumbered by the attackers, exploded the powder magazine in the castle and ordered the remaining men to take to the boats. No sooner was he on board his own ship than he gave orders for the whole fleet to depart, leaving to almost certain death those of his men who were still on shore. The Wahhabis saw off the Egyptian ships with musket and cannon fire. Then they fell on the booty, the greatest they had taken since the war began, including the entire stores, all the Turkish guns, 400 horses, and as many camels. Many of the Albanians died for lack of food and water on the ships sailing back to Jiddah, though it was said that Zaim Oglou regularly washed his hands in fresh water. Twelve Albanians who found their way by land to Mecca were rewarded by Mehmet Ali and allowed to join another corps, for they had resolved never to serve under Zaim Oglou again. The latter was appointed governor of Jiddah.

The defeat was a further blow to Turkish morale. The Turkish troops were already suffering from bad air and bad water which rendered a quarter of the army unfit for duty at any time. Their pay was also in arrears, and the Egyptian piastre was considered bad coin by the Arabs. Prices in the Hijaz were 250 per cent higher than in Cairo, and the troops could hardly afford to buy enough bread and onions, their principal diet. The booty for which they fought was nearly worthless when taken from the Bedouins and poor villagers; and Mehmet Ali prohibited the plunder of the richer townsmen. Some of the soldiers sold their horses or arms to buy food, and many decided to forfeit their pay and take ship to Egypt. Mehmet Ali caused greater resentment by prohibiting their departure and marched some of them back from Jiddah to Tayif in chains. But Finati contrived to leave Arabia for good.

Mehmet Ali paid the Bedouins twice what he paid his own men to win them round to the Turkish cause. A story was told that a Bedouin chief presented himself to the Egyptian Pasha, kissed his beard, and declared, 'I have abandoned the religion of the Muslims . . . I have adopted the religion of the heretics; I have adopted the religion of Mehmet Ali.' This caused general laughter, which increased when Mehmet Ali replied, 'I hope you will always be a staunch heretic.' But though he scoffed at religion in private, the Pasha knew its political value as well as Napoleon. In order to win over the Arabs he spent large sums on restoring the Holy Places from the damage done by the Wahhabis; he also gave generous donations to the poor.

In May 1814 the great Sa'ud, aged forty-five, died of a fever then prevalent in Najd. His eldest son, 'Abd Allah, became chief of the House of Sa'ud and defender of the Unitarian faith. Though equal to his father in courage and fighting ability, it remained to be seen whether he possessed the same intelligence and political skills. But the disappearance of the conqueror of the Hijaz appeared like a gift of Allah to the Turkish cause.

CHAPTER 6
The Passion of Shaikh Ibrahim

John Lewis Burckhardt arrived in Jiddah from Africa on the morning of 15 July 1814 with only two dollars and a few sequins sewn into an amulet he wore on one arm. He went immediately to the house of a man on whom he had had a letter of credit delivered at Cairo eighteen months before but met with a very cold reception. He habitually dressed in rags to avoid unwelcome attention, and his beggarly appearance along with the date of his letter of credit brought a flat refusal of cash, accompanied however with an offer of lodgings at the man's house. He accepted the lodgings but after two days moved to a public khan. On the fourth day he was attacked by a violent fever and was delirious for several days. He thought that he might have died had it not been for the aid of a Greek sea captain, a fellow passenger on the voyage from Africa, who procured a barber and prevailed on him to bleed the patient copiously. His lack of money seriously troubled him; the only way he could see to meet his expenses was to sell the one thing he possessed, his slave boy whom he had bought in the Sudan. He felt sorry, for he knew that the boy had some affection for him and during the African journey he had been a faithful and useful companion. Nevertheless, it had to be done: the obliging Greek captain sold the boy in the slave market of Jiddah for forty-eight dollars. As Burckhardt had bought him for only sixteen dollars, the profit defrayed the whole expense of his four months' journey through Nubia.

The Hijaz had been invaded by an army of camp followers – grooms, camel drivers, merchants, hajjis – some of them carrying arms and affecting military dress; so Burckhardt's light skin and Western features passed unnoticed. He pretended to be a reduced member of the Mamluk corps and called himself Shaikh Ibrahim ibn Abdallah. Having spent five years in Syria, Egypt, and the Sudan, he spoke Arabic well and had acquired Arab habits and manners. Yet he had been born in Lausanne, the son of an army officer who had been tried by the Bonapartists for selling secrets to the Austrians. His prospects in Switzerland thus ruined, the young Burckhardt had gone first to Germany for his education and then to England. In London he presented himself to Sir Joseph Banks of the Association for Promoting the Discovery of the Interior of Africa and was commissioned by the Association to cross the central part of Africa from Egypt through the Fezzan to Timbuctu and the Niger. It is one of the ironies of Burckhardt's career that the Association had as one of its aims the suppression of slavery in Africa.

Burckhardt was thoroughly prepared for his task. In England he had studied astronomy, mineralogy, medicine and surgery, as well as the rudiments of Arabic, and he had hardened himself by long tramps in the countryside, bareheaded, sleeping on the ground, and living on water and vegetables. In 1809 he proceeded to Syria, where for two years he studied Muslim law and theology and accustomed himself to Arab ways. Even before he left England he had assumed oriental dress, and on the voyage out he pretended to be an Indian Muslim, to explain his halting Arabic. When asked to give his shipmates a sample of Hindustani speech, he broke out in the worst dialect of Swiss–German. While in Syria he lived among the Bedouins of the desert for several months and discovered the ruins of the Nabataean city of Petra, lost to the West since the time of the Crusades.

In 1812, at the age of twenty-eight, Burckhardt felt ready to go to Cairo to await the Fezzan caravan on its return from Mecca. But the caravan had not appeared for several years, partly because of the disruption of the pilgrimage by the Wahhabis, partly because it was occupied with transporting black slaves to Barbary to replace the white slaves freed by the English navy. Disliking inactivity and anxious to prove his zeal to the Association, Burckhardt undertook an expedition to Nubia and the Sudan, where he nearly lost his life to some marauding Mamluks and discovered the temple of Ramses the Great at Abu Simbel. As there was still no sign of the Fezzan caravan, he decided to cross the Red Sea and earn the title of hajji to facilitate his journey through Muslim Africa.

The money from the sale of the slave in Jiddah was only a stop-gap, so Burckhardt decided to approach Mehmet Ali, then at Tayif. He had seen the Pasha several times in Cairo and had heard that he had expressed a favourable opinion of himself. He therefore wrote to the Pasha's Armenian physician, begging him to ask whether Mehmet Ali would accept a bill on Burckhardt's correspondent in Cairo. Meanwhile, his presence in Jiddah had come to the attention of the Syrian physician of Tusun Pasha, then governor of the port city. The physician received Burckhardt politely and in the course of conversation mentioned that he was seeking a way to send 5,000 piastres (about £100) to his family. Burckhardt took the money and gave the physician a bill upon Cairo payable at sight.

Despite his fever and financial difficulties, Burckhardt explored Jiddah and set down his findings in encyclopaedic detail. Nineteenth-century stay-at-homes were as avid for information about foreign countries as we would be today for news of life on other planets, and Burckhardt was an indefatigable explorer. He painstakingly described every quarter of the town, enumerated the kinds of shops, recorded commodities and prices, commented on the water supply, delineated the appearance and behaviour of the inhabitants, and in general painted a detailed picture of the chief port of the Hijaz in the midst of the Wahhabi war.

He found the city well built, but the madrepore of which it was constructed decayed so rapidly in the excessive humidity that there were no buildings of great antiquity. The walls, though reputed to be impregnable, were in decay and could not have withstood artillery; an immense piece of ordnance carrying a ball of 500 pounds commanded the harbour and was so celebrated all over the Red Sea that its very fame protected the city. The best water came from wells a mile from town and was so scarce that few could afford it; this was one of the causes of the constant ill health of the people. The number of wells could easily have been augmented, but most of the inhabitants were foreigners, who considered their residence as temporary and devoted all their attention to making money. Immigrants from Yemen and Hadramaut were the most numerous, living in colonies and engaged in commerce with their homelands. Upwards of a hundred Indian families had established themselves as well as a few Malays. Settlers from Egypt, Syria, Barbary, European Turkey, and Anatolia could be recognized by their features, though all lived and dressed in the Arab manner. Only the Indians remained distinct in manners, dress, and employment. They had taken the place of the Jews, who had formerly been the brokers but, having offended the Sharif, had been driven out some thirty years earlier and retired to Yemen. There were no settled Christians, though a few island Greeks occasionally brought merchandise from Egypt. In the time of the Sharif they were molested and compelled to wear distinctive dress, but Mehmet Ali had abolished these restrictions. Every pilgrimage added to the population, which was indeed necessary as the number of deaths far exceeded the number of births.

Coffee ships arrived from Yemen all year round, though the coffee trade was suffering from competition from the West Indies. The slave ships from Mozambique reached Jiddah in May and returned in June or July, taking advantage of the monsoons. Fleets from Calcutta, Surat, and Bombay arrived at the same time, bringing India goods, chiefly textiles. The Jiddah merchants collected as much money as they could in order to buy wholesale on the first arrival of the ships. The day the last ship sailed back to India, ten per cent profit could be made on re-sale; if the merchant held out for four or five months, he might count on a gain of thirty or forty per cent. Most of the goods went on to Suez, though some were sent to Mecca and Medina.

Burckhardt conscientiously counted twenty-seven coffee-shops. Respectable people were never seen in one, but they were constantly filled with the lower classes and wayfarers. It was not uncommon for a man to drink twenty or thirty cups of coffee a day. One shop was frequented by smokers of hashish, and in the African quarter there were many public women and those who sold intoxicating *bouza*. Butter sellers were numerous: every morning everyone took a coffee-cup full of clarified butter, or *ghee*, as a tonic. The higher classes drank the butter, while the lower stuffed it up their nostrils 'to stop the entry of foul air'. The lower classes also rubbed their bodies with butter to refresh the skin, as Africans did.

Jiddah depended for its labour on foreigners, chiefly Africans and men from Hadramaut. No man born in the Holy Land would consent to work as a menial servant; he would rather beg. Hence the streets were filled with beggars, encouraged by the pilgrims who showed their charity on first touching holy ground. Burckhardt thought the Arabians a proud, high-spirited nation who despised everyone who did not speak Arabic or differed from themselves in manner, especially the Turks. The latter returned an equal share of contempt. The Turkish soldier was used to treating the Egyptians with utter disdain; his hatred of the Arabian was the greater because he could not indulge his tyranny with the same impunity, being convinced that an Arabian when struck would strike back. Besides, Mehmet Ali punished severely any of his men who committed excesses against the population.

The Pasha of Egypt was about to intervene in Burckhardt's life. Having heard that the traveller was walking about Jiddah in rags, he sent a messenger with two dromedaries to the collector of customs with an order to furnish him with a suit of clothes and a purse of 500 piastres and to send him immediately to Tayif. In a postscript, the customs collector was enjoined to order the messenger to take the upper road to Tayif instead of the direct one through Mecca. The invitation of a Turkish pasha was a polite command: whatever Burckhardt's reluctance to go to Tayif, he could not but comply, and notwithstanding his aversion to receiving gifts from Mehmet Ali, he could not refuse to accept the

clothing and money without hurting the pride and exciting the resentment of a chief whose good graces it was now his principal aim to conciliate. Burckhardt understood the meaning of the postscript, though the
customs officer did not, but he flattered himself that on this point he was
a match for the Pasha.

Distrusting Mehmet Ali's intentions, he changed the whole of the
5,000 piastres he had received from the physician into gold, which he hid
in his girdle. A person with money, he reflected, had little to fear from
an Osmanli except the loss of it; and he thought he might need all he had
to facilitate his departure from Tayif. He left Jiddah with the messenger
and a band of Harb camel drivers who were carrying money to Mecca
for the Pasha's treasury. They overtook a caravan of pilgrims, whose
company was welcome, as the road was dangerous to small parties, and
a troop of Turkish soldiers, who were less welcome, as they commandeered all the sweet water at the coffee-houses and so frightened the
peasants by their requisitions that the houses were abandoned and the
fields neglected. They travelled at night not so much to avoid the heat of
day as to allow the camels to eat, which they never did at night. The
nocturnal marches did not favour observation, and during the day
Burckhardt was so worn out from lack of sleep and the effects of his
recent fever that every exertion was irksome.

At the turn-off from the Mecca road, the guide asked the reason for
his order to take the northern route. Burckhardt replied that it was
probably thought to be shorter. 'That is a mistake,' replied the guide, 'the
Mecca road is quite as short and much safer; if you have no objection, we
will proceed by it.' This was what Burckhardt wished, though he had
taken care to betray no anxiety on the subject; they accordingly followed
the great road in the company of the pilgrims. The guide, however, took
a short cut through the town, thus depriving Burckhardt of seeing the
Holy City fully.

The approach to Tayif from the coast lies through one of the most
spectacular landscapes in the world. The road passes through a series of
mound-like hills that seem to draw apart like curtains as one approaches,
revealing another line of curtain beyond. Behind the hills rises a great
escarpment some five thousand feet above the plain, a cliff so sheer, so
convoluted and striped with improbable colours that it looks at a distance
like a gigantic rosy backdrop hanging from the sky. To a devout and
impressionable believer approaching or leaving the Holy City, this
extraordinary landscape must seem a natural portent of the greatest
symbolic drama of his life. Burckhardt merely noted the geological

composition of the cliffs and remarked that the surrounding country looked very wild.

At Tayif he went straight to the house of Bosari, the Armenian physician. As it was Ramadan, the Pasha could not be informed of his arrival till after sunset. Bosari, after assurances of his entire devotion and the sincerity of his friendship, wanted to know Burckhardt's reasons for coming to the Hijaz. To visit Mecca and Medina, Burckhardt replied. The Armenian appeared doubtful and begged him to be candid as a friend, confessing that he suspected he was going to the East Indies (there to report to the English). This Burckhardt denied, saying he planned to return to Cairo. In that case, Bosari suggested, he had better remain and return with the Pasha. Nothing was said about money, though Bosari was unaware that Burckhardt's financial wants had been relieved at Jiddah.

In the evening Bosari went privately to the Pasha in his women's residence. Seated with Mehmet Ali was the qadi of Mecca, a Turk from Constantinople, who was in Tayif for his health. On hearing of Burckhardt's desire to visit the Holy Cities, the Pasha turned to the qadi and said, 'It is not the beard alone which proves a man to be a true Muslim. You are a better judge in such matters than I am.' The qadi observed that, as Burckhardt must know that only Muslims were permitted to go there, he did not believe he would declare himself a Muslim unless he was one. When Burckhardt heard these particulars from Bosari, he told Bosari that he could return alone to the Pasha, that his own feelings had already been hurt by the order not to carry him through Mecca, and that he himself would not go to the Pasha's audience if he was not to be received as a Turk. Bosari was alarmed but went reluctantly back to Mehmet Ali, who smiled when he heard the message and answered that the visitor was welcome whether a Turk or not.

Appeased, Burckhardt repaired to the castle dressed in the new clothes he had received from the Pasha. He found Mehmet Ali in the half-ruined residence of the former Sharif seated in a large saloon, the qadi on one hand, the chief of the Arnauts on the other, with thirty or forty officers forming a circle round the Pasha's sofa and a number of Bedouin shaikhs squatting on the floor. Burckhardt gave the Pasha the *sala'am alaikum* and kissed his hand; Mehmet Ali addressed him politely and bade him be seated next to the qadi. After the business with the Bedouins was completed, everyone withdrew except the qadi, Bosari, and Burckhardt. Bosari interpreted through Italian, as Burckhardt knew no Turkish and the Pasha almost no Arabic.

Burckhardt expected to be put to the test, but not a word was said about his personal affairs. The conversation was political. Mehmet Ali had just heard about the entry of the Allies into Paris and the departure of Napoleon for Elba. He was concerned that England would now seek to augment her power in the Mediterranean and invade Egypt. After two or three hours, Burckhardt took his leave.

Next day he paid a visit to the qadi just before sunset. The qadi, a true courtier, possessed an engaging manner and all the suavity of the well-bred Stambouli. Burckhardt expressed his astonishment at the Pasha's doubts as to his being a true Muslim and maintained that he had been a proselyte to that faith for many years. His host replied that Mehmet Ali had allowed that he, the qadi, was the best judge in such matters and added that he hoped they would become better acquainted. Literary subjects were broached, and the qadi asked what Arabic books Burckhardt had read. Burckhardt's studies in Syria had made him acquainted with the titles at least of commentaries on the Quran and the law, and they did not enter deeply into the subject. They broke the fast together and afterwards performed the evening prayer, Burckhardt taking care to chant as long a chapter of the Quran as he remembered. After this they both went to see the Pasha.

This became the pattern of Burckhardt's evenings in Tayif, visiting first the qadi and then the Pasha. He was never allowed to be alone for a moment and suspected that Bosari was ordered to spy on him. When asked if he kept a journal he replied that the Hijaz was not, like Egypt, full of antiquities and that he saw nothing of interest to record. He guessed that he was considered to be a spy sent by the English to ascertain the state of the country. The Pasha knew Burckhardt as an Englishman, a role he assumed when necessary, for only the English and the French enjoyed security in the East, as they were too well protected by their governments at home and their ministers at Constantinople to be trifled with by provincial authorities.

One evening the Pasha asked his visitor about his travels in Nubia. 'I understand that you treated with two of the Mamluk beys at Ibrim; was it so?' The word 'treated' startled Burckhardt, for the Pasha suspected that the English still favoured the Mamluks. Burckhardt assured him that his meeting with the Mamluks had been accidental and even dangerous, as they threatened his life.

'And, now, Shaikh Ibrahim,' said the Pasha, 'where do you mean to go?' 'I wish to perform the Hajj, return to Cairo, and then proceed to Persia,' Burckhardt replied, thinking it inadvisable to mention his design to penetrate the interior of Africa. 'May God render the way smooth to you,' replied Mehmet Ali, 'but I think it folly and madness to travel so much. What, let me ask you, is the result of your last journey?' 'Men's lives are predestined,' replied the good Muslim, Shaikh Ibrahim. 'We all obey our fate. For myself, I enjoy great pleasure in exploring new and unknown countries, and becoming acquainted with different races of people.'

Mehmet Ali returned frequently to the subject of European politics. Bonaparte, he thought, behaved like a coward; he ought to have sought death rather than expose himself in a cage to the laughter of the universe. 'The great fish swallow the small,' he said. 'And Egypt is necessary to England in supplying corn to Malta and Gibraltar. I am a friend of the English.' (This, addressed by a Turk to a Christian, Burckhardt mused, meant only that he feared him, or wanted his money.) 'My hope is that they will not fall upon Egypt during my stay in the Hijaz; if I am there myself, I shall at least have the satisfaction of fighting personally for my own dominions.' Burckhardt took the liberty of telling the Pasha that he was like a young man in possession of a beautiful girl; although sure of her affections, he would always be jealous of every stranger. 'You say well,' replied Mehmet Ali, 'I certainly love Egypt with all the ardour of a lover; and if I had ten thousand souls, I would willingly sacrifice them for its possession.'

To remain in Tayif in a sort of polite imprisonment was little to Burckhardt's liking, yet he could not press his departure without increasing Mehmet Ali's suspicions. Determined to induce Bosari to forward his plans, he began to act in the physician's house with all the petulance of an Osmanli. As it was Ramadan he fasted during the day, and at night demanded a supper apart and in the early morning an abundant breakfast. He appropriated the best room and kept the servants in constant attendance. Eastern hospitality forbade all show of resentment at such behaviour. After six days, however, Bosari asked whether his business with the Pasha would detain him much longer. Burckhardt replied that he had no business with the Pasha, though he had come to Tayif at his desire, adding that his situation was very agreeable, possessing so generous a host as Bosari. The Armenian remarked that it must be very tiresome to live among soldiers, without any comforts or amusements and being unacquainted with the Turkish language. Burckhardt agreed but added that, being unacquainted with the Pasha's wishes, he could determine nothing. This brought Bosari to the point desired. 'I will, if you like,' he said, 'speak to His Highness on the subject.' That evening the Pasha said that he understood that Burckhardt wished to pass the last days of Ramadan at Mecca (a suggestion originating with the wily Armenian); if so, he had better join the qadi, who was going there and would be glad of his company.

On the day fixed for their departure, the qadi sent word that he did not intend to set out until evening and would meet Burckhardt at Jabal al-Kura, half way to Mecca. As Burckhardt left Tayif, alone and mounted on an ass, he blessed his stars that he had left the precincts of a Turkish court in which he found it more difficult to avoid danger than among the wild Bedouin of Nubia. Burckhardt was a courageous man and not given to exaggeration. But what danger was he in? If the Pasha had suspected him of being a Christian, the worst he would have done would be to deny him access to Mecca and ship him back to Cairo. Mehmet Ali later told several Englishmen in Cairo that he had not been fooled by Shaikh Ibrahim's profession of Islam, yet he allowed him to live on in Cairo as a Muslim and even to be buried in that faith. The qadi, Burckhardt suspected, was sent to spy on Mehmet Ali and might have been pleased to report to Constantinople that the Pasha had allowed a non-Muslim to visit the Holy Cities. But he had encouraged Burckhardt to make the pilgrimage. Yet there were fanatics enough to stop him if suspicions were aroused. The fate of Ulrich Seetzen only three years before was evidence that Burckhardt's fears were not groundless. A German scholar in the pay of the Tsar, Seetzen had visited Mecca in 1811 and was poisoned in Yemen soon afterwards, probably by orders of the Imam of San'a. In a letter to the secretary of the African Association, Burckhardt wrote admiringly of Seetzen, 'It has fallen to my lot to retrace his footsteps, in many hitherto unknown parts of Syria, and Arabia Petraea, and again in the Hedjaz. . . . If he had lived to publish the mass of knowledge which he had acquired during his travels, he would have far excelled all travellers, who ever wrote on the same countries.' Seetzen's death made clear that the most careful preparations were no proof against discovery and its consequences.

On the road to Mecca Burckhardt fell in with three Arnauts who cheerfully allowed him to pay their expenses at the coffee-houses. At Wadi Mahram he donned the *ihram*. After a long day's march and a fall of rain, the light covering brought on a slight fever, but by morning it had passed. The qadi arrived during the night, but Burckhardt preferred to stay with his 'good-humoured companions', the Arnauts. On the second day, as they passed through rugged mountains, they were surprised by a violent thunderstorm accompanied by rain and hail. From a shelter on the hillside, Burckhardt saw the qadi marooned by a torrent and separated from his women by another torrent. After the storm their asses could hardly walk on the slippery ground; stumbling and falling, they reached Arafat at nightfall. The coffee-shops there had been inundated; they could not find a dry place to sit and with difficulty lit a fire. The qadi joined them, leaving his women crying from the cold in another room.

On arriving at Mecca, Burckhardt went straight to the Ka'ba to perform the prescribed prayers. It is tempting to see in his Swiss origins the source of Burckhardt's phlegmatic temper, but his description of the Bait Allah – the Holy of Holies, bourn and climax of the pilgrimage – is notably chill, even by Alpine standards. He described the building in numbered paragraphs, measured the placement of the Ka'ba in relation to the colonnade of the Holy Mosque, and took a bearing on one of the longer sides as NNW 1/2W. He criticized the architecture, remarking that the Mosque had been so often ruined and repaired that it was a thoroughly modern structure with no trace of antiquity to be seen. No two capitals of the colonnade were exactly alike; most were of 'coarse Saracen work', a few only of 'good Grecian workmanship', which had served former buildings and were placed upside down on their shafts. Parts of the walls and arches were gaudily painted in stripes of yellow, red, and blue. The Ka'ba itself was constructed of grey Mecca stone in large blocks of different sizes joined with bad cement, made impressive only by the black embroidered *kiswah*, which rippled in the slightest breeze. The Black Stone looked to him like lava of deep reddish brown containing yellowish particles and appeared to have been broken in pieces by a violent blow and reunited.

Although he betrayed no emotion in himself, he was moved by that of others. 'The effect of the joint prostration of six or eight thousand persons around the Kaaba, added to the recollection of the distance and the various quarters from which they came, and for what purpose, can not fail to impress the most cool-minded spectator with some degree of awe.' He saw a black pilgrim from the Sudan arrive on the last day of Ramadan, fall prostrate, and remain a long time in a posture of adoration; on rising, instead of reciting the usual prayer, the man exclaimed, 'O God, now take my soul, for this is paradise.' Later, when like Ali Bey he entered the Ka'ba, he noted: 'Sobbing and moaning filled the room, and I thought I perceived most heartfelt emotion and sincere repentance in many visitors.' At the Well of Zamzam he observed the hajjis drinking incredible amounts of water, for they were convinced that the water

from the well was an infallible cure for all diseases. One man with intermittent fever drank every day until he almost fainted; he then lay for
several hours on his back near the Ka'ba and returned to drink anew.
Others washed their winding sheets in Zamzam water and hung them to
dry between the columns of the Mosque.

Burckhardt settled happily in Mecca for a period of four months. On
a quick trip to Jiddah, during which he was nearly captured by a flying
squad of Wahhabis, he purchased another slave. He hired a decent apartment in an out-of-the-way quarter among other foreigners who were
not likely to make impertinent enquiries. But he hardly feared detection,
for the assumption of a false character was frequent among travellers,
especially at Mecca, where everyone affected poverty in order to escape
imposition and expense. 'During all my journeys in the East,' he wrote,
'I never enjoyed such perfect ease as at Mekka; and I shall always retain a
pleasing recollection of my residence there.'

In the early morning and late afternoon he walked about the town and
visited the coffee-houses where he treated the Bedouins to a cup of
coffee and questioned them about their country and their people. At
midday he went to the coolest spot in town, a street covered with a high
vaulted roof, where the gentlemen hajjis took their ease. He made the
acquaintance of a perfume seller and passed a couple of hours seated on
a bench before his shop, smoking a narguilah and drinking coffee. There
he heard the news, whether any great hajji had arrived during the night,
what law suits were brought before the qadi, how fared the Pasha's army,
or what big commercial deals had been made. The evenings he passed at
the Holy Mosque, seated upon a carpet spread by his slave and watching
the pilgrims praying or walking around the Ka'ba.

The Mosque was the hub of life in Mecca. During the day lectures on
religious subjects were offered in the colonnades and classes held round
the Ka'ba in which the children were taught to read and write. The
mutawifs who conducted parties of pilgrims vied in loudness to attract
customers. Public scribes set up shop with ink and paper alongside
dealers in amulets, charms, and love recipes. Women spread mats to sell
corn to the pilgrims who delighted in feeding the pigeons that circled the
square; some public women used this as a pretext to exhibit themselves
and bargain with the pilgrims. Businessmen met at the Mosque to conduct their affairs. Poor Indians and Negroes spread their mats under the
colonnades and passed the whole of the hajj eating and sleeping there,
although cooking was not allowed. The place was sometimes so full of
poor hajjis and diseased persons lying in the midst of their baggage as to

have the appearance of a hospital rather than a temple. At night the lighted lamps, busy crowds, loud conversation of idlers, and running and playing of boys gave the air of a place of amusement rather than worship. But around nine o'clock, the crowd left, and the Mosque became a place of silent meditation and prayer.

Burckhardt saw in the Holy Mosque something that shocked him so deeply that he was unable to name it. 'The Kaaba is rendered the scene of such indecency and criminal acts as can not with propriety be more particularly noticed. They are not only practised with impunity, but, it may be said, almost publicly; and my indignation has often been excited on witnessing abominations which called forth from other passing spectators nothing more than a laugh or a slight reprimand.' What can he mean? Later, when animadverting on the morals of the Meccans, he was more explicit.

Considerable sums are also lavished in sensual gratifications even more vicious and degrading [than female prostitution]. . . . It has already been observed that the temple of Mekka itself, the very sanctuary of the Mohammedan religion, is almost publicly and daily contaminated by practices of the grossest depravity: to these no disgrace is here attached; the young of all classes are encouraged in them by the old, and even parents have been so base as to connive at them for the sake of money.

Incredible as it may seem, Burckhardt saw, or thought he saw, homosexual activity in the precincts of the holiest spot in Islam.

The Mosque was served by thirty or forty black eunuchs, about a dozen of them adults, the rest boys. They were presented to the Mosque by pashas and other grandees; Mehmet Ali himself had given ten of them, each with 100 dollars as an outfit. The eunuchs of the Mosque affected great importance. Their aga was entitled to sit in the presence of the Pasha or the Sharif. They dressed in Constantinople style, in wide robes bound with a sash and topped with an elaborate headdress. Many of the lower classes, especially the Africans, kissed their hands and gave them gifts. 'Extraordinary as it may appear,' Burckhardt says, 'the grown-up eunuchs are all married to black slaves, and maintain several male and female slaves as servants.' He had evidently forgotten something he had learned in Nubia: that when a grown man was castrated by having only his testicles removed, his penis remained intact and capable of tumescence; he was therefore able to prolong the act without ejaculation, an advantage that placed eunuchs in great demand in the harems of the Turks.

The revenues of the Mosque were considerable. It owned property in most of the Ottoman provinces, left in trust by pious Muslims, although the income was often withheld or reduced in passing through the hands of corrupt officials. To this was added the donations of rich hajjis, especially the Indian princes, whose generosity was on a scale with their wealth. Little or none of this money went to help the poor hajjis but was spent on enriching the appointments of the Mosque or in lining the pockets of the eunuchs.

The sole *raison d'être* of Mecca was the pilgrimage. The streets were wide to accommodate crowds, the houses high with many windows to provide views of the Holy Places. All but the very richest houses were divided into many apartments to accommodate lodgers. But as the pilgrimage was in decline many buildings had been allowed to fall into decay. The streets were unpaved, making the dust in summer as great a nuisance as the mud in winter. The sweepings of the houses were cast into the street, where they soon became dust or mud according to the season. The streets were totally dark at night, but the different quarters were without the gates customary in Eastern towns as security for merchants and husbands; this too was for the sake of the pilgrims, who could be seen at all hours running to the Mosque in their nightclothes to pray or to drink Zamzam water. An adequate water supply was not, however, among the provisions made for pilgrims. During the hajj season sweet water sold for a shilling a skin; the conduit that brought it from wells six hours from town had not been cleaned for fifty years, and much water was lost in transit. Slaves of the Sharif were stationed at the two outlets in town to exact tolls from those filling their water-skins. These spots were surrounded day and night by crowds quarrelling and fighting for access. The infirm and indigent had to entreat the well-off for a draught.

At a place where stone benches lined each side of the street, slaves, both male and female, were exposed for sale. These benches were always surrounded by pilgrims, who often pretended to bargain with a dealer in order to view the slave-girls more closely in an adjoining apartment. The price of the handsomest slaves was 100 to 120 dollars. Male and female servants were all Negroes, concubines Abyssinians. Few families in Mecca, even the most modest, did not keep slaves. 'No wealthy Mekkawy,' wrote Burckhardt, 'prefers domestic peace to the gratification of his senses; they all keep mistresses in common with their lawful wives.' Few if any men were unmarried or without slave-mistresses, and some rich men kept several dozen concubines. If a slave gave birth to a child, the master usually married her; if he already had the legal limit of four wives, she remained in his house for life, and no distinction was made between the sons of free Arabian women and those of slaves. The middle and lower classes, however, were less scrupulous; they bought young Abyssinians on speculation, educated them, and sold them at a profit, at least if they were barren. Almost no slave girl was a virgin, the dealer himself often initiating her. Contraception was practised, and abortions frequently induced, the abortifacient being the seed of the Meccan balm.

African blood flowed in the veins of most Meccan families. The usual colour of their skins was a yellowish brown, lighter or darker according to the origin of the mother. The lower classes were stout and muscular, the higher conspicuous by their emaciation. The sharifs were extremely handsome of countenance. All Meccan men cut their moustaches short in imitation of the Prophet, blackened their eyelids with *kohl*, and polished their teeth with a branch of *arak*. Unlike the sullen Meccans of Ali Bey's time, the people loved to laugh and joke and indulged in puns, proverbs, and witty allusions. Burckhardt praised their vivacity, intellect, and suavity of manners, finding them more polite to strangers than the people of Syria or Egypt. Their pride, though 'not founded on innate worth', he found preferable to the 'cringing servility of the Levantine'. But he deplored their 'dissolute habits and extravagance', their squandering of money on high living, dress, and 'the grossest satisfactions'. A man would spend half his capital on the marriage or circumcision of his child. The houses were furnished with fine carpets, sofas of brocade, and narguilahs adorned with silver. The people ate meat every day, smoked excessively, and never allowed the coffee-pot to remain empty. The women exchanged visits, each hostess vying to surpass the others in costly show.

For the benefit of the pilgrims and other foreigners a number of public women practised in Mecca. The Sharif imposed a special tax on them. During the pilgrimage the ranks of the local prostitutes were augmented by adventuresses from abroad. The public women of Mecca were very decorous and never appeared in the streets without veils. Among them were many Abyssinian slaves, whose masters shared in their earnings.

The Meccans hardly prayed at all, leaving the Mosque to foreigners. Neither did they give alms, saying that Providence had placed them to receive charity, not to bestow it. Nearly every inhabitant of the Holy Cities received a stipend from the Porte, brought by special caravan from Constantinople under heavy guard and distributed by the qadi. Some persons received as little as one piastre (about two pence), while a few families got as much as 2,000 piastres. But the main income of the Meccans derived from the pilgrimage. 'All Mekka,' Burckhardt remarked, 'seems united in the design of cheating the pilgrims; the most adept at this being the guides, the idlest, the most impudent, and vilest individuals in Mekka.' They besieged the hajji's room day and night, sat down uninvited to meals, led him into great expense, and asked outright for money. On receiving a present they gave no thanks, saying, 'It is not you who give, but God.' Some of them performed a singular service. As Muslim law provided that no woman could make the hajj unless accompanied by her husband or a close male relative, some guides were ready to marry rich widows or wives whose husbands had died on the road. It was understood that the marriage was nominal, and the guide was expected to divorce the woman afterwards. But the law could not compel him to do so, and Burckhardt heard of two cases where the guide refused to divorce a rich widow in order to hold on to her property.

The moral atmosphere of Mecca disgusted conscientious Muslims from other lands and encouraged cynicism about the pilgrimage itself. But the excitement was nevertheless great when the ceremonies began. On the fifth day of Dhu al-Hijja 1229, that is, 21 November 1814, a horseman galloped into town and rode straight to the governor's palace, where his horse dropped dead from exhaustion. To the acclamation of the crowd the rider announced the approach of the Syrian hajj. The news had been anxiously awaited, as nothing had been heard of the caravan and rumours were circulating that it had been plundered by Bedouins on the road. Next day the Cairo caravan appeared as well, and Mehmet Ali came down from Tayif to inspect the cavalry which had come with it. The Pasha was dressed in a handsome *ihram* of two white cashmere shawls, while an officer held an umbrella over his bare head as he rode through the streets. At midday all the hajjis crowded into the Holy Mosque to hear a short sermon. That evening the town was full of bustle as everyone prepared for the journey to Arafat.

The next morning the Syrian hajj paraded through the town to martial music with all the soldiers in uniform. It was led by the *mahmal* on the sacred camel, the high swaying structure covered with embroidered cloth and adorned with ostrich plumes. The Pasha of Damascus and other grandees rode in closed litters suspended between two camels; the beasts' heads were decorated with feathers, tassels, and bells, but their necks bent down from the fatigue of the desert journey. Soon after, the Egyptian caravan paraded behind its *mahmal*, but it consisted of officials and cavalry only, as not one private pilgrim had come because of the war.

Both caravans continued on their way to Arafat, followed by all the hajjis. As the greater part of the local population went along, the city was almost deserted for four or five days. Burckhardt had hired two camels for the excursion, but he joined the exodus on foot, as this was considered meritorious; his slave boy and a companion rode the camels. Some of the other pilgrims sat on their mounts reading the Quran; some ejaculated loud prayers; while others cursed their drivers or quarrelled with hajjis who blocked their way. So great was the press that it was several hours before the pilgrims left the town.

The procession streamed through the pass and spread over the plain in search of encampment. Burckhardt reached his camp three hours before sunset, but the last stragglers did not arrive till midnight. Fires were lit for three or four miles over the plain, while clusters of brilliant lamps marked the camps of Mehmet Ali, the Pasha of Damascus, and the Amir of the Egyptian hajj. Few slept that night. Lost pilgrims wandered about; the devout sat up chanting and praying; while the irreverent Meccans made merry, drinking coffee, singing, and clapping their hands. Burckhardt wandered about observing his neighbours; just as he lay down under his carpet, two guns fired by the Syrian and Egyptian troops announced the dawn of the great day.

At sunrise every pilgrim came out of his tent to walk about and chat with his neighbour. The Egyptian and Syrian cavalry exercised their horses; the artillery pieces were discharged; and thousands of camels were let loose to feed on the dry shrubs of the plain. Burckhardt climbed the Mount of Mercy to view the scene and take his bearings, but he dared not use his compass. He counted some 3,000 tents and estimated the number of people to be about 70,000. The most magnificent encampment in sight was that of the wife of Mehmet Ali, the mother of Ibrahim and Tusun, who had come from Cairo with 500 camels to carry her baggage. Her camp consisted of a dozen tents for herself and her women enclosed by a wall of richly embroidered linen with a single entrance guarded by eunuchs. Around this were pitched the tents of her suite.

In mid-afternoon all the pilgrims pressed towards the mountain to hear the sermon at Arafat. The two Pashas – Mehmet Ali and the Pasha of Damascus – took their posts in the rear of the deep line of hajjis' camels with their cavalry drawn up in troops behind them. Further removed from the preacher stood the Sharif Yahyah with a small body of soldiers. There was not a Wahhabi in sight. All waited in silence as the two *mahmals* threaded their way through the ranks of camels and took their stations directly under the platform of the preacher.

The preacher was Burckhardt's old friend, the qadi of Mecca, seated on a richly caparisoned camel in imitation of the Prophet when he delivered the original sermon. But the Stambouli gentleman could not keep his seat when his camel became restless and was obliged to dismount. He read the sermon in Arabic from a book before him, pausing at intervals to stretch out his arms as if to implore blessings from above. At such times, the assembled pilgrims waved their *ihrams* over their heads and rent the air with cries of *Labaik, Allahum, labaik!* The white *ihrams* rippling on the side of the mountain reminded Burckhardt of a cataract of water. In the course of the three-hour sermon, the qadi frequently wiped his eyes with his handkerchief as though overcome with emotion. Some of the foreign hajjis were weeping and beating their breasts, while a few stood in silent reflection with tears in their eyes. Meanwhile many natives of the Hijaz and the Turkish soldiers were conversing and joking; they made violent gestures of ridicule whenever the pious waved their *ihrams*. Several parties of Arabs and soldiers were smoking narguilahs, and in a cavern in the hillside a woman was selling coffee to persons whose laughter and riotous behaviour interrupted the devotions.

As the sun began to set the qadi shut his book, and the crowd rushed down the mountain. In former times when the strength of the Egyptian and Syrian caravans was nearly balanced, bloody affrays broke out as each party tried to outrun the other and carry its *mahmal* in advance; as many as two hundred lives had been lost in supporting the honour of the respective caravans. But now, in the presence of the Pasha of Egypt, the Syrians displayed greater humility.

In the confused rush, many pilgrims lost their camels. Burckhardt was among them, and he was obliged to walk to the next station, Muzdalifah. The procession swept along in great disorder and deafening clamour, as the artillery fired its guns, the soldiers discharged their muskets, and two military bands played simultaneously; sky rockets exploded, and torches trailed sparks across the darkling plain. After two hours the pilgrims reached Muzdalifah, but no tents were pitched, everyone lying down on the first clear spot he could find. After several hours of searching for his party, Burckhardt gave up and lay down on the ground covered only by his *ihram*. The artillery boomed without intermission through the night.

At dawn the qadi delivered another sermon, but hardly anyone listened, as most of the hajjis preferred to stay with their baggage. The pilgrims then decamped to Mina, where they stoned the devil and killed six to eight thousand sheep bought at inflated prices from the Bedouins. The pilgrimage was now over, and the pilgrims were free to have their heads shaved and to don ordinary clothes. But Burckhardt had still not found his camels and baggage and was forced to spend the day in his *ihram*. It was not till after sunset that he found his party, who said that they had been under great anxiety about him.

Now the great fair of Mina began, with booths set up for the sale of goods and everyone, men, women, and children, dressed in new clothes. Few ventured to sleep at night on account of thieves. A hajji was robbed of 200 dollars, and several dozen camels were stolen by Bedouins. Two of the thieves were caught and brought before Mehmet Ali, who ordered them beheaded. Their bodies lay before his tent for three days under guard to prevent their friends from taking them away. Burckhardt heard a Bedu exclaim, 'God have mercy on *them*; but no mercy upon him who killed them!' Meanwhile the troops held manoeuvres and displays of arms. The two Pashas exchanged visits, and their followers were admitted to kiss hands and receive gifts. When a group of Negro pilgrims tried to present their compliments to Mehmet Ali, however, they were beaten by his officers. Day and night were enlivened by rockets, gunfire, and bonfires.

By the second day the putrefying carcasses of the slaughtered animals became offensive, as the hajjis could not consume all they had sacrificed. In the mosque of Mina where a crowd of poor Indians had taken up their quarters the pavement was covered with carrion, and slices of meat were hung to dry on cords extended between the columns. The sight and smell disgusted many of the more delicate pilgrims, who expressed surprise that such indecencies were allowed. Foreigners were often offended by the shameful practices permitted in the Holy Cities; but, Burckhardt remarked, the Christian Holy Land was open to the same censure.

Burckhardt planned to leave for Medina with the Syrian caravan ten days after the feast, when the camels would have been rested. Mehmet Ali, however, seized 12,000 of the Syrian camels to transport military supplies. As the Egyptian caravan contained no civilians, it was wholly detained for active service, the *mahmal* being sent back to Suez by sea. When the Syrian caravan was at last allowed to leave, Burckhardt found that the Bedu guide he had hired had disappeared. So he was obliged to remain another month in Mecca. He heard later that many of the Syrian camels had died from exhaustion on the return journey and that the Syrian Pasha had become delirious and died shortly before reaching Damascus.

After the departure of the Syrians, Mecca was nearly deserted. Rubbish and filth covered the streets, and on the outskirts the dead carcasses of camels rendered the air so offensive that people stuffed their nostrils with pieces of cotton. Moreover the Meccans were in the habit of emptying their privies after the pilgrimage, but, being too lazy to cart the contents beyond the town, they merely dug a hole in the street before the very door of their dwellings and there deposited the ordure under a thin layer of earth. The consequences, Burckhardt remarked, could easily be imagined.

The Holy City was a macabre mixture of festival and charnel house. The Meccans always celebrated their nuptials and circumcisions after the pilgrims had departed, leaving their money behind them. Burckhardt saw more funerals than weddings, however, as among the hajjis disease and mortality succeeded the excitement of the hajj. The Holy Mosque was filled with the dead and dying. The sick hoped to be cured by the sight of the Ka'ba or at least to expire within the sacred enclosure. Poor hajjis, worn out with hunger and disease, dragged their emaciated bodies among the columns; when no longer able to extend their hands for charity, they placed a bowl to receive alms near the mat where they lay. When they felt their last moments approaching, they covered them-selves with their tattered garments, and often a whole day passed before it was discovered they were dead. Burckhardt, with the help of a Greek hajji, closed the eyes of a poor Maghrabi who had crawled into the Mosque to breathe his last. He intimated by signs his wish to be sprinkled with Zamzam water; as this was done, he expired and half an hour later he was buried. The Mosque employed several men to bury all poor and friendless persons who expired at Mecca and to wash the spot where they died.

Mehmet Ali remained at Mecca, preparing to lead his troops person-ally against the southern Wahhabis. To encourage his men he staged an execution of twelve 'heretics' on the plain of Arafat, in clear defiance of the law forbidding the shedding of blood in such a holy place. It mattered even less to him that the victims were not in fact Wahhabis but twelve peaceful members of the 'Ataibah tribe captured on an innocent expedi-tion to Jiddah. An immense crowd came out to the plain to watch the execution. The prisoners were forced to kneel while a Turkish soldier stood behind each of them armed with a broad sword. One of the victims, just as his hands were untied to receive the blow, knocked down his executioner and escaped into the crowd. As he dodged across the plain, the Arabs encouraged him with shouts and applause. But a Turkish pilgrim mounted on a horse chased him and cut him down to the hisses and execration of the crowd.

Mehmet Ali marched out of Mecca at the head of a column of men and camels newly arrived from Egypt. He had sent other troops ahead to engage the Wahhabis, but the enemy refused to meet the Turks head on and used hit-and-run raids that took a steady toll in dead and wounded. A few Turkish soldiers deserted and ran back to Mecca spreading the rumour that the Pasha had been defeated and the Wahhabis were marching on the Holy City. The frightened people of Mecca put on Bedouin rags to escape detection and paid exorbitant prices for old and tired camels to take them away. Even the Sharif prepared once more to fly to Jiddah. Burckhardt gathered a supply of biscuits and repaired to the Holy Mosque with his slave and carpet, convinced that the Wahhabis would respect the right of asylum.

Far from being defeated Mehmet Ali lived up to his reputation for skill and daring as a commander in the field. Knowing that he could not beat the Wahhabis in the mountains, he determined to draw them into the plain. He advanced on their stronghold at a place called Bissal, shelled them with artillery and then retreated in apparent disorder. The Wahhabis set off in pursuit, and Mehmet Ali ordered his cavalry to wheel about and face the enemy. The Wahhabis were cut to pieces and their allies fled. When he saw the Arabs in retreat, Mehmet Ali proclaimed a bounty of six dollars on every head brought to him; soon a pile of 5,000 heads rose before his tent. Four days later the Turkish troops appeared under the walls of Taraba, the stronghold of the 'sorceress' Ghaliyah. This time her magic failed: Faisal, brother of 'Abd Allah ibn Sa'ud, fled from the field and the local inhabitants capitulated. The Turks plundered the town, finding little of value except some handsome Arab women who were, however, restored to their families on the Pasha's orders. Ghaliyah escaped to the desert and found refuge among the Bedouin tribes, refusing to give herself up despite Mehmet Ali's fair promises. Sharif Yahyah was sent to take Qunfudah, completing the rout of the southern Wahhabis. Mehmet Ali was now free to march on Yemen if he had wanted to; but his soldiers refused to go on and, being a realist, he returned to Mecca. The entire operation had taken fifteen days.

But Turkish losses were heavy. Of 4,000 men who set out, only 1,500 returned, worn out and nearly without clothes or equipment. The toll of animals was even greater, only 300 of the 4,000 camels and horses surviving. Nevertheless the Pasha sent messengers to Cairo and Constantinople with the news of his victory, and he staged another Roman holiday in the Hijaz. At his express orders, 300 Wahhabis had been taken alive by men who rode after them and offered them quarter, as none of them would

beg for it. As celebration of his victory, the Pasha had fifty of them im-
paled before the gates of Mecca and a dozen others similarly executed at
each of the coffee-houses on the road to Jiddah. Their bodies were left to
be devoured by vultures and dogs. The Arab allies of Mehmet Ali,
horrified by this conduct, remonstrated with the Pasha but to no avail.

When the news of the Egyptian victory was known, the caravans
dared to move again. Burckhardt left Mecca on 15 January 1815 with a
small group of Malay pilgrims. As usual the caravan travelled by night,
although the road was infested with robbers. Twice, walking ahead in
the dark, Burckhardt was set upon but was saved in the nick of time by
the arrival of the caravan. Sometimes the robbers, dressed as Turkish
soldiers, joined the caravan at night, and made off with horses and other
loot. Others would jump on a camel behind a sleeping traveller, stop his
mouth with their *aba*, and throw down to their companions whatever
valuables they found. If discovered, they drew their daggers and cut their
way out, for they could expect no mercy. The usual mode of punishment
was to impale the robbers at the moment the caravan departed for the
next station, leaving them to perish on the stake or to be devoured by
wild beasts.

And yet Burckhardt met several poor hajjis who had nothing whatever
of their own and lived entirely on the generosity of the Bedouins.

He disliked the Malays with whom he travelled. Their broad features,
short stature, and decayed teeth were in striking contrast to the physical
refinement of the Arabs. Although sober and quiet, they were avaricious
in the extreme. Several poor Malays, travelling among them on foot, fell
behind and straggled into camp an hour or two after the rest. One day
one of them was found wandering in the desert by two long-haired 'Awf
tribesmen, notorious robbers, who brought him into camp and demanded twenty piastres for his release. The other Malays disclaimed the
man and refused to pay. The Bedouins threatened to take his meagre
clothing and to hold him prisoner until some other Malay should pass
and redeem him. As the caravan prepared to start, the prisoner was led
away, speechless with terror. The camels were loaded, the pilgrims
mounted, and the leader gave the signal to start when the poor wretch
found his voice and broke into loud lamentations.

At this Burckhardt seized the leader's camel and made it lie down,
declaring that the caravan should not proceed till the man was released.
He then went from load to load, collaring each man and calling down
curses upon him until he had collected twenty paras (about three pence)
from him. After a long contest he made up twenty piastres. Appealing to

the honour of their tribe, he induced the Bedouins to take only ten piastres. The rest he gave to the poor Malay, to the mortification of his countrymen and with the consequence of having the man on his hands for the remainder of the journey.

On the last night of the march, a heavy thunderstorm struck the travellers but, having no tents, they marched on. After ten hours they arrived at the gate of Medina to find it shut for the night. The rain was followed by a severe frost. Soaked to the skin and unable to light a fire on the wet ground, they waited until daybreak for admission to the town.

Burckhardt found lodgings, but provisions were scarce. Medina was then governed by Tusun, whose high-handed measures had frightened away the camel drivers who usually supplied the town. It was three days before Burckhardt's slave could find coal, and he felt the want keenly. Hearing that Yahyah Effendi, Tusun's Syrian physician, was in town, Burckhardt paid him a call, to his later regret. For the physician returned the visit and seeing Burckhardt's stock of medicine asked for half a pound of bark to treat the Pasha and his suite, who were ill with fever. Burckhardt owed the man a favour and, being in good health himself, gave him his entire stock of bark.

Two days later Burckhardt was attacked by fever. When he asked for the return of some bark, Yahyah Effendi told him that it had all been distributed. The fever grew worse, accompanied by vomiting and profuse sweating. He treated himself with emetics and let the disease run its course. After a month it abated for a few days only to return with greater violence, accompanied by fainting and ending in total prostration. He was unable to rise from his carpet without the assistance of his slave, who by habit and nature was more fitted to take care of a camel than to nurse his drooping master.

Lacking all hope, Burckhardt prepared to die at Medina. He became despondent with apprehension that when the news of his death reached London his whole Hijaz journey would be condemned as unauthorized and imprudent. He had but one book to divert him, a pocket edition of Milton which he had borrowed from an English captain at Jiddah. Apart from his slave, his sole society consisted of his landlady, an old Egyptian woman, who used to converse with him every evening for half an hour from her retreat on an upper storey without ever being seen by him. His guide paid him an occasional visit in order, he suspected, to seize his luggage if he died. Yahyah Effendi, who might have come to him, had left in March with the army of Tusun Pasha.

In April the returning warmth put an end to his fever, but it was nearly a fortnight before he could walk abroad, and every breeze made him fear a relapse. The streets were full of fellow sufferers emerging pale and tottering from their sickbeds. He was now anxious to leave Medina. His original intention was to remain there a month, then to cross the desert to Aqaba, seeing the ruins of Madain Salih on the way, before taking ship to Suez. But this was impossible in his present state, and he was convinced that only a change of air would cure him. He therefore determined to go to Yanbu' as soon as he could mount a camel and from there embark for Egypt.

But first there was the City of the Prophet to explore, measure, and describe. Burckhardt was the first Westerner to report on the second city of Islam since Joseph Pitts nearly two centuries earlier. Unfortunately his illness prevented him from doing as thorough a job as he had in Mecca or Jiddah. The city consisted of an inner town enclosed in high, thick walls flanked by thirty towers and surrounded by a protective ditch dug by the Wahhabis. Some of the central streets were paved, a rarity in the East. Of the three gates to the inner town, Bab al-Misr – the gate of Egypt – was one of the finest he had seen in Muslim countries, surpassed only by Bab al-Futuh in Cairo. The suburbs surrounding the inner town contained large courtyards called *hosh*, enclosing thirty or forty family dwellings, a well, and a place in the middle for cattle; each *hosh* had a single gate which was locked at night, for the inhabitants of these walled hamlets often engaged in bloody feuds with each other. The palm groves around the city produced over a hundred varieties of dates celebrated throughout Arabia. Burckhardt did not go far into the countryside, but he noted that it looked as if it had been burned by fire. Only after his return to Cairo did he learn of the volcanic eruption in the thirteenth century that had threatened Medina with a great flood of lava but had stopped abruptly near the present airport as if it had been frozen by divine reprieve.

The Prophet's Mosque, built like the Holy Mosque of Mecca as an open space surrounded by colonnades, did not impress him. At first it dazzled the eye with its gaudy colours, tiled columns, fine carpets, and gilt inscriptions; but it was a display of tinsel and not of real riches. The jewels and gold vessels formerly presented by the faithful had been stolen by a corrupt governor, and the Wahhabis had despoiled the rest. Tusun Pasha, the only devout member of Mehmet Ali's family, had bought back some of the gold vessels and restored them to the shrine, but he had been unable to revive its former splendour.

The ceremonies, less elaborate than those at Mecca, amounted to no more than a pious visit to the tomb of Muhammad. At every spot where visitors were expected to pray people sat waiting to receive gifts. At the tomb of Fatimah a party of women spread their handkerchiefs for alms, while the eunuchs of the Mosque waited till the last prayer had been said to wish the visitor joy of his visit and to receive their fee. The eunuchs of Medina were even more richly dressed than those of Mecca and assumed greater airs. They were emaciated, their hands those of skeletons, their faces nothing but bones emerging from the rotund contours of their padded dress. Their harsh voices had none of the fine feminine tone so much admired in the castrati singers of Europe in Burckhardt's day.

The people of Medina were largely of foreign origin, as in Mecca and Jiddah. Among the ancient families were a number of families, including descendants of the Prophet, who were known to be sectaries of 'Ali. There were also a few descendants of the Abbasid caliphs, living in extreme poverty. It was the custom of some Medinans to make mendicant journeys to Constantinople at least once in their lives, living there at the expense of pilgrims they had met on the hajj, accepting alms and investing in merchandise with which they returned home fairly rich men.

The principal wife of Mehmet Ali, after performing the pilgrimage, had also come to Medina, to see her son Tusun. She brought him presents valued at £25,000, among them two beautiful Georgian slaves. In her retinue was another Georgian of such beauty and rare accomplishments that Mehmet Ali had married her himself at Mecca. But as she had not yet borne any children, she was much inferior in rank to Tusun's mother, who counted three pashas among her sons. The beautiful Georgian had belonged to the qadi of Mecca, but Mehmet Ali, having heard his women praise her, obliged the qadi to part with her for the sum of 50,000 piastres. So great were her accomplishments that soon after the Pasha of Egypt presented her with a marriage contract.-

Tusun's mother spent most of her nights in Medina at devotions in the Mosque. When she returned to her quarters, her son paid her a short visit, then left her to repose and ordered a carpet spread in the street near her door, where he slept. Burckhardt admired his filial respect and humility but regretted that he was much inferior to his father and brother Ibrahim in intellectual ability.

After three months' recuperation, Burckhardt felt strong enough to mount a camel again and start for Yanbu'. As he left Medina he brooded over the differences three months had made: 'Then I was in full health and spirits, and indulging in the fond hopes of exploring unknown and interesting parts of the desert on my return to Egypt; but now, worn out by lingering disease, dejected, and desponding, with no more anxious wish than to reach a friendly and salubrious spot, where I might regain my health.' But his troubles were not over. On the third day's march, the fever returned accompanied by profuse sweating and followed by shivering fits. As the caravan would not halt, he could not change his damp linen, and often they camped on wet ground. His camel driver was ill-natured and surly, and insisted that Burckhardt help to load the animals. When the route was rocky and steep, he was obliged to walk, though he could hardly muster the strength to reach the summit. Nevertheless, he conscientiously observed and recorded the terrain. At Badr he examined the tombs of the Prophet's companions who had fallen in battle, all systematically ruined by the Wahhabis. On the sixth day violent vomiting and profuse sweating made the night hideous, and a quarrel with his guide about victuals increased his fever. At last a few saline shrubs appeared, and soon after the ground was covered with a salt crust and the air impregnated with sea-vapours. At sunrise the travellers could see Yanbu' in the distance. But it was still fifteen painful hours before their camels waded across a shallow inlet of the sea and they reached the gate of Yanbu'.

The town was filled with soldiers and pilgrims trying to leave Arabia. Four ships were being prepared to transport the principal wife of Mehmet Ali and her suite. All other vessels had been commandeered by the army. Burckhardt learned with dismay that he would have to wait at least a month for passage.

While sitting at a coffee-house near the port, he saw three funerals pass and learned that many people had died in the last few days from feverish complaints. During the day he saw several more funerals, and at night heard voices raised in those heart-rending cries that mark the parting breath of friend or relation in the East. The thought crossed his mind that the plague might have broken out. Next morning he voiced his fear to the Arabs in his khan, but they called him to order, asking him if he was ignorant that the Almighty had forever excluded the plague from the Hijaz. Such argument admitted of no reply. He walked out in search of some Greek Christians he had seen the previous day, and they confirmed his fear. The plague had broken out ten days before; it had been raging in Cairo for several months; at Suez a large part of the population had died of it, and from there it had been brought by ship to Yanbu'. As the plague had not been seen in the Hijaz within living memory, the inhabitants could not believe that it had come now, especially when the Holy Cities had been recovered from the Wahhabis.

Six days later deaths had risen to forty or fifty a day in a population of five or six thousand. The people fell into a panic, and many fled into the desert; but the disease followed them and they returned. They excused their flight, saying 'God in His mercy sends this disease, to call us to His presence; but we are conscious of our unworthiness, and felt that we did not deserve His grace; therefore we think it better to decline it, for the present, and to flee from it.' Burckhardt denied that the Muslim religion forbade its followers to take any precaution against the plague. It forbade men to avoid the disease once it had entered a place, but it warned them not to enter where the plague was raging, and it permitted quarantine. But the belief in predestination was so deeply rooted among the people of Yanbu' that not the slightest preventive measures were taken. Burckhardt himself recommended bleeding and a plaster applied to the neck as prophylaxis. More poetically and perhaps just as effectively, the people of Yanbu' avoided the trunk of a palm tree where they suspected the angel of death was lurking; and when the plague was at its height, they led a she-camel decked with feathers and bells through the town to attract the plague into its body. Having reached the burial ground, they killed the beast and threw its flesh to the vultures and the dogs.

Burckhardt offered bribes to obtain passage to Suez, but the ships were crowded to excess and full of diseased soldiers and hajjis. Then he tried the expedient of staying shut up in his room. But in the very yard of his khan an Arab lay dying, and the master of the khan, while seated on Burckhardt's carpet, told how his son had died the previous night in his arms. Burckhardt's slave in particular put all his precautions to naught. Having missed him several mornings, Burckhardt enquired the cause of his absence and was told that the boy had gone to assist in washing the bodies of the dead that were exposed each morning on biers near the seashore before prayers were said over them in the mosque. The slave thought it meritorious to join in this office. Burckhardt ordered him to stay at home at that hour to prepare his breakfast, but he could not prevent his walking about and could not himself avoid this necessity. The main street of Yanbu' was lined with men begging for charity in the very agony of death.

For the poor of Yanbu' the plague was a continual feast, for every family that could afford it killed a sheep on the death of any of its members and entertained the whole neighbourhood. The women entered the apartments of the deceased and embraced all females of the family, thus exposing themselves to infection. Because of the custom of burying the dead a few hours after decease, two cases occurred of persons being buried alive, the stupor into which they had fallen being mistaken for death. One of them gave signs of life at the moment of burial and was saved; the body of the other, when the tomb was opened several days later to admit the corpse of a relative, was found with bloody hands and face, the winding sheet torn by his efforts to rise. The people said that the devil, unable to hurt his soul, had disfigured his body.

The ravages of the plague were even greater at Jiddah, where as many as 250 died every day. Many of them were foreigners, whose deaths increased the treasury of Mehmet Ali, for when a foreigner died anywhere in Turkish dominions the governor had the right to seize his property. Burckhardt suspected that this practice inspired official complacency in regard to epidemics.

Unlike the other citizens of the Hijaz, the people of Yanbu' were totally Arab and close to the Bedouins in dress and manner. They all carried firearms as well as a heavy bludgeon to enforce their rights. They hated both the Wahhabis and the Sharif, and were learning to hate the Osmanlis. The Turkish soldiers, being at a distance from the Pasha and his son, behaved worse in Yanbu' than they dared in Jiddah or the Holy Cities. Every *bimbashi*, or company commander, who landed with his soldiers here took temporary control of the town. Affrays between Turks and Arabs broke out constantly. One Turkish officer made an infamous proposal to a young Arab in the street at midday; when the Arab rejected his advances, the Turk shot him and took refuge in the quarters of his *bimbashi*, whose guards defended the importunate officer from the fury of the populace.

After eighteen days in the infested town, Burckhardt procured passage in an open *sambouk* bound for Qusair with a load of corn, paying double fare for his own and his slave's passage. As the commander of Yanbu' had a share in the boat, it was allowed to leave without soldiers, and the master told Burckhardt that there were only half a dozen Arabs on board. When he came aboard, however, Burckhardt found he had been deceived: above thirty passengers, mostly Syrian and Egyptians, were crowded into the hold with about ten sailors. The master, his younger brother, the pilot, and the steward had established themselves behind the helm, in the space Burckhardt had been promised for his inflated fare. But to return to Yanbu', the abode of death, was not advisable, and as he saw no sign of the plague on board, he submitted to his lot.

It was not till after the boat had sailed that Burckhardt realized the true situation, for in the hold lay a dozen sick, two of them in violent delirium. One died in the night, and his body was thrown overboard. Little doubt remained in Burckhardt's mind that the plague was actually in the boat, though the sailors maintained that it was a different illness. On the third day, the master's brother felt pains in his head and insisted on being set ashore. They stopped in a small bay, and the master engaged a Bedu to take his brother back to Yanbu'.

The only precaution that Burckhardt could take was to place his baggage around him to form an island in which he had just room to sit. But he was compelled to come into contact with the boat's company. Only one more passenger died, though several came down with the malady. He thought that perhaps the seasickness and vomiting were salutary. He himself was tormented by the ague. He took a disgust to all solid food; whenever they entered a port he bought a sheep in order to make broth; by distributing the meat among the crew he won their goodwill and their help in raising his awning against the sun and filling his water-skin on shore. In addition to the plague, he feared the boat might be dashed against the shore, which it hugged in Red Sea fashion; at night, when the boat entered a cove, he was on his guard against thieves who might swim out from shore. During the long hot days, insulated by his baggage, he surreptitiously observed the passing shore and made notes.

Burckhardt survived the sea journey and finally reached Cairo. The last that the African Association had heard from him was a letter dated 7 August 1814 written just after his arrival at Jiddah. Now, nearly a year later, the Association received one from Cairo dated 25 June 1815, informing it of his successful journey through the Hijaz. He devoted the next nine months to mending his health and to preparing his journals on Nubia and Arabia. In the heat of a Cairo summer, he suffered several relapses and often could not work because of depression and listlessness.

But he grew stronger and looked impatiently for a way to travel to Niger. When the Fezzan caravan failed to arrive, it aroused his concern lest the African Association suspect he was malingering. 'Yet I cannot prevail upon myself,' he wrote to the secretary, 'to take a false, inconsiderate step; and I would rather expose myself to a temporary imputation of a neglect of duty, than to act with rashness against my conviction.' Although he mixed with Europeans, he continued to live in the Turkish quarter and to appear as a devout and learned Muslim. Living with him was a slave of English origin, Osman, whom he had arranged to have released from slavery, and he kept several male and female household slaves. The Muslim way of life seemed to have become a habit in which he was completely at ease.

For three successive years the plague had raged in Cairo, returning every spring and lasting through the summer. 'I shall neither imitate my Mussulman neighbours,' he wrote, 'in taking no precautions against the attacks, nor the Greeks and Franks who shut themselves up for three or four months in their houses as close prisoners; but I shall leave the infected borders of the Nile, and seek refuge among the Bedouins.' He left for Sinai in April 1816 and spent two months in pursuit of his re-searches into Bedouin life. On his return to Cairo he had a recurrence of an ophthalmic complaint, but he seemed immune to the plague and recovered from his intermittent fever.

At last a caravan from West Africa passed through Cairo on its way to Mecca, and Burckhardt determined to join it on its return. The prospect of accomplishing his long-delayed mission of reaching Timbuctu filled him with elation, as he prepared for a journey more arduous than any he had yet made. But the angel of death, who had tracked him so long, now claimed him. His fever returned and with it a violent dysentery. On 15 October 1816, he sent for Mr Salt, the British consul general, who described his condition to the secretary of the African Association:

I went over immediately and cannot describe how shocked I was, to see the change that had taken place in so short a time. On the Tuesday before, he had been walking in my garden with every appearance of health, and conversing with his usual liveliness and vigour; now he could scarcely articulate his words, often made use of one for another, was of a ghastly hue, and had all the appear-ance of approaching death.

Burckhardt dictated his will to the consul general. He left 2,000 piastres to his companion Osman, as well as his household goods and slaves. He sent 1,000 piastres to the poor of Zurich and left his collection of books and manuscripts to the University of Cambridge. 'Give my love to my friends,' he said, enumerating several persons with whom he was intimate in Cairo and Alexandria. He then paused and seemed troubled. At length, with great exertion, he said, 'Let Mr Hamilton acquaint my mother with my death, and say that my last thoughts have been with her.' Immediately thereafter, according to Mr Salt, he added, 'The Turks will take my body, I know it, perhaps you had better let them.' Six hours later he died. He was thirty-three years old.

The funeral was Muslim – 'Upon this point I had no difficulty in deciding,' asserted Mr Salt, 'after his own expression on the subject' – and conducted with proper regard to the respectable rank he held in the eyes of his neighbours. Forty years later, according to Burton, his tomb was revered as that of a Muslim saint, and for this reason the European residents of Cairo refused to subscribe for a monument to the discoverer of Abu Simbel. For Burckhardt's conversion to Islam pricked the conscience of Christians; he was so obviously a good and upright man. It is still somewhat enigmatic. Burckhardt was deeply European in character, imbued with Protestant habits of truthfulness, hard work, and self-reliance. The character of a renegade – an unsavoury adventurer – must have been repugnant to him. Yet he adapted easily to the life style of the Turks. His ownership of slaves seems particularly significant at a time when this unequal relationship between men was beginning to trouble Christendom. The petty differences between cultures that loom so large in the complaints of other Westerners in the East meant nothing to him. His strictures on the superstitions and hypocrisy of Muslim individuals and institutions did not reflect on the core of the religion; in fact, they implied a desire to reform and strengthen the faith. Yet he never stated clearly and unequivocally his belief in Islam.

Perhaps the enigma lies in our own attitude. To most Christians Islam appears alien, even inimical. But to Muslims, Christianity is familiar ground, for Islam contains Christianity as Christianity contains Judaism. From the Muslim point of view there is no sharp dividing line between the three semitic religions. Perhaps Burckhardt felt that he had crossed no gulf in becoming a Muslim, that he did not thereby cease to be a Christian. His death-bed instructions to Mr Salt on the disposal of his body were so casual as to suggest that the distinction meant little to him. Perhaps it should not matter to us.

CHAPTER 7
Viceregent of Asrail

In the spring of 1815, relations between the Pasha of Egypt and his son were nearly at breaking point. Mehmet Ali had appointed Tusun governor of Medina, but he denied him sufficient revenue and appointed a member of his own court to oversee the administration. Tusun, now a pasha of three tails and thus equal in rank to his father, asserted his independence by beheading the adviser sent by his father and marching into the Qasim to deal with the Wahhabi chief on his own account. On his departure he made Thomas Keith acting governor of the second holiest city in Islam – the strangest office, it has been observed, to which even a Scot has attained. When Mehmet Ali went to Medina to take charge in April, the first thing he did was to send Keith with 250 horsemen to join Tusun. On the road a contingent of Wahhabis ambushed the Turkish troop; Keith brought down four of the enemy with his sword; but the Turks were outnumbered and all of them killed, including the doughty Scot. The great Sa'ud said that Keith was one of the two bravest men in the Turkish army, and Burckhardt predicted that, had he lived to return to Egypt, he would have been made a pasha of two tails.

'Abd Allah ibn Sa'ud came in force to meet Tusun's army in the Qasim, but the confrontation was a stalemate. Tusun could not trust his Bedouin allies, and his own officers were reluctant to fight a battle they might lose, leaving their men cut off in the desert without a secure line of retreat. For his part, 'Abd Allah realized that even the destruction of Tusun's army would not end the war, but only bring Mehmet Ali's inexhaustible supply of men and arms into Najd. The two sides therefore agreed to negotiate. Tusun sent Yahyah Effendi, who as a Syrian spoke fluent Arabic, to the Wahhabi camp, and after three days he returned with an agreement. 'Abd Allah renounced all claims to the Holy Cities, declared himself a dutiful subject of the Sultan, and agreed to permit free passage of caravans through his domains. Tusun agreed to abandon all towns of the Qasim then in his hands and to allow 'Abd Allah control over all tribes that pastured in the north. The two sides exchanged hostages to ensure a safe retreat, and by the end of June Tusun was back in Medina.

He did not find his father there. News of Napoleon's fall and of an Ottoman fleet cruising off Alexandria had induced Mehmet Ali to imitate his hero, Bonaparte, and decamp. With only a few trusted officers he took ship from Yanbu' on 19 May and sailed to Qusair; there, finding neither horse nor camel, the Pasha's party mounted asses to cross the desert to Qena on the Nile, arriving by river boat in Cairo on 19 June. Not knowing that Tusun had signed a peace treaty with 'Abd Allah, Mehmet Ali falsely announced the taking of Dar'iyah and the destruction of the Wahhabis. For a fortnight all Cairo fêted the famous victory. But that summer, when discontented troops returned and pillaged the city, the Pasha shut himself up in the Citadel till the insurrection ended.

In Arabia the truce held. Caravans moved freely through Najd for the first time in ten years, and hordes of Wahhabis made the pilgrimage in December 1815. But when 'Abd Allah's envoys arrived in Cairo to confirm the agreement, they were placed under surveillance and kept waiting. At last Mehmet Ali gave them a letter to 'Abd Allah in which he made the impossible demand that he be ceded the fertile province of al-Hasa in return for peace. Tusun arrived in Egypt in November to an enthusiastic public welcome but a cold reception from his father. Ill and in disgrace, he was placed in charge of the coastal defence at Rosetta, where he died in the plague of 1816.

Mehmet Ali was already in correspondence with the Porte in which he represented Tusun's treaty with 'Abd Allah as a mere truce and declared his intention of destroying Wahhabi power at its source in Dar'iyah. His position demanded total victory over the Unitarians, and the disbanded Egyptian forces, especially the unruly Arnauts, required employment outside of Egypt. The Wahhabi chief provided a pretext for further intervention by punishing the towns and tribes that had collaborated with the Turks, taking prisoners, pulling down walls, cutting palm groves, and filling in wells. The people of the Qasim sent urgent messages to Cairo demanding protection against Wahhabi revenge. Soon 'Abd Allah's presents and requests for renewal of the peace were coldly received by the Egyptian Pasha.

This time he entrusted the mission to his older son, or stepson, Ibrahim, who had served him well in his climb to power. At an early age Ibrahim had spent a year as hostage for his father's loyalty at the court in Constantinople, a school for ruthlessness and intrigue. During the war against the Mamluks he had led a force of 300 cavalry and killed all the beys he could lay hands on, including those who gave themselves up to his protection. He was a curious mixture of traditional Osmanli tyrant and

forward-looking administrator. As governor of Upper Egypt he collected revenues, parcelled out the villages to a new gang of tax farmers,
and enhanced the yield of both crops and taxes by investing large sums
in agricultural improvements. During this period he employed a number
of Copts as clerks and accountants; suspecting some of them of taking
bribes, he had one roasted on a spit, another burnt alive on a bed of
chopped straw soaked with oil. For his services to the state he was
created a pasha of two tails in 1813.

Ibrahim had difficulty in assembling troops for the new expedition. As
the number of volunteers was insufficient, he had his father issue an order
requiring all troops to serve under him and preventing any man from
seeking a discharge. Each horse soldier was expected to provide a camel
as well as a horse to transport baggage and serve as an auxiliary mount,
for the Egyptian horses were no match for the Arab steeds and had to be
kept fresh for combat. The troops grumbled, but the army was strengthened by the arrival of 1,500 horsemen from Libya. Their horses were of
miserable appearance but good performance; and at full speed in a
charge, setting up a yell, firing their pistols and muskets and brandishing
their sabres, the Libyans made a formidable show. Moreover they fought
without pay, being content with their pillage.

Ibrahim supervised the embarkation of his infantry at Qusair, then
hurried back to Cairo to consult with his father and to see off the first
contingent of cavalry by road from Suez. Returning to Qusair, he set
sail for Yanbu' with only a few officers, among them two Frenchmen,
one of whom had served as commodore with Napoleon at Rochefort.
On his arrival in the Holy Land, Ibrahim, who had acquired Western
ways in Constantinople, destroyed the whole stock of wine he had
brought with him. After waiting forty days at Yanbu' for supplies
promised by the Arabs, he sent out a raiding party which captured 1,000
camels and 2,000 sheep, killing 150 of the defaulting Bedouins against
only two Turks wounded. On the other hand, 400 of his men died in the
first weeks from disease caused by the insanitary conditions in the
Turkish camp.

But the loss was more than made up by the arrival of a small occupying
force that had been left at Medina under an able officer, Auzun Ali. With
these reinforcements Ibrahim was able to forge a striking force of 600
Turkish cavalry, 200 Maghrabi horsemen, and 900 foot soldiers, with
artillery consisting of three cannon slung between pairs of camels. In a
phrase much quoted at the time, but dating from at least 1683 when the
Turks failed to take Vienna, Ibrahim commenced the slow but steady

process of rolling up the desert carpet to reach the apple in the middle – Dar'iyah.

The hem of the carpet consisted of the Bedouin tribes in and near the Hijaz. To obtain more supplies, Ibrahim raided the Harb tribe, seizing 500 camels, 6,000 sheep, and a quantity of dates. In the face of such arguments, other Bedouin shaikhs flocked to enlist under his banner. One tribe, however, the 'Ataibah, refused to submit to him; filling in their wells and destroying what they could not carry, they took flight with their herds. Enraged, Ibrahim rode personally in pursuit and catching up with seventeen of the 'Ataibah commenced the slaughter with his own sabre. On his return to camp he received news of the death of his brother Tusun in Rosetta and his own elevation to the rank of pasha of three tails. He proceeded at once to Medina to receive the pelisse of honour and to publish the *firman* of his appointment.

It took Ibrahim two years to roll up the carpet and reach the apple in the middle. First blood of the Wahhabis was tasted by Auzun Ali at the wells of Mawiyah in March 1817, when 'Abd Allah came to meet him with 10,000 men on dromedaries. But the Wahhabi cameleers were no match for the Turkish artillery, and the number of Arabs killed was said to have exceeded the tally of Auzun Ali's troops. Ibrahim arrived at Mawiyah when the fight was over but he joined in the slaughter of prisoners and the collecting of ears to send to Cairo to substantiate enemy losses.

The next large-scale action took place at Rass, a walled town near the borders of Najd and the Qasim, which the Turks besieged. But the Turkish cannonballs had no effect on the walls, merely lodging in the yellow earth of which they were built. When at last a breach was made, Ibrahim's men threw themselves into the ditch under the walls but could not scale the other side. When they tried to retreat under enemy fire, Ibrahim and a few trusted Mamluks shot them in the ditch; afterwards Ibrahim refused to allow the bodies to be buried. The siege of Rass lasted three and a half months, and Ibrahim was finally forced to come to terms, guaranteeing the neutrality of the townspeople for the rest of the campaign. The battle of Rass cost the Turks 400 camel-loads of ammunition, 3,000 artillery charges, and 900 men killed and 1,000 wounded, against the town's losses of 50 killed and 75 wounded. But casualties meant little to Ibrahim, as reinforcements were now flowing in from all over the Ottoman world, including a contingent from Iraq.

Other walled towns – Khabrah, 'Unaizah, Buraidah, Shakrah – fell to the Turks by assault or by the threat of assault. Those troops who surrendered were allowed to part with their arms. Dhurmah, however, the strongest town in Najd after Dar'iyah, resisted for four days of heavy fighting before surrendering. Three hundred Wahhabis commanded by an uncle of 'Abd Allah barricaded themselves in a strong house and were allowed to leave, without their arms. The rest of the town was put to pillage: for seven days the Turkish soldiers had their way, killing two-thirds of the male citizens, filling their purses with plunder, and collecting a reward for every pair of ears they turned in. When enough blood had been shed, Ibrahim rounded up 3,000 women and children and sent them unmolested to Dar'iyah, an act of chivalry, but one that added many useless mouths to be fed there.

The apple of Dar'iyah stood in an oasis of densely planted date palms deep in Wadi Hanifa, a valley running north-south, about four miles long and only 500 yards across at some points. Protecting cliffs rose to a height of 100 feet on one side, and at the highest point stood the citadel of Turaif, containing the houses and mosques of the intertwined families of Sa'ud and 'Abd al-Wahhab. Strewn among the palm groves, villages and hamlets lay surrounded by gardens of figs, apricots, grapes, and pomegranates.

February 1818 was cold in Najd, and heavy rains fell, flooding Wadi Hanifa. 'Abd Allah spent the pilgrimage season preparing his defences, setting up his front lines at the north and south entrances to the valley, with other strong points manned and fortified along the cliffs. One of the forts was entrusted to a contingent of black slaves commanded by a freedman of Sa'ud. The entire defending force numbered about 4,000 men, irregularly armed. The townspeople, numbering perhaps another 10,000, huddled in their cold, damp mud-brick houses, while the combatants stood guard in their rain-drenched battle stations, awaiting the Turkish advance through Najd.

Ibrahim appeared at the north end of the wadi on 11 March and immediately launched an attack. The Turkish forces were nearly double the defenders in manpower and vastly superior in firepower, with 5,000 infantry and 2,000 cavalry, the artillery strengthened with two mortars, a Swedish cannonade, a howitzer, four twelve-pounders, and five Turkish guns, manned and supported by 150 gunners, 200 pioneers, and a company of miners and artificers (preparers of shells). For ten days the Turkish guns bombarded the Wahhabi front lines, forcing the defenders back to their secondary positions. An unexpected respite from the guns occurred when the Turkish magazine was accidentally blown up and Ibrahim was obliged to wait two months for fresh shipments of ammunition. But the siege went on, preventing food and ammunition from reaching the town and Arab losses from being replaced, while Turkish reinforcements arrived continually. The attackers forced the Wahhabis to fall back again to prepared positions; at each set-back the defenders rallied but were unable to regain lost ground. Wahhabi forces were further depleted as deserters began to slip away.

Nevertheless, 'Abd Allah held off the vastly superior forces of Ibrahim for six months. In September, his strength reduced to 2,000 fighting men, the Wahhabi chief held only the citadel of Turaif. Ibrahim, who knew the state of the defence from some of the deserters, ordered a general assault and took Turaif by storm. 'Abd Allah with 200 supporters retreated into the castle. Seeing the hopelessness of his situation, the Wahhabi leader sent emissaries to Ibrahim, but the Pasha refused to discuss terms unless 'Abd Allah appeared before him in person. After three days of bombardment of the castle, 'Abd Allah came under truce to the Egyptian commander's tent. Ibrahim received him haughtily, presenting his hand to be kissed. Although he had not yet surrendered, 'Abd Allah kissed the proffered hand in token of submission. Ibrahim demanded total surrender but offered pardon to the defenders of Dar'iyah including members of the House of Sa'ud. He could not guarantee the safety of the town, however, and as for 'Abd Allah himself, Ibrahim could pledge for his life only until he reached Cairo. The Wahhabi chief retired to the castle to reflect on these melancholy terms. On 11 September he surrendered.

True to his word, Ibrahim sent 'Abd Allah to Cairo along with other members of his family. Mehmet Ali received the defeated Wahhabi and sent him on to Constantinople under Tartar guards. Turkish imams tried to convince him that the Unitarian faith was in error; when this failed he was paraded through the streets for three days and then beheaded at the gates of the Serail. As if to destroy the ideas it contained, his head was crushed in a mortar, while his body was hanged with a copy of the death sentence attached to it by a dagger piercing the flesh.

In Dar'iyah, Ibrahim arrested all persons whom he suspected of having hidden money and valuables and, through torture and stratagem, extorted large sums. He allowed his soldiers to enter the town, pillage the houses and ill-treat the citizens. Turkish vengeance was particularly directed against the religious leaders of the town. The qadi had his teeth pulled out before he was executed, and a grandson of Muhammad 'Abd al-Wahhab was forced to listen to the hateful music of a guitar before being dragged before a firing squad.

Ibrahim entered the citadel with only a few confidential servants, but found nothing of value except a few religious books and copies of the Quran, which he sent to Medina to be examined for heresy. After the soldiers had had their way with it, the town of Dar'iyah was systematic-ally destroyed. The walls and houses were mined, while squads of soldiers broke or burned everything that survived. Other troops cut down all the date palms and fruit trees and filled in all the wells. The surviving inhabitants fled to neighbouring towns, while a few made their way to the petty shaikhdoms of the Persian Gulf, where the Wahhabis had always found a welcome. The centre of the Unitarian faith was obliterated as completely as Carthage was by the Romans. It has never been rebuilt, and to this day the site of Dar'iyah is a wilderness of tumbled houses, gaping walls, rubble-choked streets, stunted, un-watered groves, and a few feathery, dust-covered tamarisk trees.

When the news of Ibrahim's victory reached the English in India, the Marquis of Hastings, the Governor General, proposed that the Egyptians be invited to join the English fleet in putting down the pirates of the Persian Gulf. The Wahhabis had intimate relations with these pirates, and from the perspective of Bombay the Ottoman-Egyptian army appeared to represent reason and progress bringing law and order to the Arabian peninsula. Word had reached India that the Turkish army had occupied Qatif and that Ibrahim might have designs on the pearl banks of Bahrain. The Governor General therefore thought it useful to send an emissary to Dar'iyah bearing a letter to the Pasha congratulating him on 'the brilliant success of the arms of the Ottoman Empire' accompanied by a sword of honour of fine Indian workmanship. The letter also included an invitation to the Egyptian government to join the British in inflicting on the vexatious pirates 'that chastisement which their cruelties justly deserved'.

The man chosen by Lord Hastings to undertake this delicate mission was a fellow Anglo-Irishman, Captain George Foster Sadleir of the 47th Regiment of Foot. Sadleir had been born in Cork of stock transplanted by Cromwell from Stratford-upon-Avon and was connected by marri-age to the family of Shakespeare. At the age of sixteen he had entered the 47th Foot as an ensign and had seen action at Montevideo and Buenos Aires before being posted to India. The 47th had already grappled with the Persian Gulf pirates in 1809, and Sadleir himself had been attached to a military mission to Persia to train the troops of the Shah. Three members of previous missions to Persia had been murdered, two by Persians and one by a Russian officer. Captain Sadleir had not only survived but had been presented with a sword of honour by the Shah on his departure.

In 1818, at the start of his mission, Sadleir was thirty years of age, just two years older than Ibrahim and, like the Pasha, he had spent the greater part of his life in government service. His devotion to duty and deference to his superiors were unqualified. Self-discipline and will-power seemed to clothe and support him as completely as the braided, high-collared uniform he wore throughout the heat of an Arabian summer, revealing only occasional hints of the discomfort, illness, and frustration of the suffering human being underneath. For Ibrahim eluded him across the breadth of Arabia, missing several rendezvous, and in the end snubbing and quarrelling with him violently. By force of circumstance and his own sense of duty, this gruff, unimaginative soldier made the first journey across the Arabian peninsula recorded by a European, travelling seventy days and 1,000 miles from Qatif to Jiddah. In his diary and letters to his superiors he described the state of Najd after the destruction of Dar'iyah, regretting that he had 'been dragged a reluctant witness to the devastations of the Pacha's army' and to 'a series of the most barbarous cruelties, committed in violation of the faith of the most sacred promises'.

Sadleir sailed from Bombay in the brig-of-war *Thetis* and reached Muscat after fourteen days. As part of his mission, he treated with the Imam of Muscat, who, though willing to join the British in curbing the pirates of the Gulf, wanted nothing to do with the Turks. The Imam reviled Ibrahim's conduct of the war and his cruelty towards the Arabs, and suspected him of having designs on his own domains. Politely but firmly he refused to further Sadleir's plan to go to Dar'iyah. Sadleir therefore sailed to Bushire on the coast of Persia, where the British Resident helped him forward. Taking a pilot who claimed to know the Arabian coast, he sailed on the cruiser *Vestal* for Qatif. The weather was sultry with baffling winds, and the Bushire pilot managed to run the *Vestal* on a sandbank, delaying Sadleir's arrival by two days.

The Turkish governor of Qatif, Khalil Aga, was very morose, as he and his Turkish assistants had been recalled and the sixty Arabs who worked for him discharged. He was planning to join Ibrahim at Dar'iyah and invited Sadleir to accompany him, warning the Englishman not to trust the Bedouins for transport or protection. But Sadleir reckoned that Khalil's power had ceased and, not wishing to burden himself with so useless a companion, he hired animals from a shaikh of the Beni Khalid tribe and set out for the oasis of al-Hasa. Although he was accompanied by his own servants, a mixed bag of Persians, Indians, Portuguese, and Armenians, Sadleir hardly mentioned them in his reports and appears to have held aloof from them on the road.

The first day's march would have turned back a lesser man. The travellers rode across the thick crust of *sabkhas* – depressions where rainwater collects underground – their animals' pads sinking to the viscous mud below; the heat was intolerable and a hot wind blew so strongly that breathing was difficult. Once into the desert, the Bedouin shaikh demanded immediate payment for his animals, though this had not been in the agreement, and threatened to march off leaving Sadleir without water. Sadleir paid up, but when they reached an encampment of the Beni Khalid he tried to shame his guide by publicly denouncing his conduct. This merely caused more argument, and Sadleir, already ill from bad water, cursed 'the procrastination, duplicity, falsity, deception, and fraudulence of . . . these hordes of robbers'. But, as he remarked on another occasion, 'by being very obstinate I carried the point', and the party continued on its way.

When he reached Hufuf, the capital of al-Hasa, he found the Turkish officers there preparing to depart as well. It was clear that Ibrahim was about to withdraw from eastern Arabia and had no interest in further action in the Persian Gulf. Sadleir sent a letter to Bombay, saying,

With respect to my further proceeding, I find myself in a most perplexed and embarrassing situation. Was I not dubious of incurring the displeasure of the most noble Marquis of Hastings, I should be inclined to abandon the hope of proceeding on the mission with which I have been entrusted, but as the motives which induced the Governor General to open a communication with the Pacha may not be solely confined to the destruction of [the pirate lair of] Ras-al-Khima, I conceive it my duty to make every effort in my power to carry His Lordship's orders into effect . . .

Hopefully, he sent his letter to Qatif where the *Vestal* awaited his communications, but the messenger did not reach the coast for four months.

Having been assured by Ibrahim's representative in al-Hasa that the Pasha would await the arrival of the Turkish column at Sudair, ten or twelve days' march to the west, Sadleir agreed to accompany the Turks there. But he also contacted the shaikh of the Beni Khalid to ensure his return to Qatif. The Bedouin's reply was 'laconic'.

The Turks marched from al-Hasa in a convoy of 600 camels, as a precaution against marauding Bedouins. They marched by night, an advance guard carrying a large lantern fixed to a pole like the top-light of a commodore's ship. Pistols were discharged at intervals from front to rear of the column to prevent the convoy from becoming over-extended. The moon provided a cheerful light, but not enough for Sadleir to read his compass by. He found the Turkish soldiers disagreeable company as they took every opportunity to pilfer.

As usual the Turkish soldiers took no precautions in their use of water. Soon supplies ran out, while the wells at which they filled their skins in disorderly fashion soon failed. At one place Sadleir noted drily, 'Four Arabs unfortunately fell into one well; only two of them were saved.' The Turks would not permit their Bedouin guides to lead their camels out of camp to graze for fear of defections; the camels were therefore starving, the Bedouins grumbling, the Turks cursing. Several camels were in fact ridden off by their owners, who had received payment in advance. One of Sadleir's animals complete with its baggage strayed or was stolen; he sent one of his men with two Bedouins to recover it. The guides returned a couple of hours later without the man or the camel, saying that the man had been seized by Arabs from another tribe and his life threatened. Four days later the man stumbled back into camp; he had been stripped by his captors and forced to return on foot with only a little camel's milk to sustain him.

One Turk died on the march and several horses. Some Persian and Kabul mendicants who had joined the convoy on foot in hope of making their way to Mecca died of fatigue and lack of water. Meat was so scarce that whenever a camel showed signs of illness, the *Bismillah* was recited, the knife brought out, the animal's throat cut, and the meat separated from the bones, leaving the skeleton to mark the route of the convoy. As the Turks proceeded further into Najd they found the villages barricaded against them; the people appeared on the flat roofs and extorted high prices for whatever produce was available, including a little bad camel meat. Ibrahim's soldiers had consumed the year's crop of wheat and barley. Not a horse was to be found, as the Pasha had requisitioned them all.

Learning that the Sa'dah tribe was on the warpath, the *kashif* in charge of the convoy changed the route of march, adding two days to the journey. Another ten days were lost because of Ibrahim's breach of faith. The Pasha had extended mercy and a promise of future protection to four shaikhs of the House of Sa'ud at Salamiyah in exchange for their cooperation in governing the district. Having decided to abandon Najd, Ibrahim ordered his men at Salamiyah to kill the four shaikhs. As there were only fifty Turks in the area, the governor decided to resort to treachery and invited the shaikhs to a feast which ended in their assassination. A few days later 1,600 Arabs besieged Salamiyah and would have massacred the fifty Turks had not the *kashif* sent half his detachment to lift the siege. All the Arabs with whom Sadleir conversed declared themselves to be implacable enemies of the Turks and adherents of the Unitarian faith. They confirmed that several of their relatives were living at Ras al-Khaimah.

The convoy reached what was left of Dar'iyah on 13 August, Sadleir noting in his diary that there was not a single family inhabiting the ruins. The miseries of war cut deeply into the social fabric. Sadleir saw several Bedouin girls who had joined the train of the convoy. 'They proceed generally on foot, dependent on the occasional attention of a Turk, who probably shared their favours, and in return permitted them to ride on one of his camels, thus forsaking the life of innocence for the most horrid state to which human nature can be debased – that of a common prostitute, following a Turkish camp through the deserts of Arabia.'

The convoy was plagued with continual brawling between Bedouins and Turks. On learning that members of the 'Ataibah tribe had carried off all the camels belonging to a town on their route, the *kashif* sent a party in pursuit; the Turks killed twenty of the robbers on the plain and brought in five prisoners, whose heads they struck off in camp. This caused great alarm among their guides, the Beni Khalid, because the 'Ataibah would certainly retaliate against them on their return journey to al-Hasa. The guides attempted to escape with their animals and, though Sadleir placed a guard on his, two of his camels disappeared with their owners. But the Turks took revenge on the Bedouins who remained. When they reached the limits of the territory of the Beni Khalid, they insisted on keeping their camels to make up for the losses sustained on the road. The Bedouins, who were really entitled to double pay as the march had taken twice as long as stipulated, were turned adrift in the midst of deserts surrounded by their enemies. The *kashif*'s breach of faith also made it impossible for Sadleir to return to Qatif by the same route, for he could no longer count on the Beni Khalid tribe for protection.

Daily reports reached the convoy that Ibrahim awaited it at the town of Rass. Sadleir sent messages to apprise the Pasha of his arrival and pushed confidently on, sure of reaching his goal. Near Rass he entered a confused medley of tents, some belonging to Turks, some to Bedouins of Arabia, some to Bedouins of Barbary, and a few to Arnauts. But he learned that Ibrahim had set off for Medina two days before, leaving a secretary in charge. Sadleir now gave up all hope of accomplishing his mission and demanded an escort to Basra. Ibrahim's secretary replied that the route was too dangerous and that he could not provide the escort without orders. Sadleir stormed and argued, but for once his obstinacy did not carry the day. 'I was obliged to desist,' he wrote wearily, 'and to look forward to the Red Sea in place of the Persian Gulf to obtain a release.' The convoy proceeded, passing the wells of Mawiyah where the valley was still strewn with the bleached skeletons of fallen Wahhabis.

On 6 September, seventy days after starting out from Qatif, Sadleir saw the lights of Ibrahim's encampment at Bir Ali, three miles from Medina. As he entered the valley his horse dropped from exhaustion, and he was obliged to enter the camp on a camel almost as worn out as his horse. He was conducted to the tent of Ibrahim's doctor, Antonio Scotto, an Italian in charge of the Pasha's family, who were with him at Medina. It was late, and the doctor served Sadleir a Turkish meal before sending him off to sleep.

At nine o'clock the next morning the Pasha rode up and alighted at Scotto's tent, having no personal accommodation other than the tents of his harem. His retinue, though not numerous, was richly clothed and armed. Coffee and pipes were brought, as this first meeting was purely social. The Pasha's cup rested in a silver holder set with diamonds; those of the others were 'intended to pass as silver'. He offered Sadleir a pinch of snuff from a diamond snuff box. Ibrahim apologized for the inconvenience of the long march, saying that urgent business had obliged him to quit Rass before the arrival of the convoy. Sadleir politely regretted not having reached the Pasha at Dar'iyah to offer the congratulations of the Governor General of India 'on the very spot where the arms of the Ottoman Empire, under the command and guidance of His Excellency, has obtained a signal victory'. The Egyptian was highly gratified to hear that the news of his victory had reached Calcutta and declared that 'he was very desirous to be known personally to the English in India, with whom his father had always been on the most friendly terms'. In such compliments and prevarications the interview stretched to three hours before Ibrahim retired to his harem.

The following morning the Pasha walked over to Dr Scotto's tent bearing his eldest son in his arms, while his daughter was carried by an officer of his retinue. The Pasha sat in an armchair, with Sadleir and Scotto sitting on each side, the Italian acting as interpreter. Sadleir presented the despatches from the government of India, and Ibrahim appeared to peruse them. Then Sadleir presented the sword of honour. After directing his retinue to withdraw, Ibrahim entered into a long explanation of the destruction of Dar'iyah, claiming that it had originated in orders from Constantinople. The entire policy of his expedition, he said, had been directed by his father under orders of the Porte, and he himself had been entirely ignorant of the ultimate views of the Ottoman court. As for the invitation to join the English fleet in chastising the pirates of the Persian Gulf, he was not at liberty to reply on a subject of such importance without referring the matter to his father. He would forward the letters to Cairo from Jiddah, where Sadleir might await his return from the hajj he was about to undertake.

Sadleir tried to force a decision, but in the end had to agree to await a reply from Cairo. Meanwhile, he himself would communicate with Mr Salt, His Majesty's consul general in Cairo, and request him to use his influence with the Pasha of Egypt. The deliberations ended, breakfast was announced, and the three men took their places at table. Ibrahim dexterously made use of his spoon, fork, and knife to make a hearty meal. The only part of an English breakfast he did not relish was tea, so a bowl of sherbet was brought instead. The Pasha then retired to his harem till the afternoon, when he set off for Medina.

Sadleir prepared to go to Jiddah to await the results of his mission, but news of an attack by bandits on a party of Turks only three miles from Bir Ali forced him to change his plans. Instead he joined a well-guarded convoy for Yanbu' accompanying the Pasha's harem at the start of its return to Egypt. Also in the train was Ibrahim's stud of 300 Arab horses, which the Pasha had seized from the tribes wherever he went, leaving Arabia practically destitute of horses for years to come. The remnants of the Maghrabi Bedouins also rode in the convoy, returning to Barbary and driving before them the fruits of their pillage in the form of camels and horses, women, children, and slaves. The Moors were muttering against the Pasha, who had dismissed them without distributing a single dollar of bakshish among them.

Although the plague had subsided, Yanbu' had not improved in the last three years. Sadleir found it 'a miserable seaport' surrounded by tottering walls, the waste spots within the town 'appropriated for dunghills, burying grounds, and receptacles of dead horses and camels'. The water supply was still precarious from without, and the town wells produced water which emitted 'as abominable a smell as the bilge-water of ships'. Sadleir fell ill with fever and could obtain no medicine or medical assistance. The courier from Cairo brought the unpleasant news that Mr Salt was absent. But as letters from Mehmet Ali to his son arrived in the same packet, Sadleir immediately hired an open boat to take him to Jiddah.

The port of Mecca was crowded with homeward bound hajjis, some of them sleeping in the streets. Sadleir was unable to find accommodation until two days after his arrival; and the Pasha, though aware of his presence, did nothing to help him. In fact Ibrahim had no time to see him, as he was occupied in investigating the accounts of the governor of Jiddah, a procedure that involved the torture of those involved in order to extract confessions of malfeasance. When Sadleir at last obtained an interview, Ibrahim refused to discuss the reply from Cairo. After many days they met again. Ibrahim excused the delay by saying that he had been unable to find a scribe capable of drawing up a letter in Arabic, but added that the intended reply would express regret that the Governor General's letter had not been received earlier, thus permitting him to unite his views with those of the British government. Sadleir, though still ill from the effects of fever, contained his disappointment at the failure of his mission and agreed to convey a present from the Pasha to the Governor General of India, namely an Arab horse and mare complete with saddle furniture.

Relations between the Egyptian pasha and the Indian Army officer, never cordial, now deteriorated into an undignified squabble. The first bone of contention was the wording of Ibrahim's letter to Lord Hastings. In India the proper form of address to so exalted a person was *ashraf al-ashraf*, 'noblest of the noble', but to the Arabs and Turks this was a term applied only to God. Sadleir suggested as an alternative *amjad al-amjad*, 'most glorious of the glorious', but this was also rejected on religious grounds. The impasse was not resolved before the affair of the saddle furniture broke off all relations between the two men.

The gift horses, along with one for Sadleir himself, were placed aboard a ship that was about to leave for Mocha. The trappings, consisting of a headstall, a breastplate, a saddle-cloth all silver-mounted and gilt, and a pair of silver stirrups, were sent round for Sadleir's inspection. He noticed that the saddle-cloth had been used and was in a tattered condition. Without hesitation he deferred acceptance of the gift and requested a meeting with the Pasha. This being refused, he sent a message to the Pasha stating that 'articles which had been used could not be considered a suitable present to a nobleman filling as high an official situation under the British government as the Marquis of Hastings now fills'.

Sadleir's pent-up anger and frustration, perhaps aggravated by his illness, show clearly in the justification he later wrote to his superiors.

It did not appear to me that in offering an opinion on a subject on which I had been previously consulted there could be any risk of offending against the rules of Turkish politeness, and of which I do not propose to plead total ignorance. . . . It appeared evident to me from His Excellency's deportment that he aimed at lessening the dignity of the British authorities in the eyes of his court and of the people of Jiddah, and that he wished to arrogate to himself a superiority, not an equality, to which latter title a Pacha could have no just claim. . . . So long as their contempt was personally confined to myself, I felt bound to appear insensible to it, but it was impossible for me to feign ignorance of a custom which is so well known to the meanest Turks. . . . Garments or vestments that have been worn are offered only to dependents and servants, and His Excellency would not presume to offer to His Minister or to his Silikdar any article which bore such traces.

But offence was taken, and Ibrahim coldly replied:

That as I had offered an objection on the subject of the trappings, His Excellency had ordered the horses to be disembarked, that the reply was annulled, and the letters ordered to be destroyed; and that His Excellency directed me to depart on the morrow in a boat which had been prepared to take me to Mocha; that His Excellency on arriving in Cairo would address a letter to the Governor General, returning the sword which he had presented.

Not to be outdone by a Turkish pasha in pride and obstinacy, Sadleir responded in kind: 'That there remained only one reply to offer, that under any other circumstances I should have accepted the accommodation of the buggalo [boat]; that I should now procure a vessel at my own expense to convey me to the destination I might now prefer, and at such time as would best suit my convenience.' He also sat down and wrote another letter to Mr Salt in Cairo setting forth in fourteen numbered paragraphs the insults and injuries he had received at the hands of Ibrahim culminating in the affair of the saddle-cloth. He requested His Majesty's consul general to inform Mehmet Ali of his son's infamous deportment.

Considering Ibrahim's absolute power in the Hijaz and his reputation for ruthlessness, Sadleir showed great courage in the affair, the Pasha himself remarkable restraint. But that is about all the credit that emerges on either side. The brave ride across Arabia came to naught because of the clash of two stiff-necked individuals. It was already clear that the English could expect no help from the Egyptians in putting down the pirates of the Persian Gulf, an area in which Cairo had no interest. But relations between the ruler of Egypt and the British in India were of wider importance. The feud between Ibrahim and Sadleir was only a pin prick, but it did not dispose the British government more favourably towards the government of Mehmet Ali.

A few days later Ibrahim, without seeing Sadleir again, departed by ship for Qusair and Cairo. All the guns in Jiddah, afloat and ashore, boomed out in farewell salute, reminding Sadleir wryly that 'the Turks of Egypt are not unmindful of the importance attached to public compliments'. He was gratified, however, to note the joy shown by the inhabitants of Jiddah on the departure of the high-handed Pasha, revealed on their countenances and expressed openly in all ranks of society. The new governor of the town and other dignitaries called on Sadleir to explain that their previous neglect of so distinguished a visitor was entirely due to Ibrahim's attitude, and to express their entire devotion to Britain's interests and British trade.

Sadleir stayed on in Jiddah for another nine weeks, awaiting a reply from Mr Salt and the arrival of an English ship. The reply never came, but on 21 January 1820 the *Prince of Wales* entered port on its way from Qusair to Mocha. Sadleir went aboard with relief and, after another long delay at Mocha, arrived back in Bombay on 8 May, a year and a month after his departure. The failure of his mission to Arabia was evidently not held against him, for he continued to serve in various capacities both political and military in India and fought in the Burma campaign. Later his regiment, the 47th Foot, was posted back to Edinburgh, Ireland, and Gibraltar, and Sadleir probably went with it. In 1837 he retired, selling his majority for £1,400, a substantial sum in those days, and becoming sheriff of Cork. At the age of sixty he married for the first time, and a few years later emigrated to New Zealand, where he died in December 1859.

Ibrahim Pasha arrived back in Cairo in December 1819, and the city was given over for seven days to celebrating the conqueror of the Wahhabis. His success did not diminish his deference to his father, or stepfather, and he continued as Mehmet Ali's right-hand man in the modernization of Egypt and expansion of Egyptian power. The two Pashas, whether related in blood or not, were of like mind and methods. Sadleir, not noted for his poetry or humour, in the last entry in his diary of the journey across Arabia, described the character of Mehmet Ali in terms that could as well be applied to Ibrahim. Recording the fact that the Shah of Persia had sent letters to the Pasha of Egypt requesting his permission for the Persian Shi-ites to visit Mecca and Medina and to offer prayers in the Shah's name at the Prophet's tomb, Sadleir proferred the following advice:

As I entertain sentiments of the highest respect for the king of kings, I would recommend to him to affect his salvation through the medium of Ali, at whose shrine his diamonds, emeralds, rubies and feroosahs [topazes] will be eagerly accepted, and through whose intercession he has equally as good a chance of inducing the divine providence to defer the visit of Asrail [the angel of death], of whose approach it would be treason to offer the most distant hint to His Majesty. I fear if this pious king should ever fall into the hands of Mahomed Ali, he would discover too late, that the Pacha had been one of that angel's most active and expert viceregents.

PART III
AFTERMATH

And proclaim the Pilgrimage
Among men; they will come
To thee on foot and mounted
On every kind of camel,
Lean on account of journeys
Through deep and distant
Mountain highways . . .

The Quran
(translated by Abdullah Yusuf Ali)

CHAPTER 8
Jets of Flame Against the Night

Mehmet Ali was nearly fifty when the Wahhabi war ended, and his health had suffered from his unaccustomed exertions in a debilitating climate. According to Burckhardt, the victory over the Wahhabis also affected his character. The affability that had distinguished him from other Turkish pashas changed to haughtiness. In place of the simple soldierly establishment he had formerly maintained, he began to indulge in pomp and show. He was now the strongest political leader in the Ottoman empire, and his possession of Egypt was at last unchallenged. Although the English continued to distrust him, the French offered him aid and encouragement. With the help of French advisers, he turned the ramshackle Egyptian army into a semblance of a modern war machine and ran the economy of Egypt as a private concern dedicated to the production of a single commercial crop, cotton.

In the Hijaz he exercised his power through an army of occupation and the appointment of a relative by marriage as governor in Jiddah. When the Grand Sharif died it was the Pasha of Egypt who named his successor. Even in Najd, where the House of Sa'ud gradually reasserted leadership, he tried to impose his own candidate, a Saudi prince raised in Cairo, but Egyptian arms could not force the people to accept an Egyptian puppet for long. As the Wahhabis revived, they occasionally sent a raiding party into the Hijaz, but this was an old Bedouin tradition inspired more by necessity than by religion. The Unitarians no longer posed a threat to the Holy Cities, and the pilgrim caravans, as long as they paid passage money and bought the protection of powerful tribes, crossed the desert with impunity.

The Egyptian occupation of the Hijaz lasted for nearly a quarter of a century and ended only with the collapse of Mehmet Ali's fortunes elsewhere. After helping the Porte to reimpose Ottoman control over the Greeks in 1826, Mehmet Ali, convinced that Constantinople was too weak to oppose him, sent Ibrahim into Syria in 1831 to enforce his long-withheld claim to that pashalik. Ibrahim defeated a Turkish force at Homs and occupied Damascus. Now in open revolt against the Sultan, he crossed the Taurus into Anatolia where he routed another Turkish army and captured the Grand Vizir himself. Ibrahim was within 150 miles of Constantinople when his father ordered him back to Syria. Mehmet Ali had counted on French support in his bid for the Sultanate, but in the last resort France was not prepared to sacrifice her own interests to those of her Egyptian protégé. Fearing a threat to capture the Sultanate itself, the Porte attempted to satisfy Mehmet Ali by confirming him as Pasha of Syria as well as of Egypt. For eight years Ibrahim governed in his father's name, bringing order to a turbulent region of rival chieftains and developing the agriculture and industry of the region, especially the production and manufacture of silk.

While Ibrahim was occupied in conquering Syria, the Turkish cavalry in Jiddah revolted for the classic reason of arrears in pay. The leader of the rebellion was a Georgian Mamluk nicknamed Turçe Bilmez, meaning 'he does not know Turkish'. Posing as a loyal servant of the Sultan, Turçe Bilmez proclaimed himself governor of the Hijaz and marched on Mecca. The Porte recognized the rebellious Georgian and urged him to strike northwards to attack Ibrahim in Syria. But Mehmet Ali sent reinforcements to the Hijaz and routed the rebels. Turçe Bilmez turned south, plundering Qunfudah and the Asir on his way to Mocha. There the Arabs put up a fierce resistance to the rampaging Turks, killing many of them. The remnants were carried off by English ships to Bombay, whence they made their way back to Constantinople.

The English remained the implacable enemy of Mehmet Ali and his ambitions. Lord Palmerston considered Mehmet Ali's control of the overland route a threat to India and the production of Egyptian cotton a threat to English markets. France failed to support her protégé against the English as she had against the Sultanate, and by military threats and pressure on the Porte, Palmerston forced Mehmet Ali to abandon his nascent empire in Syria and the Red Sea and to withdraw within the confines of Egypt. Perhaps the Pasha was losing his grip. In 1848, at the age of eighty, he suffered a mental breakdown and Ibrahim became regent. But the tough old Macedonian recovered until a second collapse a year later induced the Porte to confirm Ibrahim's succession. The new reign did not last long, for the two Pashas died within ten months of each other in 1848 and 1849. The government passed to Hilmi Pasha, Tusun's morose and reclusive son, and the English tutelage of Egypt, so feared by Mehmet Ali, loomed nearer.

The Porte replaced the Egyptian presence in the Hijaz with its own vizir and a Turkish army to maintain a semblance of order. But Constantinople was further away than Cairo and hardly able to stem the endemic chaos. The government of the Hijaz was deep in debt and the pay of the Turkish garrison more than a year in arrears. In 1855 when a *firman* from Constantinople banning the slave trade was read out in Jiddah the people rose in indignation, killing the French and English consuls. Mecca for a time proclaimed its independence and the Hijaz seethed with unrest. Only an epidemic of cholera in 1856 abated the rebellion. Asiatic cholera was brought to the Holy Cities by pilgrims from the Ganges almost every year and transmitted from there to Europe and even to America.

The heroic age of European exploration was over, but travellers from the West continued to turn up in the Holy Cities throughout the nineteenth century. Among them was a professor of Arabic at the University of Helsingfors, George Augustus Wallin, who explored northern Arabia in 1845 and again in 1848, and who visited Medina and Mecca, although he felt they had already been adequately described. Two Frenchmen from Algeria, one a diplomat, Léon Roches, the other a photographer, Gervais-Courtellemont, made the hajj disguised as Muslims in 1841 and 1894 respectively. In the 1860s Baron Heinrich von Maltzan borrowed the passport and persona of an Algerian hashishi and briefly visited Mecca. Two Englishmen, both coming from India and posing as converts to Islam, also made the pilgrimage: Dr Herman Bicknell in 1862 and John F. Keane in 1877. Among his other adventures, Keane claimed to have met an Englishwoman living in Mecca, a former Miss McIntosh of Devon, who had been carried off by a rebel at the siege of Lucknow and taken by him into exile. Most of these men had exciting adventures which attracted attention in their own day and make entertaining reading today, but few of them added greatly to the knowledge acquired by their predecessors.

One latter-day traveller, however, stood out by force of his outsize personality and his extraordinary empathy with alien cultures. The swashbuckling Captain Richard Burton of the Indian army made the pilgrimage in 1853, during the heyday of Ottomanism in the Holy Land. He relished its mixture of liveliness and decay, its moral laxity and social rigidity, its gratification of the senses within a framework of religion and custom. In fact, he seemed more at home in the atmosphere of the hajj than he did in Victorian England.

Although he had spent ten years in the Indian army, Captain Burton was not on an official mission to Arabia in 1853. He was then, and habitually, in bad odour with his superiors. He had asked for a three-year leave of absence in order to cross the Empty Quarter – that white space on the map which he considered a reproach to English exploration – but had been refused, he said, for his 'impolitic habit of telling political truths . . . upon the subject of Anglo-Indian misrule'. (His criticisms were justified a few years later by the Indian Mutiny.) Instead he had been allowed a furlough of one year to improve his Arabic, and had decided the best way to accomplish this task was to make the pilgrimage to Mecca disguised as a Muslim from the subcontinent.

Burton was already a master of disguise and dissimulation, aided by his unusual appearance and upbringing. Though born in Torquay in 1821 of English parents, he had been taken at an early age to live in France and Italy. A continental boyhood gave him facility in languages, but it also made him seem un-English, a disparaging term in nineteenth-century England. There was said to be gypsy blood in his veins, and he did not look Anglo-Saxon or even Celtic. His portraits show him as dark and saturnine with high cheek-bones and an intensity in his eyes that needed only a deep sunburn or a stain of walnut juice to allow him to pass as non-European. He reminded Wilfrid Blunt of 'a black leopard, caged and unforgiving'. Arthur William Symons took an even more romantic view: 'Burton's face has no actual beauty in it, but it reveals a tremendous animalism, an air of repressed ferocity, a devilish fascination. There is almost a tortured magnificence in this huge head, tragic and painful, with its mouth that aches with desires; with those dilated nostrils that drink I know not what strange perfumes.'

Sent down from Trinity College, Oxford, because of an under-graduate escapade, Burton joined the Indian Army at the age of twenty-one. He was an atypical soldier and unpopular with his fellow-officers, who called him Ruffian Dick, the White Nigger. For one thing, he studied languages eight to ten hours a day, mastering five Indian languages as well as Arabic and Persian in seven years, and wrote or gathered material for four books, not to mention numerous reports for the Indian government and the Asiatic Society. Some of this material he obtained by passing himself off as a native in the bazaars and coffee-houses of Sind. But he went too far: one of his reports concerned Indian boy-brothels, an indiscretion that was to dog him all his life, for it was a subject that Victorian England thought contaminated anyone who touched it.

But Burton was at his happiest and most effective as an outcast, wandering beyond the pale of civilization in search of the unknown. A year after his pilgrimage to Mecca he got leave to explore Somaliland and to visit the then forbidden city of Harar. During an attack by a band of natives he received a lance through the jaw and one of his companions was killed. Invalided home, he persuaded the authorities to send him to the Crimea. Later he returned to Africa with John Speke, and together they discovered Lake Tanganyika, although illness kept Burton in camp while Speke alone reached Lake Victoria. The ensuing quarrel as to which of the two erstwhile friends had discovered the true source of the Nile became a public scandal and ended in the apparent suicide of Speke. In 1859 Burton explored West Africa and a year later he crossed the Atlantic to pay an admiring visit to the polygamous Mormon community in Utah.

In the summer of 1856 he had become engaged to Miss Isabel Arundell, an English Catholic, who had marked him for her own some eight years earlier. The engagement was spent by him thousands of miles away in desert and jungle, by her reading of his exploits in the popular press. In 1861 they married, despite family objections, and thanks to Isabel's exertions Burton was appointed British consul in various outlandish posts: Fernando Po in Spanish Guinea, Santos in Brazil, Damascus and Trieste. Burton and his wife were forced to leave Damascus in haste, accused of fomenting religious unrest. While at Trieste Burton obtained leave to return to Arabia to search for gold in Midian for the Khedive of Egypt.

Burton did not attain the recognition he and Isabel hoped for, partly because of the notoriety he acquired. He made little secret of his willingness to try every experience – opium, aphrodisiacs, yoga. He was far in advance of his time in the keen interest he took in the science of anthropology; but his scientific attitude did not exclude phrenology, the theory of humours, a concern with measuring the penises of different races, or belief in the inferiority of Negroes. Frank Harris, no mean connoisseur of strange scents himself, wrote of Burton: 'His ethnological appetite for curious customs and crimes, for everything singular and savage in humanity was insatiable. A Western lynching held him spellbound; a *crime passionel* in Paris intoxicated him, started him talking, transfiguring him into a magnificent story-teller, with intermingled appeal to pathos and rollicking fun, camp-fire effects, jets of flame against the night.' Besides the spate of travel books that flowed from his pen, he found time to translate *A Thousand and One Nights* and the medieval Arab sex treatise *The Perfumed Garden*. The egregious Isabel cleaned up the former for a family edition and burned the manuscript of the latter after Burton's death in 1890. The aura of scandal thus pursued him beyond the grave. Lady Burton (he had been knighted in 1887) buried him in the Roman Catholic cemetery in Mortlake near London, though there was no evidence that he was a Catholic (as she was) or even a Christian. Over his grave she erected a tomb for the two of them in the shape of an Arab tent carved in stone, complete with camel-bells.

But all this was in the womb of the future when Captain Burton, aged thirty-two and single, set off for the Hijaz dressed as a Pathan and calling himself Hakim (that is, Doctor) Abdallah. He gave out that he had been born in India of Afghani parents and educated in Rangoon; sent by his parents to wander in early youth, he had lived in England, France, and other European countries, and therefore spoke many languages but none with the accents of a native. To this disguise he had added another for purposes of travel to the Holy Land, that of a dervish. In the Muslim world, he reasoned, it was a character

assumed by all ranks, ages, and creeds; by the nobleman who has been disgraced at court, and by the peasant who is too idle to till the ground; by Dives who is weary of life, and by Lazarus, who begs his bread from door to door. Further, the Darwaysh is allowed to ignore ceremony and politeness, as one who ceases to appear upon the stage of life; he may pray or not, marry or remain single . . . and no one asks him – the chartered vagabond – why he comes here? or wherefore he goes there?

As a dervish Burton knew that the appearance of disguise was part of the disguise. It was a character that suited him well.

Let us join him on the beach at Suez among pilgrims waiting to board *The Golden Wire* bound for Yanbu'. Burton is in his element amidst the hurly-burly of the crowd, sardonically aloof but assuming a hearty bonhomie, relishing the outrageous behaviour of his fellow pilgrims, and button-holing his readers with recourse to the present tense. It is a fiery hot July day. People are rushing about, friends weeping farewell, shopkeepers claiming debts, boatmen demanding fees, women shrieking as they are carried to the boats in brawny arms, children howling, men scolding and swearing. Once in the boats everyone finds something missing – a pipe, a box, a servant, a watermelon, a child. The sailors are enraged at being made late for a second trip.

First the boats are poled to a pier where the bey makes a final examination of passports. Passengers found without the necessary documents are bastinadoed and sent back to Cairo. Then sails are hoisted and the boats run down to where *The Golden Wire* stands waiting. On the way a boat crammed with Maghrabis runs alongside Burton's, and a score of these ruffians pour into the other vessel. They outnumber Burton's party and are armed, so their insolence must be borne at present.

For Burton is not alone: with his usual gregariousness he has picked up a motley crew of travelling companions. First there is the boy Muhammad, a beardless youth returning to Mecca from Cairo and Constantinople, where he has acquired a taste for questionable women and strong waters. He is selfish, affectionate, easily offended, half brave, coveting other men's goods but generous with his own. Then there is Omar Effendi, a Circassian, grandson of a mufti and son of a shaikh, with a small plump body, yellowish complexion, grey eyes, soft features, beardless, looking fifteen and admitting to twenty-eight. He dresses respectably, prays regularly, and hates the fair sex. Pressed to marry by his parents, he has fled to Cairo and entered al-Azhar university as a pauper-student. His family has sent a confidential man to fetch him home, by force if necessary.

This man is a Negro, born a slave in Omar's family and nicknamed Sa'd the Demon. After manumission he joined the Sharif's army, then turned mercenary and wandered as far as Russia and Gibraltar. A pure African, he is merry one moment, sulky the next, affectionate and abusive, brave and boastful, crafty, quarrelsome, and unscrupulous. He dresses like a beggar whilst his boxes are full of handsome apparel for himself and his three wives at Medina.

Shaikh Hamid as-Suman, a town Arab, squats on his box full of presents for 'the daughter of my paternal uncle' (a circumlocution for the too-intimate 'my wife'). His face is a dirty brown, his goatee untrimmed, his feet bare, and his only garment an unclean blouse tucked into a leathern belt. He will not pray as he is unwilling to take clean clothing from his box. But from his bosom he draws a little dog-eared manuscript full of serious romances and silly prayers, which he devoutly kisses with all the veneration of the vulgar for a book. He is returning from Constantinople, where he has squandered the money given him by noble ladies whom he has guided round the Prophet's tomb.

Stretched out on his carpet smoking a Persian pipe all day is Salih Shakkir, a Turk on his father's side, an Arab on his mother's. A lanky youth of sixteen, he has the ideas of a man of forty-six and is as coldly supercilious as a Turk, as energetically avaricious as an Arab. His yellow complexion makes people consider him a superior person. Friendly enough on the road (he even borrowed a little money from Burton), at Medina he will cut his wayfellows mercilessly.

Completing this band is Burton's Indian boy, Nur, a brave at Cairo, an arrant coward in Arabia. The Bedouins despise him for his effeminacy in making a camel kneel to dismount, and he cannot keep his hands from picking and stealing. But his swarthy skin and chubby features convince the Arabs that he is an Abyssinian slave, which furthers his master's disguise.

As was customary, *The Golden Wire* had been overbooked. Piles of boxes filled it from stem to stern, and a torrent of hajjis poured over the sides like ants into a sugar bowl. The poop, where Burton and his friends had reserved places, was covered with baggage and passengers. Presently, however, there appeared Sa'd the Demon, who had signed as a seaman to obtain free passage; he speedily cleared the poop by throwing the intruders and their baggage into the hold. Those who remained settled down as comfortably as they could: three Syrians, a Turk and his family, the captain and part of his crew, and Burton's party, a total of eighteen persons in a space ten feet by eight. The cabin, a miserable box three feet high, was crammed like the hold of a slave-ship with fifteen women and children. Eighty or so passengers were crushed into the hold, sitting on their luggage or squatting on the bulwarks.

Among them were the Maghrabis, fine-looking animals from the deserts round Tunis and Tripoli, tall, broad-shouldered, and large limbed, with frowning eyes and voices in perpetual uproar. An argument soon developed between them and a few Turks, ragged old men from Anatolia and Caramania, who contemptuously elbowed and scolded their wild neighbours. The latter retorted willingly and in a trice nothing was to be seen but a confused mass, pushing and pulling, scratching and biting, butting and trampling, with cries of rage and pain. A Syrian on the poop incautiously leapt down to aid his countrymen and sank immediately below the surface of the living mass; when fished out his forehead was cut open, half his beard was gone, and a fine sharp set of Maghrabi teeth had left their mark on his calf. The Maghrabis showed no love of fair play, five or six of them setting upon a single man. The weaker drew their daggers. In a few minutes five men were wounded, and the victors began to fear the consequences.

A deputation went to wait on the owner of the vessel. After three hours he appeared in a rowboat, preserving a respectful distance, and announced that anyone who pleased might quit the ship and take back his fare. No one, of course, would leave, and the owner rowed back to shore. This was the signal for a second fray, and this time those in the poop were summoned to share their space. Sa'd the Demon rose with an oath and gave each of his party a stave, six feet long and thick as a man's wrist, shouting 'Dogs and sons of dogs, now you shall see what the sons of the Arabs are !' The Maghrabis surged forward like angry hornets with cries of '*Allahu Akbar* – God is great!' But the poop was four feet above them, and their short daggers could do nothing against the terrible quarter-staves of the defenders.

At first Burton laid on at half strength fearing to kill someone, but he soon saw that the heads of the Maghrabis could bear the full brunt. A large earthenware jar of drinking water weighing about a hundred pounds stood at the edge of the poop. Burton crept up to it and with his shoulder rolled it down on the assailants. A shriller shriek rose from the din, as heads, limbs, and bodies were bruised, scratched, and wetted. Defeated, the Maghrabis slunk off to the end of the vessel. Later they sent a delegation to the poop to solicit peace. The victors' hands and shoulders were penitently kissed, and the fellows retired to the hold to bind their wounds in dirty rags.

At three o'clock in the afternoon on 6 July 1853 *The Golden Wire* shook out her sail, and as it bellied in the wind the passengers recited the *Fatihah*, or opening verse of the Quran, raising their hands and drawing them down to their faces filled with the blessing of God. Hakim Abdallah joined them fervently in their prayers.

Settling in, Burton paid a crewman a dollar for his cot, four feet long and broken, which he lashed over the side where it was out of the way but continually at the mercy of the waves. To his chagrin he found that his box, containing his provisions and his opium, was at the bottom of the hold. His companions invited him to join their mess, but it was not till they reached al-Wijh that he was able to buy an ounce of opium 'at a Chinese price'. There was nothing to do all day except to doze and watch the passing shore. The heat – it was July on the Red Sea: truly the pilgrimage is a penance – was intense. The wind reverberating from the flowing hills was like a blast from a limekiln. All colours melted away; the sky was a dead milk-white and the mirror-like sea so reflected the tint that one could hardly distinguish the line of the horizon. After noon even the wind slept; there was a deep stillness, the only sound being the melancholy flapping of the sail. Men were not so much sleeping as half-senseless; they felt as if one more degree of heat would be death.

Omar Effendi alone had the courage to pray, but after such exertion he looked an altered man. Even the boy Muhammad forgot to chatter, scold, and make himself disagreeable. The Turkish baby appeared to be dying but was too weak to wail. The most pleasant trait in the Arabs' character was the consideration they showed the mother and her children. Whenever one of them drew forth a little delicacy – a few dates or a pomegranate – he shared it with the children, and most of them took turns to nurse the baby. The sole exception was the half-Turk Salih Shakkar, who gorged himself on dates till he was threatened with dysentery.

In the evenings they revived a little and at night slept on the beach. One of their night landings was shared by a shipload of Persians, whom the orthodox Arabs baited as heretics. When the Persian muezzin led them in prayer, the Arabs howled in derision and, snatching up their weapons, offered them the opportunity of martyrdom. The Maghrabis crowded round fiercely to do a little *jihad*.

But among the Persians was an inquisitive Pathan who severely tried Burton's alias. The man could speak five or six languages and had travelled far and wide. To his questions Burton replied that he no longer had a name or nation, being a dervish. When the man insisted he must have been born somewhere, Burton asked him to guess. To his relief, the man claimed him for a fellow Pathan and complained that he had been abused as a Sunni Muslim by his fellow travellers. Burton immediately offered to arm himself and his party with cudgels to avenge his compatriot, and this thoroughly Afghani style of doing business completely convinced the man.

Wading ashore at one of the stops, Burton felt an acute pain running into his toe and extracted a thorn, apparently a prickle from a poisonous sea-urchin. From then on he suffered the physical disability that seemed to be obligatory for all Arabian travellers. He hobbled through the Holy Land, trying many cures, including a bandage of onion skins, but every remedy failed until his return to Cairo, when the wound healed of itself. When, after twelve days' sailing, *The Golden Wire* reached Yanbu' his foot was so inflamed that he could scarcely place it on the ground. But traveller's duty was to be done, so leaning on his servant's shoulder he set off to see the town. The people lived up to their reputation for pugnacity. They were all armed, the civilian with loaded pistol in his waist-shawl, the irregular Turkish soldier strutting down the street with a small armoury, the grim Bedouins 'wild as their native wastes and in all the dignity of their pride and dirt', armed to the teeth. But Captain Burton admired the people of Yanbu' for 'their independent bearing, proud without insolence . . . manly without blustering'.

At Yanbu' his wayfellows met friends and relations starting out on a *Wanderjahre* of their own. These informed them that the desert between Yanbu' and Medina was infested with bandits. Nothing daunted, the pilgrims proceeded to hire camels, lay in provisions, and polish their arms. On the advice of his camel-broker, Burton discarded his Afghani clothes and assumed yet another layer of disguise, dressing as an Arab to avoid the capitation tax levied on foreigners by the Arabs on the road. Although it was considered unmanly, he bought a *shugduf*; his excuse was his lameness, but the real reason was secrecy: it was much easier to take notes in the privacy of a litter than in a saddle. Before leaving Cairo he had had the case of his pocket Quran fitted out for a watch, compass, pencil, and penknife, and slips of paper could be concealed in the hollow of his hand. The sketches he made were cut into squares which he numbered and hid in the canisters containing his medicines.

On the day of departure from Yanbu' there was a struggle over the loading, the cameleers complaining about the unconscionable weight, the owners of the goods swearing that a child could carry them, while the beasts themselves moaned, reared, bit, and started up suddenly, throwing the half-secured boxes to the ground. In three hours all was ready, but now the travellers had disappeared. Some had forgotten an article of vital importance; others wished to drink a last cup of coffee with friends; still others had heard of the arrival of a ship in the harbour and wished to see if it carried any friends or relations. Then the sun set and prayers had to be said. The brief twilight had almost faded before they mounted. They threaded their way through the dusty streets, past heaps of rubbish higher than the houses, and out through the Medina gate. The moon rose full and clear, dazzling them as they emerged from the shadowy streets; the sweet air of the desert replaced the offensive smells of the town. The Arabs began to sing.

Their little caravan consisted of twelve camels marching Indian file, head tied to tail, with only one outrider, Omar Effendi, whose rank required him to mount a dromedary with showy trappings. Their escort consisted of seven Irregular Turkish cavalry tolerably mounted and armed. The guards were privately derided by the Arabs, who had a sneaking fondness for the Bedouins, however loath they might be to see them among their boxes. They travelled through desolate country, past huge blocks and boulders, clefts choked with sand, dark caves and crevices, where not a bird or a beast was to be seen. By day a sky of polished steel glared down on the brass-coloured circle of earth, scorching their faces and dazzling their eyes.

On the third day they joined forces with a caravan coming from Mecca, and Burton witnessed an affecting reunion between the boy Muhammad and his elder brother. Although now much bigger and stronger, the combined caravans that night were ignominiously hailed by a band of Bedouins who manned a gorge and refused to let them pass.

On hearing that they were sons of the Holy Cities the Bedouins relented on condition that the military escort should not proceed. Upon this, the Turkish troops, now swollen to 200 men, wheeled round and galloped back towards home. Captain Burton of the Indian army saw the remedy for such lawlessness: 'By a proper use of the blood-feud; by vigorously supporting the weaker against the stronger classes; by regularly defeating every Badawi who earns a name for himself; and, above all, by the exercise of unsparing, unflinching justice, the few thousand half-naked bandits, who now make the land a fighting field, would sink into utter insignificance.' In the absence of such a forceful policy, Burton foresaw 'the day when the Wahhabis or the Badawin, rising *en masse*, will rid the land of its feeble conquerors'. He was in no doubt as to who would take the Turks' place: 'The day shall come,' he predicted, 'when the tide of events will force us [the British] to occupy the mother-city of Al-Islam.'

On the seventh day, as they approached Medina, the excitement was great. They climbed a huge flight of steps cut into a ridge of black basalt and filed through a lane between walls of dark lava. When a full view of the city opened to them, they halted and feasted their eyes on the Holy City. The Arabs broke into poetical exclamations: 'O Allah! this is the harim (sanctuary) of Thy Apostle; make it to us a protection from Hell fire, and a refuge from Eternal Punishment. O open the Gates of Thy Mercy, and let us pass through them to the Land of Joy!' As they descended, people came out to meet them, and the travellers dismounted and walked for the better convenience of kissing, embracing, and shaking hands with relations and friends.

Burton was conducted to the house of Shaikh Hamid as-Samun, who had hurried in that morning to receive the embraces of 'the daughter of my paternal uncle' and to prepare for his guest. Shaikh Hamid's appearance had totally changed from the dirty, unkempt state in which he travelled. The razor had passed over his head and face, and he now wore a neat little moustache and beard. The filthy shirt had been exchanged for an outer cloak of pink merinos, a caftan of flowered stuff, a fine silk shirt, and a plaid sash elaborately fringed. On his head he wore a muslin turban wound round a new embroidered cap. His purified feet were encased in two pairs of slippers, the inner of supple leather in place of stockings, the outer of lemon-coloured leather of Stambouli cut. His manners had also changed from the vulgar and boisterous to a staid courtesy, as he took Burton and led him up to the *majlis*, or sitting-room.

The honoured guest was placed in a cool window while visitors poured in to congratulate the travellers on their safe arrival. They sat and smoked and drank coffee, asking all manner of questions about foreign parts, and after half an hour rose abruptly, embraced, and departed. The great topic of conversation was the *jihad* against the Russians, the Crimean War. The gossip of Jiddah was that the Sultan had ordered the Tsar to become a Muslim. The Tsar had sued for peace and offered fealty and tribute, but the Sultan had exclaimed, 'No, by Allah! Al-Islam!' The Ottoman army was expected to dispose of the Russians in a short time; then the Turks would turn against the idolators of Europe, starting with the English. The Bedouins had decided that there would be an Arab contingent and were looking forward to the spoils of Western Europe. This caused quarrels, as all the men wanted to go, and not a ten-year-old would be left behind.

The *majlis* was soon invaded by a plague of children, who rushed in treading on toes, pulling things to pieces, and using language that would have shocked an old man-of-war's man. Adults in the Hijaz amused themselves by grossly abusing children in order to excite their rage and to judge their dispositions. This supplied the infant population with a large stock of ribaldry. One urchin scarcely three years old threatened to slit Burton's throat with his father's sword; another caught up a loaded pistol and clapped it to his neighbour's head; fortunately it was at half cock and the trigger was stiff. Ruffian Dick admired these 'manly, angry boys, who punched one another like Anglo-Saxons in the house, whilst abroad they were always fighting with sticks and stones'.

During the month Burton spent in Shaikh Hamid's house he never once set eyes on the face of a woman, except for two African slave girls, who drew their ragged veils over their sable charms and would not answer the simplest questions. He never even heard the voice of 'the daughter of my paternal uncle', who stayed all day in the upper rooms. But he entered fully into the social life of the men, dining, praying, receiving and paying visits with his host and friends. Some evenings, dressed in common clothes, Burton and his host shouldered a stave and went to a café on what were clearly regarded as slumming expeditions.

Like his predecessor Burckhardt, Burton was disappointed in the Prophet's tomb, finding it 'an old Curiosity Shop' decorated with 'pauper splendour'. The celebrated jewel suspended over the tomb looked to him like the stopper of a glass decanter, but he admitted he thought as little of the Koh-i-noor diamond. He was not even convinced that the tomb was the actual resting place of Muhammad's body, suspecting it to be 'as doubtful as the Holy Sepulchre in Jerusalem'. But Burton's most original contribution to Western knowledge of the Holy Land was his exploration of the sites associated with the Prophet's life in Medina. At one spot Muhammad's she-camel had stopped of her own accord after the flight from Mecca, and there he ordered the first place of public prayer to be built. At another, he received a revelation to turn and face Mecca, rather than Jerusalem, in prayer. At a third, the Mosque of the Date Liquor, several of his companions first learned of the prohibition of intoxicants and promptly emptied their cups on the ground. At the dome of Kuwwat al-Islam (the Strength of Islam) the Prophet planted a dry palm stick which immediately blossomed and bore fruit. In the same place on one occasion, when his followers were unable to perform the pilgrimage, Muhammad produced a simulacrum of the Ka'ba and Mount Arafat. Burton warned his readers 'not to condemn the founder of Al-Islam for these puerile inventions'.

On the outskirts of the town, 10,000 of the Prophet's companions were said to have been buried in the cemetery of al-Bakia, but the Wahhabis had destroyed many of the tombs, and time and later interments had completed the confusion. Burton, however, was able to distinguish a few graves, such as that of Muhammad's daughter Fatimah and those of fourteen of his fifteen wives (the first, Khadijah, lies at Mecca). The Bedouin wet-nurse of the Prophet was honoured at one spot, and Ibrahim, the Prophet's son who died in infancy, was interred beside his mother, the Coptic Christian girl Mariyah. Hassan, the son of 'Ali and Fatimah, was thought to lie under a handsome dome built by an Abbassid caliph, but Burton found it difficult of approach because of the crowd of weeping Persians and importunate beggars.

But Burton was more interested in the present than in the past. With the rest of Medina, he anxiously awaited the arrival of the Damascus caravan bringing pilgrims from Anatolia and Muslim lands to the north. Its arrival was heralded by the appearance one night of three of Shaikh Hamid's brothers, who had entered as guides with the hajj. They leapt off their camels, kissing, embracing, and weeping bitterly for joy of being home. The next morning Burton rose early to gaze from the windows of Shaikh Hamid's house on the square below.

What had been a dusty waste spotted with a few Bedouin tents had been transformed during the night into a town of tents of every size, colour, and shape, from the shawl-lined pavilion of the pasha to the little green rag of the tobacco-seller. Burton described the scene in loving detail: huge white Syrian dromedaries, bells jingling and *shugdufs* swaying on their backs; gorgeous litters carried between two camels or mules with scarlet and brass trappings; Bedouins astride naked-backed *daluls* (riding camels), clinging like apes to their hairy humps; Arnaut, Kurd, and Turkish Irregular cavalry, fiercer looking in their mirth than Roman peasants in their rage; fainting Persians forcing their camels to kneel so they could dismount; sherbet sellers and ambulant tobacconists crying their wares; country people driving flocks of sheep and goats through lines of horses which were snorting and biting, kicking and rearing; townspeople seeking their friends; devout hajjis in their hurry to reach the Prophet's Mosque, jostling, running under the legs of camels, tumbling over tent ropes; cannon roaring from the citadel; water carriers and fruit vendors bargaining; boys bullying heretics; a well-mounted party of fine old Arab shaikhs preceded by their varlets performing the *ardah*, or war-dance, firing their duck-guns upwards or blowing powder into the calves of those before them, brandishing swords, leaping frantically with bright-coloured rags floating in the wind, tossing long spears tufted with ostrich feathers in the air, reckless where they fell; servants seeking their masters and masters seeking their tents; grandees preceded by their crowd-beaters shouting to clear the way; here the shrieks of women and children whose litters were bumping and rasping against one another, there the low moan of some poor wretch, seeking a corner to die in; and over it all a thick dust that blurred the outlines like a London fog while the flaming sun drew sparkles of fire from the burnished weapons and the brass balls of tents and litters.

A Persian nobleman had pitched his tent directly under Shaikh Hamid's window so that the whole of his private life was public to those above. The Persian's pretty wife did not veil when the boy Muhammad gazed at her, thereby showing that she considered him a mere child. To rouse her shame he asked her to marry him, but the fair Persian never ceased fanning herself. For once the boy Muhammad was confounded.

The Prophet's Mosque was now crowded at night and brightly illuminated. The pilgrims went through the visitation ceremonies or sat overcome with emotion. The boys and beggars were inspired with fresh energy; the eunuchs were surlier than ever; the young men-about-town swaggered and chattered more freely than usual. The unhappy Persians were learning lessons about the brotherhood of man. The doorkeepers charged them five piastres where others entered free. Whenever one stood in the way of an Arab or a Turk he was rudely shoved aside. All eyes followed the Persians as they approached the tombs of Abu Bakr and 'Umar, for the Sunnis believed that every Shi-ite was bound to defile them if he could. 'Hail 'Umar, thou hog,' exclaimed a Medinan as he passed a heretic, a demand more outrageous than requiring a black

North Protestant to bless the Pope. Nothing but a furious contraction of the brow and a twitching of the mouth denoted the wrath within the Persian as he obeyed. But before the tomb of Fatimah, tears trickled down the Persians' hairy cheeks and their brawny bosoms heaved with sighs.

There were Arab heretics living at Medina who traced their line back to the *Ansar*, or helpers of Muhammad. They had their own imams, married only among themselves, and performed such low offices as slaughtering, sweeping, and gardening. They were not allowed to enter the Prophet's Mosque in life nor to be buried from it in death. Reports were current about their horrid customs and their sharing of their women with the Persian pilgrims. The greater part of the population was of foreign origin, and Burton counted settlers from the Maghrib, Takruris from eastern Africa, Egyptians, Kurds, Afghanis, Circassians, Javanese, and Indians. The ruling caste were the *Sufat*, the sons of Turkish fathers and Arab mothers, who occupied the most lucrative posts and had the worst manners.

The slave market injected a constant stream of African blood into the veins of Medina. Burton's nostrils flared as he investigated this branch of commerce. A little black boy perfect in all his points cost about 1,000 piastres (about £20). Girls were dearer and eunuchs fetched double. The older the child the less his value, and no one would purchase an adult slave, for one was never sold but for some incurable vice. Abyssinian girls were highly prized because their skins were thought to be cool even in the hottest weather; their price sometimes reached £60. Burton never heard of a white girl being sold in Medina; their prime cost was £200 to £400, and few Hijazis could afford such a luxury.

With all this intermingling of races, the Medinans were remarkably fair, their cheeks often lit with red, their hair a dark chestnut. The Meccans, a dark people, said that the hearts of the Medinans were as black as their skins were white. Burton found the Medinans the most manly of Easterners, but they displayed a curious mixture of generosity and meanness. Their personal conceit was strong – 'I am such an one, the son of such an one' was a common boast. Their mouths were as full of religious expressions as of indecency; they abused their own children in terms injurious to themselves – 'Thou dog and son of a dog . . . thou child of an unworthy mother.'

As a supposed physician, Burton investigated disease and treatment wherever he went. Although it was the boast of Medina that the plague had never crossed her frontier, she was frequently visited by the 'Great

Mercy', or Asiatic cholera, which carried off whole households. It was treated with mint, lime-juice, and copious draughts of coffee. Smallpox was endemic and swept through Arabia with devastating violence. Inoculation had recently been introduced from Yemen, where a century earlier Niebuhr had seen Bedouin mothers prick their children's arms with a thorn. Jaundice was treated by exorcism, and cautery was a popular treatment for dysentery. Almost everyone had haemorrhoids. When the vena worm attacked the legs, it was extracted by being gradually wound round a splinter of wood; if the worm broke and re-entered the flesh the patient was thought to be doomed. When a man was bitten by a mad dog, his friends poured boiling water mixed with ashes over him, 'a certain cure, I can easily believe', Burton remarked. In cases of severe wounds or chronic disease the patient was sent to the Black Tents to live among the Bedouins, drinking camel's milk and doing nothing. Burton thought that this compared favourably with the fashionable cures of Europe.

The Damascus caravan was due to set out for Mecca on 1 September. As a famous robber was on the warpath, all other pilgrims joined it, as did all the available soldiers. To Burton's joy it was decided to take the eastern road named after Harun ar-Rashid's queen Zubaidah, rather than the usual route, the Sultan's road, which Burckhardt had taken. The boy Muhammad was sent to buy another *shugduf*, as the previous one had not survived the trip from Yanbu', while Nur, the Indian boy, was set, sleeves tucked up, to make large saddlebags for provisions and to mend the water-skins, which had been eaten by rats. Burton bought provisions for the way: wheat flour, rice, turmeric, onions, dates, unleavened bread, cheese, limes, tobacco, sugar, and coffee. Shaikh Hamid busied himself with hiring the camels. He found a Bedu named Mas'ud of the Harb tribe, a short, thin, well-built old man with a white beard, cool clear eyes, and limbs covered with scars. After long mannerly discussions agreement was reached for two camels and the services of Mas'ud and his son as guides. The Bedu delighted Burton by calling him Father of Moustaches, the nickname of the great Sa'ud. Shaikh Hamid warned Burton not to allow twenty-four hours to elapse without dipping hands into the same pot as his camel-men so that the party might always be *malih*, on terms of salt.

The town was in utter confusion as the pilgrims prepared to depart. Random shots from the hills reminded them of the dangers they faced. Burton was ready with his baggage an hour before sunset; it was reported that the caravan would take off at midnight; at two o'clock in the morning he went to bed. At breakfast next day Mas'ud appeared accompanied by his son, a bold lad of fourteen who fought sturdily over the weight of every package as it was thrown onto the camels' backs, and a nephew, a poor pock-marked lad too lazy even to quarrel and an extra mouth to feed. Shaikh Hamid, Omar Effendi, and Burton's other Medinan acquaintances accompanied him to the Egyptian gate and had to be dissuaded from going all the way to Mecca with him. After an hour's march the caravan stopped and everyone turned to gaze for the last time on the venerable minarets and the green dome of the Prophet's tomb.

The caravan consisted of about 7,000 souls divided into seven classes. The lowest hobbled on foot with heavy staves. Then came the riders of camels, asses, and mules. Respectable men, especially the Arabs, were mounted on dromedaries, and the soldiers on horses. Women, children, and the poorer invalids sat upon rugs spread over the two large boxes that made up a camel's load. The richer occupied *shugdufs,* and the truly noble lay in litters carried between pairs of camels or mules. A saddled horse was led for every grandee, ready whenever he wanted to leave his litter. The guard of about 1,000 Irregular horsemen, half bandit, half soldier, each dressed and armed after his own fashion, was exceedingly dirty, picturesque, brave, and of no use whatsoever.

Even on the first march the animals began to sink in numbers. Soon the fresh carcasses of asses, ponies, mules, and camels dotted the wayside. This was a constant feature of Arabian travel: the beasts were overloaded, underfed and under-watered, and driven beyond endurance. Considerations of humanity aside, it seemed an uneconomical way of doing business. Those that died naturally were left to the carrion birds, but those whose throats were cut before death were immediately surrounded by a crowd of Takruris. These half-starved wretches from East Africa carved steaks from the warm corpses, flung them over their shoulders, and marched on. Most of the Takruris were destitute and carried wooden bowls which they filled with water by begging. They dressed in a long dirty shirt or sometimes a mere rag covering the loins, an old skull cap, and a strip of leather tied to each foot; their only weapon was a small knife tied above the elbow in a sheath. Some were perfect savages, others fine looking men, broad-shouldered, thin-flanked, and long-limbed. Many were lamed by fatigue and thorns. Looking at them Burton fancied he saw death depicted in their forms and features. They seemed quite happy.

At every water-stop the two boys Muhammad and Nur set off for the well, leaving Burton to write up his journal. The water had to be paid for, as the wells were guarded by soldiers whose only income was what they got from the travellers. It also had to be fought for at times; the boy Muhammad, having snapped his pistol at a Persian's head, came away with two skins and was in his glory. That night Muhammad drank copiously of clarified butter and ate dates mashed with flour, and was violently sick. At certain hours of the day ambulant vendors offered sherbets, hot coffee, and water-pipes to those who could afford them. At the stops the pilgrims cooked their own meals of rice plain or mixed with pulse, eaten with chutney or lime pickle, and varied occasionally with a little tough mutton or goat.

The way was hard. They toiled over ridges of broken blocks of basalt; the camels stepped gingerly from block to block, assuring themselves of their forefeet before trusting all their weight to advance. Not a camel fell, but the animals moaned piteously, for the sudden turns puzzled them, the ascents were painful, and the rocks sharp. The acacia barrens were a hazard dreaded by all. Here the *shugdufs* were bodily pulled off the camels' backs and broken on the hard ground. The animals dropped to their knees, the whole line was deranged, and everyone lost his temper and attacked his neighbour. Sometimes pillars of sand scudded over the plains, huge yellow shafts with lofty heads bent back like clouds, and more than one camel was thrown by them. The Arabs believed them to be *jinns*, or spirits, and, stretching a finger, exclaimed, 'Iron! O thou ill-omened one!'

When the hot *samun* blew, the travellers' tempers frayed. A Turk, who could not speak a word of Arabic, violently disputed with an Arab, who could not speak Turkish. The pilgrim insisted on adding a few sticks of firewood to his camel's load, and the camel-man persisted in throwing off the extra burden. They screamed with rage, shoved each other, and at last the Turk dealt the Arab a heavy blow. During the night the pilgrim's stomach was ripped open with a dagger. When Burton asked what had become of him, he was assured that he had been comfortably wrapped in a shroud and laid in a half-dug grave. This was also the practice when illness or accident prevented the poor and solitary from continuing. Burton contemplated such a fate with horror: 'The torturing thirst of a wound, the burning sun heating the brain to madness, and – worst of all, for they do not wait till death – the attacks of the jackal, the vulture, and the raven of the wild.' Truly he was a master of the campfire effect, the jet of flame against the night.

On the fourth day they fell in with the Baghdad caravan, about 2,000 strong, Persians, Kurds, people from northeastern Arabia, Wahhabis and others, escorted by the fierce mountaineers of Jabal Shammar. At the next stop the patter of muskets sent the pilgrims scattering. Burton had never seen such a pugnacious lot; a look sufficed for a quarrel. Once a Wahhabi stood before him and pointed his finger in hatred at the *chibuk* the other was smoking. To chastise his insolence, Burton offered him the pipe. The Wahhabi drew his dagger, but Burton and his party showed their pistols, and the dagger was sheathed.

On the ninth day they donned the *ihram*, shaved their heads, washed and scented themselves, and began chanting the *Labbaik*. The Turkish women appeared in white robes and exchanged their coquettish veils for hideous masks of split, dried, and plaited palm leaves with two holes for light. Burton could not help laughing and, to judge by the shaking of their shoulders, the women were laughing too. Soon after, they fell in with a band of Wahhabis guided by a kettle-drum and following a green flag with the Muslim creed written upon it. They were wild looking, dark and fierce, their hair twisted in plaits, each armed with a spear, a matchlock, and a dagger. They sat on wooden saddles without cushions or stirrups. The women disdained veils and either rode their own camels or sat pillion fashion, clinging to their men.

At sunset the caravan stumbled along a dry river bed between a stony buttress on one hand and a precipice on the other. The loud *Labbaiks* gradually ceased, and the chatter of the women and children sank into silence. While speculating on the cause, Burton saw a small curl of smoke like a lady's ringlet on the top of the buttress and simultaneously heard the echoing crack of a matchlock. A high-stepping dromedary in front of him rolled over on the sand, throwing his rider in a somersault of six yards. Terrible panic broke out. Women screamed, children cried, men vociferated, each trying to urge his animal out of this place of death. The pilgrims only succeeded in jamming themselves into a solid, immoveable mass. At every shot a shudder ran through the whole body. The Irregular horsemen galloped to and fro over the stones, shouting to one another and ordering everyone about. The leader of the Baghdad caravan had his carpet spread at the foot of the precipice and debated over a pipe with his officers what ought to be done. 'No good genius whispered "Crown the heights",' mused Captain Burton.

But help came from another source. A troop of Wahhabis galloped up, their hair tossing and their firing matches casting a lurid glow on their faces. Taking up a position, one group fired on the robbers while another two or three hundred dismounted and swarmed up the hill. Presently the firing was heard from the rear – the robbers had taken flight. So did the pilgrims. Camels lurched up the river bed; boxes and baggage strewed the shingle. Some people had been killed, but the reports were contra-dictory and doubtless exaggerated. The robbers were said to be of the 'Ataibah tribe; although their object was plunder, their principal aim was to boast, 'We, the 'Ataibah, on such and such a night, stopped the Sultan's *mahmal* one whole hour in the pass.'

At the start of the skirmish Burton had primed his pistol, but seeing there was nothing to be done and wishing to make an impression, he called aloud for his supper. Nur could not move for fear; the boy Muhammad cried only 'Oh, sir!' and the people around exclaimed in disgust, 'By Allah, he eats!' A Meccan shaikh, whom Burton had invited to share his *shugduf* and his opium, was amused and asked if these were Afghani manners. Yes, his Pathan friend replied, 'In my country we always dine before an attack of robbers, because that gentry is in the habit of sending men to bed supperless.' The shaikh laughed but those around looked offended. Burton decided his bravado was *mal placé*, but he was later gratified to hear the boy Muhammad relating the incident to enhance his prestige.

As they approached Mecca they entered Wadi Laimun, the Valley of Lemons, a paradise after the desert, where Bedouin girls leaned laughing over the garden walls and offered the travellers sweet water, limes, pomegranates, and fresh dates. The Grand Sharif came out to meet them, a dark beardless man with African features derived from his mother, who was a slave. He was plainly dressed in white garments and turban and rode on an ambling mule, his only emblem of dignity a green satin umbrella held over his head by an attendant. Slaves surrounded him, and he was followed by four sons, all splendidly dressed in bright coloured silks, armed with swords and gold-hilted daggers, and mounted on swift dromedaries. They were all young men of light complexion and true Meccan features.

Night fell before they reached the Holy City, and Burton was dozing in his *shugduf* when he was awakened by cries of 'Mecca! Mecca! . . . Labbaik! Labbaik!' Peering through the curtains of the litter he saw by starlight the dim outline of a large city a shade darker than the surround-ing plain. Descending the last ridge, the caravan threaded its way through darkened suburbs crowded in places with rude cots and dusky figures. At two o'clock in the morning Burton found himself at the door of the boy Muhammad's house.

By dint of violent kicks and testy answers to twenty cautious questions the sleeping Indian porter was induced to swing open the huge gates of the house. The boy Muhammad rushed upstairs to embrace his mother, and soon the shrill *lulululu* could be heard welcoming the wanderer home. When the youth returned his manner had changed from the boisterous and jaunty to the gravely courteous as he led his guest into a gloomy hall and seated him upon the *mastabah*, a large carpeted platform. Meanwhile the shuffling of slippered feet above indicated that the *kabirah*, or mistress of the house, was intent on hospitable thoughts. When the camels were unloaded there appeared a dish of *kanafi*, fine vermicelli browned and powdered with sugar, into which Hakim Abdallah, the boy Muhammad, and Nur dipped their right hands. Then they procured cots from a neighbouring coffee-house and lay down to sleep for an hour or two before visiting the Ka'ba.

The sceptic Burton was in ecstasy:

There at last it lay, the bourn of my long and weary Pilgrimage, realising the hopes and plans of many a long year. The mirage medium of fancy invested the huge catafalque and its gloomy pall with peculiar charms. There were no giant fragments of hoar antiquity as in Egypt, no remains of graceful and harmonious beauty as in Greece and Italy, no barbarous gorgeousness as in the buildings of India; yet the view was strange, unique – and how few have looked upon the celebrated shrine! I may truly say that, of all the worshippers who clung weeping to the curtain, or who pressed their beating heart to the stone, none felt for a moment a deeper emotion than did the Hajji from the far-north. It was as if the poetical legends of the Arabs spoke the truth, and that the waving wings of the angels, and not the sweet breeze of the morning, were agitating and swelling the black covering of the shrine. But, to confess to the humbling truth, theirs was the feeling of high religious enthusiasm, mine was the ecstasy of gratified pride.

Conducting his guest through the ceremonies, the boy Muhammad displayed a fiery zeal against heresy and schism by foully abusing every Persian in his path; Burton wondered that none dared turn and rend him. To reach the Black Stone the boy collected half a dozen stalwart Meccans, with whose aid they wedged their way into the crowd. The Bedouins turned on them like wild cats, but they had no daggers and as it was autumn they had not drunk milk for six months and were living mummies. Despite popular indignation, Burton and his crew monopolized the Stone for ten minutes; while kissing and rubbing it Burton examined it closely and decided that it was a meteorite. The Circuit of the Ka'ba reminded him of the movement of the planets round the sun, and he wondered if it was not a remnant of solar worship.

Day and night the Holy Mosque was crowded with pilgrims. Now and then a corpse on a wooden shell circled the Ka'ba borne on the shoulders of four friends, whom other Muslims relieved occasionally. A devout man with arms flung high so that his whole body might touch the Ka'ba sobbed as though his heart would break. A Takruri was in a state of *malbus*, or religious frenzy, held down by his friends as he threw his arms about, swayed his body, and waved his head from side to side, uttering shrill cries and deep groans like a chained and furious elephant.

On the day of the Standing at Arafat Burton joined the throng of white-robed pilgrims leaving the city. On the way some of the camels, worn out from crossing the desert, dropped to the ground and died. Burton saw no fewer than five men die as well. Exhausted and moribund, they had dragged themselves out of the city to give up the ghost where it might depart to instant beatitude. It seemed easy to die in these latitudes: each man suddenly staggered, fell as if shot, and after a brief convulsion lay as still as marble. The corpses were taken up and carelessly buried the same evening, in vacant spaces amidst the crowd encamped on the plain.

The boy Muhammad had long chafed at the pretensions to poverty of his dervish friend. Determined to be grand, he had brought with him two cousins, fat youths of fifteen or sixteen, a family friend, and his mother's Indian servants. When they reached Arafat he directed the servants in pitching the tent, carpeting it with Persian rugs, and disposing a divan of silk cushions round the interior. In the centre he placed highly polished water-pipes and at the entrance a large copper fire-pan with coffee-pots singing a welcome to the visitor. The youth insisted that his guest cover his travel-stained garment with a rich red cashmere shawl left behind some years before by the son of the king of Delhi. The shawl was later to lead Burton into an episode of gallantry.

Burton climbed the Mount of Mercy to survey the plain and estimated about 50,000 persons to be present, a falling off from previous years. His companions, however, assured him that 150,000 angels were also there in human shape. It was difficult to decide which these were. In one place a drunken Arnaut stalked, elbowing peaceful passers-by and frowning fiercely in search of a quarrel. In another a knot of Egyptians in red tarbushes were noisily smoking the forbidden hemp. There was great confusion and frequent brawls. Many had lost their companions and went about shouting their names. The frequency of female names puzzled Burton till the boy Muhammad explained that Egyptian and 'other bold women' unable to join the pilgrimage paid to have their names shouted at Arafat to ensure their presence the following year.

Thieves were active; a woman surprised one of them and held him by the beard till men ran to her assistance. Burton's party was obliged to defend their encampment against grave-diggers who would bury a little heap of bodies next to their tent. Burton was struck by the difference in cleanliness between a camp of town-dwellers and one of Bedouins. Mas'ud sat holding his nose in disgust and derided the Meccans. The polyglot Pathan consoled the old Bedu by reciting the celebrated song of Maysunah, the beautiful Bedu wife of the Caliph Mu'awiyah:

> O take these purple robes away,
>   Give back my cloaks of camel's hair,
> And bear me from the tow'ring pile
>   To where the Black Tents flap i' the air.
> The camel's colt with falt'ring tread,
>   The dog that bays at all but me,
> Delight me more than ambling mules—
>   Than every sort of minstrelsy;
> And any cousin, poor but free,
>   Might take me, fatted ass! from thee.

Mas'ud, delighted, clapped him on the shoulder and exclaimed, 'Verily, O Father of Mustachios, I will show thee the black tents of my tribe this year!'

As the preacher began the sermon at Arafat, the most solemn moment of the hajj, stillness fell over the mass of pilgrims. But where was Burton? He was in his tent, held there by a pair of pretty eyes. We have seen Burton in the character of Indian Army officer, Afghani doctor, explorer, dervish, and pilgrim, but not yet in the role of romantic lover.

I had prepared *en cachette* a slip of paper, and hid in my Ihram a pencil destined to put down the heads of this rarely heard discourse. But unhappily that red cashmere shawl was upon my shoulders. Close to us sat a party of fair Meccans, apparently belonging to the higher classes, and one of these I had already several times remarked. She was a tall girl, with regular features, a skin somewhat citrine-coloured, but soft and clear, symmetrical eyebrows, the most beautiful eyes, and a figure full of grace. There was no head thrown back, no straightened neck, no flat shoulders, nor toes turned out – in fact, no 'elegant' barbarisms: the shape was what the Arabs love, soft, bending, and relaxed, as a woman's figure ought to be. Happily she wore, instead of the usual veil, a 'Yashmak' of transparent muslin, bound round the face; and the chaperone, mother, or duenna, by whose side she stood, was apparently a very unsuspicious or complaisant old person. Flirtilla fixed a glance of admiration upon my cashmere. I directed a reply with interest to her eyes. She then, by the usual coquettish gesture, threw back an inch or two of head-veil, disclosing broad bands of jetty hair, crowning a lovely oval. My palpable admiration of the new charm was rewarded by a partial removal of the Yashmak, when a dimpled mouth and rounded chin stood out from the envious muslin. I entered upon the dangerous ground of raising my hand to my forehead. She smiled almost imperceptibly, and turned away. The pilgrim was in ecstasy.

This idyll was interrupted by preparations to descend the mountain, although the sermon was only half over. Burton ordered Mas'ud to keep the party of the fair Meccan in view, but though his own party worked with a will their animals were not ready till sunset. The plain was in utter confusion as the pilgrims rushed towards Muzdalifah. The ground bristled with tent-pegs, litters were crushed, pedestrians trampled, camels overthrown. Guns roared and re-echoed from the stony hills. A shower of rockets burst in the air, throwing the mob of women and children into panic. Martial music wailed, and the stouter-hearted pilgrims shouted their *Labbaiks* and *'idkum mubaraks* ('may your festival be blessed'). In the confusion the sentimental lover lost sight of his Flirtilla forever.

Burton did not bother to attend the rites at Muzdalifah, but he was not one to miss the Stoning of the Devil. The fiend was malicious enough to appear to Adam, Abraham, and Ishmael in a narrow pass, which was now crowded with pilgrims all struggling like drowning men to reach the devil's pillar. Among them horsemen on rearing chargers competed with Bedouins on wild camels and grandees on mules and asses accompanied by outrunners. Scarcely had Burton entered the crowd than he was thrown off his ass by a dromedary and found himself under the stomping beast's stomach. By judicious use of his knife he avoided being trampled and escaped. Presently the boy Muhammad fought his way out of the crush with a bleeding nose. They waited on the edge of the surging mass till they found an opening, approached the pillar, and threw their seven stones. Then they repaired to a barber's shop, where their heads were shaved, their beards trimmed, and their nails cut. 'We could now safely twirl our mustachios and stroke our beards, placid enjoyments of which we had been deprived by the laws of the Pilgrimage.'

Returning to Mecca to bathe and change from the inconvenient *ihram*, Burton was invited to the opening of the Ka'ba, a privilege that cost him eight dollars. All pilgrims did not wish to enter the sacred cube, as it imposed obligations, among them never to tell lies again – a restriction, Burton remarked, which most Orientals could not afford.

The pilgrims returned to Mina for the sacrifice of blood. As it was not obligatory, Burton was content to watch his neighbours bargaining with the Bedouins for a victim. Some dragged their purchase to a smooth rock, whose sides were soon dripping with blood. Others stood before their tents and, twisting the animal's face towards the Ka'ba, ejaculated a prayer and slit its throat. The mild Indians hired Arabs to do the deed, to the contempt of the boy Muhammad. Parties of Takruris sat like vultures waiting to fall upon the bodies and cut them up.

The following day the heat was intense; flies swarmed and the blood-soaked earth reeked with noisome vapours; nought moved in the air save kites and vultures. Burton spent the day in a torpor in his tent. The next day Burton and Muhammad fled the revolting scene in the company of other pilgrims of tender sensibilities.

Back in Mecca again the pilgrims repaired to the Holy Mosque for the final ceremony of the hajj. Worshippers packed the vast quadrangle so that nothing was to be seen but a pavement of heads and shoulders. The preacher, staff in hand, stood on a pulpit above the crowd. All was silence as he spoke; then, at the end of a long sentence, the worshippers intoned a general *amin* (amen). Towards the end of the sermon every third or fourth word was followed by the rise and fall of a thousand voices. Even Burton was impressed: 'I have seen the religious ceremonies of many lands, but never – nowhere – aught so solemn, so impressive as this.'

An Arab proverb says 'Evil dwelleth in the two Holy Cities', and no wonder, since plenary indulgence was so easily secured. After the hajj all were whitewashed, the book of their sins was a *tabula rasa*, and they lost no time in opening a fresh account. Burton, with his nose for curious customs and crimes, wandered at night in the city. Vice was less overt than in Burckhardt's time. It was only by starlight in the northern out-skirts of the town that citizens could be seen with light complexions and delicate limbs, dressed in coarse turbans and Egyptian woollen robes, speaking disguise and the purpose of disguise.

But it was time for the new hajji to leave for Jiddah. The *kabirah*, as fond of little presents as a nun, laid firm but friendly hands on a brass mortar and pestle of Burton's as she took affectionate leave and begged him to be careful of her son, who was to accompany him to the port. Sending his boxes ahead with Nur by camel, he and the boy Muhammad mounted their asses and rode in leisurely fashion, stopping every five miles to refresh themselves at a coffee-house. Arriving at Jiddah without funds, Burton repaired to the British vice consulate to cash a draft on the Royal Geographical Society, which partly funded him. The dragoman at the consulate would not allow the ragged dervish to enter, but a note to the vice consul secured him a warm welcome.

His stay in Jiddah was enlivened by the appearance at his door one morning of Omar Effendi, who had fled his family once more in order to return to Cairo. Burton fed and succoured him, and hid him in a dark hole covered with grass. Omar's father appeared, questioned Burton, and left with a grim smile. That evening, returning from the baths, Burton found the boy Muhammad furious with rage and Nur trembling with fear. The father had returned with a posse of friends and relations. They had beaten the boy Muhammad, who had defended Burton's baggage from their prying, and had found Omar Effendi's hiding place and taken him away. Burton pacified the boy Muhammad by offering to sally forth with him to rescue Omar by force, but the offer was declined. The escapade was not serious; the father did not punish his son but merely bargained with him to stay at home a few more days. Burton afterwards met Omar Effendi in the streets of Cairo.

Finding an English ship bound for Suez, Burton boarded it, accompanied by the boy Muhammad, to secure passage. With the money Burton had given him, the boy had already laid in a store of grain for sale; he had also secured all of his guest's disposable articles and had hinted that a present of twenty dollars would find him at Mecca. But he took his leave with a coolness Burton could not account for. Some days later Nur explained. On the ship he had seen how Burton had been received, and a suspicion of the truth had crossed his mind. 'Now I understand,' the boy Muhammad said to Nur, 'your master is a sahib from India; he hath laughed at our beards.' The mask fell.

Epilogue

The destruction of the Ottoman empire, contemplated by Napoleon in 1798 and nearly accomplished by Mehmet Ali in the 1830s, was finally achieved at the end of the First World War, which the Turks had unwisely entered on the side of Germany. In the Hijaz, British agents, including Colonel T. E. Lawrence, persuaded the Grand Sharif to mount an Arab revolt against the Sultan with promises of Arab independence under sharifian rule if the Allies won the war. The Sharif's forces harried Turkish troops in the Hijaz and marched into Damascus at the end of the war. The defeat of the German-led coalition deprived Constantinople of its provinces, and Sharif Husain claimed his reward. But the British had made other promises, to the French and the Zionists, and at the Treaty of Versailles the victors created a system of mandates by which they were to control most of the Arab East, Britain, however, recognized Husain as King of the Hijaz and placed two of his sons on the thrones of Iraq and Transjordan under British protection. Notwithstanding, Husain proclaimed himself King of the Arabs.

Although born in Mecca, Husain had been raised in Constantinople and was an urbane and cultivated prince bearing a family likeness to his predecessor Ghalib in ambition and guile. In Najd the House of Sa'ud had also thrown up a leader in the mould of an earlier generation, that of the great Sa'ud. When 'Abd al-'Aziz ibn 'Abd ar-Rahman Al Faysal Al Sa'ud – better known in the West as Ibn Sa'ud – was born, his family's fortunes were again at low ebb. In 1891 a rival house, that of the Ibn Rashids of Jabal Shammar, drove his father out of Riyadh, the Saudi capital since shortly after the destruction of Dar'iyah. 'Abd al-'Aziz therefore spent his childhood eating the bread of exile, first among the wandering tribes of the Empty Quarter and then in the court of the ruler of Kuwait, while the Ibn Rashids extended their rule over Najd. When the Ibn Rashids attacked Kuwait, the Sa'uds, father and son, took the field in defence of their host. During one of these campaigns the young 'Abd al-'Aziz disappeared into the desert leading a band of forty friends and relatives. After wandering in the desert for several months seeking allies, he appeared suddenly at the gates of Riyadh and in a daring night raid with a handful of men captured the castle and killed Ibn Rashid's governor on 16 January 1902. Although he had recovered the Saudi capital at one stroke, he had now to win back Najd and the Qasim in a series of arduous campaigns that lasted nearly two decades. Like his famous ancestor, 'Abd al-'Aziz was a great desert warrior, a devout Wahhabi, and an inspiring leader of men able to rally the tribes and the pockets of Unitarian faith to the House of Sa'ud once more. In 1904 he demolished an army of Ibn Rashid supported by eight Turkish battalions and artillery. In 1913 he drove the Turks out of al-Hasa, which they had re-occupied forty years before. The British, then in control of most of the Persian Gulf amirates, were impressed enough by his successes to sign a treaty with 'Abd al-'Aziz at the outset of the First World War similar to the one they had reached with Sharif Husain. Saudi forces attacked Hayil, the capital of the pro-Turkish Ibn Rashids, but did not otherwise play an active part in the fighting.

With the return of world peace the stage was set for a contest in the Hijaz strongly reminiscent of events that had taken place there a century before. The Sharif, determined to increase his power, attacked the tribes east of Mecca in the vicinity of Khurmah, where Ghalib had met defeat at the hands of the Wahhabis in 1798. The people of Khurmah, after beating back the sharifian forces three times, called on 'Abd al-'Aziz for protection. In May 1919 Husain's son 'Abd Allah led an army of 4,000 men on a fourth raid against Khurmah; but before they could reach the oasis the Wahhabis launched a devastating night attack from which only 'Abd Allah and about 100 of his men escaped alive.

The worried British tried to reconcile their warring allies at a conference in Kuwait in 1923, without success. By then 'Abd al-'Aziz had captured Hayil and won the towns of Khaybar and Taymah on the northeastern frontier of the Hijaz. In March 1924 the Republic of Turkey, having supplanted the Sultanate, abolished the office of the caliphate as well, and Husain on a visit to his son in Amman, declared himself Caliph of all Islam. This was anathema to the Wahhabis, who still condemned what they considered to be the heresy and corruption of the Holy Cities. In September 'Abd al-'Aziz attacked the city of Tayif then under the jurisdiction of Husain's eldest son 'Ali. 'Ali fled to Mecca, abandoning Tayif to Wahhabi troops, who massacred 200 of the townspeople in a manner recalling that of a century before.

Husain was now an old man, and the people of the Hijaz prevailed upon him to abdicate. He sailed from Jiddah to Aqaba in October 1924 and then went into honourable retirement in Cyprus until his death. 'Ali, now king of the Hijaz, decided that Mecca was untenable and sought safety behind the walls of Jiddah. Mecca surrendered to the Wahhabis without a fight, and 'Abd al-'Aziz entered the Holy City clad in the white *ihram* of a simple pilgrim. As of old, his followers set about dismantling the tombs and purifying the Holy Places.

The walls of Jiddah withstood a Wahhabi siege for a year. But in December 1925 Medina surrendered to a Wahhabi force, and two weeks later Jiddah capitulated. 'Ali sailed to Iraq where his brother Faysal was king. On 18 January 1926 'Abd al-'Aziz was proclaimed King of the Hijaz in the Holy Mosque of Mecca. The House of Sa'ud was at last in sole possession of the Hijaz, and the stern pieties of Unitarianism in command of the Holy Cities.

One of 'Abd al-'Aziz's first acts following his conquest of the Hijaz was to call an Islamic congress in Mecca to hear the advice of Muslims from other countries on the conduct of the pilgrimage. By imposing his authority on the tribes he eliminated many of the dangers that threatened caravans crossing the interior, and he began to improve facilities for the pilgrims. For a few years the Saudi government subsisted largely on pilgrim receipts augmented by a British subsidy. Oil, however, was discovered near al-Hasa in the 1930s, although large revenues from that source did not begin to flow into the treasury until after the Second World War. Then the Hijaz, in common with the other provinces of Saudi Arabia, began to benefit from wealth inconceivable to previous generations of Arabs.

In the eighteenth and early nineteenth centuries the pilgrimage was on the wane. Burckhardt noted that parts of the city of Mecca had fallen into ruin even before the Egyptian campaign, and he estimated that only about 70,000 pilgrims stood at Arafat in 1814, many of them soldiers. Forty years later Burton reckoned he saw about 50,000 pilgrims, half of them residents of Arabia. The tide of Islam seemed to be ebbing, partly because of the dislocations imposed on the Muslim world by European imperialism. But soon a reaction set in as Muslims began to rebel against their alien masters. The triumph of Wahhabism in Arabia was part of the resurgence of Islam that has been a marked phenomenon of our own time. This revival is reflected in the hajj. Since the Second World War the number of pilgrims has increased annually until now more than a million and a half of the faithful make the *tawaf* round the Ka'ba and stand at Arafat every hajj season. About half the pilgrims come from abroad, from some seventy countries and all the continents.

This enormous augmentation is partly due to improved transport. The majority of pilgrims now arrive by air. At the height of the hajj season the airport of Jiddah receives over 100 flights a day. The hajjis stream through the reception gates and transit halls, some already wearing the white *ihram*, others in native dress, others still in lounge suits and ties or even the international uniform of blue jeans and sport shirts. Pilgrims from Kabul and Pakistan sometimes bring rugs which they display for sale on the railings round the airport; those from Yemen peddle silver jewellery in the souks and hotels; the well-to-do Indonesians buy European products in the shops. Bigger deals involving thousands of dollars are concluded by pilgrims from Lebanon and Egypt. African, Malaysian, and Moroccan villages spring up in the waste ground near the port.

Not all the hajjis come by air; some from the north still cross the desert where the old caravan trails have become paved four-lane highways. They come by air-conditioned bus, in limousines and jalopies, some of them crammed in the back of open pick-up trucks. The vehicles stop along the way, and peasants from Anatolia or Aleppo descend to kneel in rows by the roadside to pray in the direction of Mecca. On the zigzag highway that clings vertiginously to the sheer cliffs between Mecca and Tayif the urgent rush of pilgrim traffic recalls a scene by Doré of all mankind fleeing catastrophe, the Flood perhaps, or the end of the world. It has been said that it is now difficult to die on the hajj, but oriental fatalism and reckless driving can still achieve the longed-for holy death that was once provided by thirst, disease, or hostile Bedouins.

The Saudi government does everything in its power to avoid catastrophe and to ensure the smooth running of the pilgrimage. And because of oil, its power is great. It provides reception centres, guides, accommodation, local transport, medical services, police, and sufficient water and food supplies to ensure that most pilgrims survive. To perform its task it uses the most advanced techniques of radio, telephone, closed-circuit television, helicopters, antibiotics, cameras, computers, and soon no doubt the silicon chip. At first the Wahhabi imams opposed such innovations as the work of heretics and the devil; but 'Abd al-'Aziz, by having the Quran read on the first radio broadcast in the kingdom, convinced them that modern inventions were good when used in the service of Allah. But the Saudi government still enforces the moral standards of its Unitarian origins. Tobacco and music are now permitted, but alcohol, prostitution, and unseemly dress and conduct are strictly forbidden. The laws of religious observance, shorn of superstition and corruption, are also enforced. But it is no longer merely the letter of the law that is observed. A spirit of voluntary submission – the literal meaning of Islam – infuses the mass of pilgrims following the hajj.

Much has been lost in the process of modernization. The hard-won independence of the Bedouins is gone; the town walls and gates and the handsome old houses of Jiddah have been razed; electricity has replaced the candles and oil lamps round the Ka'ba; the words of the Quran are transmitted electronically from the minarets. One might shed a tear for the passing of the camel caravans, the Irregular Turkish cavalry in their absurd uniforms, the glittering litters of the grandees, the swaying ostrich feathers of the *mahmal*, the military bands and sky rockets, the lovely Ethiopian women, the eunuchs and dervishes, the footsore Takruris happily dying of hunger and fatigue. But these things would have vanished in any case. The Hijaz was never cut off from history and change. But who would have thought a hundred years ago that the followers of Muhammad 'Abd al-Wahhab, who sought to revive the simplicity of the past, would bring the twentieth century to the Muslim Holy Land?

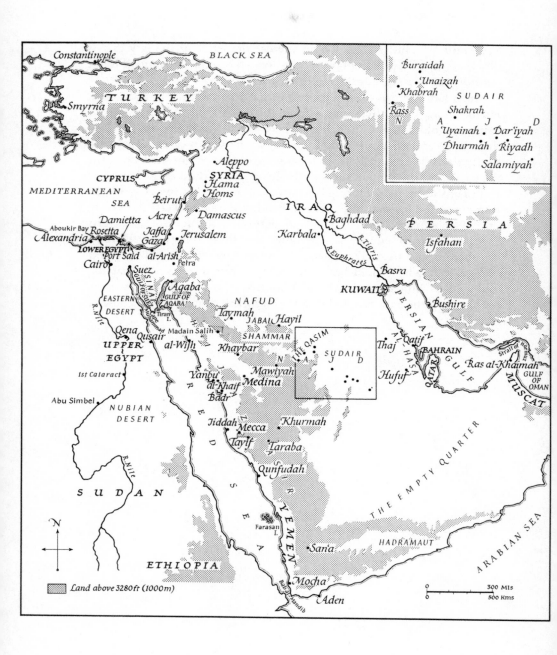

Map of the Middle East

212

Note on Sources

General Works

Bernard Lewis: *The Arabs in History*. London, 1964

Philip K. Hitti: *History of the Arabs*. London, 1956

Rom Landau: *Islam and the Arabs*. London, 1958

Alfred Guillaume: *Islam*. Middlesex, 1954

H. A. R. Gibb: *Mohammedanism*. London, 1949

Albert Kammerer: *La Mer Rouge*. Cairo, 1947–49

M. T. Houtsma, *et al*: *Encyclopedia of Islam*. Leiden, 1954

H. A. R. Gibb and J. H. Kramers: *Shorter Encyclopedia of Islam*. Leiden, 1953

P. M. Holt, Ann K. S. Lambton and Bernard Lewis (eds): *Cambridge History of Islam*. Cambridge, 1970

H. W. Hazard: *Atlas of Islamic History*. Princeton, 1952

R. Roolvink, *et al*: *Historical Atlas of the Muslim Peoples*. Amsterdam, 1957

D. G. Hogarth: *Arabia*. Oxford, 1922

H. St John Philby: *Sa'udi Arabia*. London, 1955

K. S. Twitchell: *Saudi Arabia*. Princeton, 1958

R. Bayly Winder: *Saudi Arabia in the Nineteenth Century*. New York, 1965

Lord Kinross: *The Ottoman Centuries*. London, 1977

Travellers

D. G. Hogarth: *The Penetration of Arabia*. London, 1904

R. H. Kiernan: *The Unveiling of Arabia*. London, 1937

Jacqueline Pirenne: *A la Découverte de l'Arabie*. Paris, 1958

Robin Bidwell: *Travellers in Arabia*. London, 1976

Chapter 1

In addition to the general works cited above, this chapter is based on: Alfred Guillaume: *Life of Muhammad* (London, 1955); W. M. Watt: *Muhammad at Medina* (Oxford, 1956); W. M. Watt: *Muhammad at Mecca* (Oxford, 1953);

Gerald de Gaury: *Rulers of Mecca* (London, 1951); John Lewis Burckhardt: *Notes on the Bedouins and the Wahabys* (London, 1831). The story of Reynald de Châtillon is taken from Steven Runciman: *History of the Crusades* (Cambridge, 1951–54). Shafik Ghorbal's remark about the Mamluks is quoted from his *The Beginnings of the Egyptian Question and the Rise of Mehemet Ali* (London, 1928). The Hakluyt Society's *Voyages* is the source of the story of the Portuguese traveller cited in Albuquerque's *Commentaries* and of the report of an anonymous Englishman's pilgrimage to Mecca in 1586. Varthema's story is told in *The Nauigation and Vyages of Lewes Vertomannus, Gentelman of the Citie of Rome, to the Regions of Arabia, Egypte, Persia, Ethiopia, and East India . . . Translated out of Latine into Englyshe, by Richarde Eden, in the Yeare of Our Lord 1576* (London, 1811). Joseph Pitts' *True and Faithful Account of the Religion and Manners of the Mahometans*, describing his captivity and pilgrimage, was published in Exeter, 1704.

Chapter 2

Brian Gardner: *The East India Company: a History* (London, 1971) has furnished useful background information for this chapter. The episode concerning Sir Henry Middleton's landing at Mocha is to be found in Kerr's *Voyages*, viii (Edinburgh, 1811–24), while that of Major de la Grélaudière comes from La Roque's *Voyage de l'Arabie Heureuse* (Amsterdam, 1716). The murder of fourteen English traders at Jiddah in 1743 is mentioned in Bruce's *Travels* . . . (see below). The account of the King of Denmark's mission to Arabia is based on Carsten Niebuhr: *Travels through Arabia and Other Countries in the East*, translated by Robert Heron (Edinburgh, 1792), with biographical material from Thorkild Hansen: *Arabia Felix* (London, 1964). Additional information about the Wahhabi movement comes from Burckhardt's *Notes* . . ., Philby's *Sa'udi Arabia*, and the *Encyclopedia of Islam*. The account of Bruce's visit to Jiddah is taken from his *Travels to*

Discover the Source of the Nile (London, 1803), with biographical material from F. B. Head: *The Life of Bruce* (London, 1836). The Ottoman *firman* restricting English ships in the Red Sea and James Capper's remarks on the importance of the overland route to India are to be found in *Observations on the Passage to India through Egypt* (second edition, London, 1785). The voyage of four Englishmen of the East India Company through Arabian waters and Egypt is recounted in Eyles Irwin: *Series of Adventures in the Course of a Voyage up the Red Sea, on the Coasts of Arabia and Egypt, in the Year 1777, in Letters to a Lady* (London, 1780).

Chapter 3

The French occupation of Egypt and British and Ottoman counter-measures are set forth in C. de la Jonquière: *L'Expédition d'Egypte 1789–1801* (Paris, 1899–1901); F. Charles-Roux: *Bonaparte, Governor of Egypt* (London, 1937); P. G. Elgood: *Bonaparte's Adventure in Egypt* (Oxford, 1931); and Christopher Herold: *Bonaparte in Egypt* (London, 1963). A useful collection of documents relating to the expedition is contained in Christopher Lloyd: *The Nile Campaign: Nelson and Napoleon in Egypt* (New York, 1973). The French savants' *Description de l'Egypte* was published in Paris, 1809. The career of Mehmet Ali is described in Félix Mengin: *Egypte sous le Gouvernement de Mahomet Ali* (Paris, 1823); Henry Dodwell: *The Founder of Modern Egypt* (Cambridge, 1931); J. C. Richmond: *Egypt 1798–1952* (London, 1977); and Shafik Ghorbal: *The Beginnings of the Egyptian Question and the Rise of Mehemet Ali* (London, 1928).

Chapter 4

The Wahhabi raids on their neighbours and the attempts of the Sharif of Mecca and the Pasha of Baghdad to contain them are related in the sources cited above, especially Burckhardt: *Notes . . .* and Philby: *Sa'udi Arabia.* Lord Valentia's description of the Hijaz under the Wahhabis is taken from his *Voyages and Travels to India, Ceylon, the Red Sea, Abyssinia and Egypt* (London, 1809). Ali Bey's account of his pilgrimage comes from the English edition of *Travels of Ali Bey in Morocco, Tripoli, Cyprus, Egypt, Arabia, Syria and Turkey Between the Years 1803 and 1807* (London, 1816); biographical material concerning him is taken from

the editor's preface to the same volume and from Burckhardt's letters to the African Association printed in his *Travels through Nubia* (London, 1819). The story of Ali Bey's 'Christian' death appeared in the Catalan edition of his *Travels,* cited by Hogarth in *The Penetration of Arabia.*

Chapter 5

Finati's account of his life and his part in the Egyptian-Wahhabi war can be found in *Narrative of the Life and Adventures of Giovanni Finati . . . Translated from the Italian, as Dictated by Himself, and Edited by William John Bankes, Esq.* (London, 1830). Further information concerning the massacre of the Mamluks, the conduct of the Egyptian campaign, and the part played by the Scottish renegade Thomas Keith comes chiefly from Burckhardt's *Notes . . .,* with some details from the modern sources cited above.

Chapter 6

The entire chapter is based on John Lewis Burckhardt: *Travels in Arabia* (London, 1829), with additional material from *Travels in Nubia* (London, 1819) and *Notes on the Bedouins and the Wahabys* (London, 1831). The account of his life and death is contained in the editor's Memoir printed in *Travels in Nubia*; other biographical material comes from Katharine Sim: *Desert Traveller* (London, 1969). An account of Ulrich Seetzen's travels can be found in *Reisen Durch Syrien,* edited by F. Kruse (Berlin, 1854).

Chapter 7

The account of Ibrahim's campaign in the Qasim and Najd is based on Burckhardt, Philby, and Sadleir. John Foster Sadleir's *Diary of a Journey Across Arabia from El Katif in the Persian Gulf to Yambo in the Red Sea* was first published in Bombay, 1866; a reprint of this edition by Falcon–Oleander, 1977, contains an introduction by F. M. Edwards providing biographical material of interest.

Chapter 8

The Egyptian occupation of the Hijaz and the further career of Mehmet Ali and his son Ibrahim can be found in Burckhardt (*Notes . . .*),

Dodwell, and Richmond. Wallin's report on his travels in Arabia is printed in the *Journal of the Royal Geographical Society*, vol. 24, 1854. John F. Keane told the story of the English-woman residing at Mecca in his *Six Months in the Hijaz* (London, 1887). The basis of most of this chapter is Richard Burton: *Personal Narrative of a Pilgrimage to Al-Madinah and Meccah*, Memorial Edition (London, 1893). Biographical material comes from Isabel Burton: *Life of Sir Richard Burton* (London, 1893); Byron Farwell: *Burton* (London, 1963); and Fawn Brodie: *The Devil Drives* (London, 1967). The quotations from Frank Harris and A. W. Symons are taken from Thomas Assad: *Three Victorian Travellers* (London, 1964).

Epilogue
The historical information comes from Philby: *Sa'udi Arabia*; Elizabeth Monroe: *Britain's Moment in the Middle East: 1914–1956* (London, 1963); T. E. Lawrence: *The Seven Pillars of Wisdom* (London, 1935); James Morris: *The Hashemite Kings* (London, 1959); and *Aramco Handbook*, edited by George Rentz (Dhahran, 1968). The description of the modern pilgrimage is based partly on the author's observations, partly on Saudi Government publications, newspaper accounts, and G. H. Jansen: *Militant Islam* (London, 1979). An authoritative account of the pilgrimage is contained in *Aramco World Magazine*, vol. 25, no. 6, November–December 1974.

List of Illustrations

Index

Numbers in italics refer to illustrations